COL

Kristy and her friends love babysitting and when her mum can't find a babysitter for Kristy's little brother one day, Kristy has a great idea. Why doesn't she set up a babysitting club? That way parents can make a single phone call and reach a team of babysitting experts. And if one babysitter is already busy another one can take the job. So together with her friends, Claudia, Mary Anne and Stacey, Kristy starts THE BABYSITTERS CLUB. And although things don't *always* go according to plan, they have a lot of fun on the way!

Catch up with the very latest adventures of the Babysitters Club in these great new stories:

91 Claudia and the First Thanksgiving

92 Mallory's Christmas Wish

93 Mary Anne and the Memory Garden

94 Stacey McGill, Super Sitter

95 Kristy + Bart = ?

96 Abby's Lucky Thirteen

97 Claudia and the World's Cutest Baby

98 Dawn and Too Many Sitters

99 Stacey's Broken Heart

And coming soon...

100 Kristy's Worst Idea

COLLECTION 15

Book 43
STACEY'S EMERGENCY

Book 44
DAWN AND THE BIG SLEEPOVER

Book 45
KRISTY AND THE BABY PARADE

Ann M. Martin

Scholastic Children's Books,
Commonwealth House, 1–19 New Oxford Street,
London, WC1A 1NU, UK
A division of Scholastic Ltd
London ~ New York ~ Toronto ~ Sydney ~ Auckland ~
Mexico City ~ New Delhi ~ Hong Kong

Stacey's Emergency
Dawn and the Big Sleepover
Kristy and the Baby Parade
First published in the US by Scholastic Inc., 1991
First published in the UK by Scholastic Ltd, 1993

First published in this edition by Scholastic Ltd, 1999

Text copyright © Ann M. Martin, 1991
THE BABY-SITTERS CLUB is a registered trademark of Scholastic Inc.

ISBN 0 439 01259 7

All rights reserved

Typeset by M Rules
Printed by Cox & Wyman Ltd, Reading, Berks.

1 2 3 4 5 6 7 8 9 10

The right of Ann M. Martin to be identified as the author of this work has been asserted by her in accordance with the Copyright, Designs and Patents Act, 1988.

This book is sold subject to the condition that it shall not, by way of trade or otherwise, be lent, resold, hired out, or otherwise circulated without the publisher's prior consent in any form of binding or cover other than that in which it is published and without a similar condition, including this condition, being imposed upon the subsequent purchaser.

CONTENTS

Stacey's Emergency   1

Dawn and the Big Sleepover   141

Kristy and the Baby Parade   279

STACEY'S
EMERGENCY

The author would like to thank
Dr Claudia Werner
for her sensitive evaluation of this book

1st CHAPTER

I looked up from my homework. I watched Charlotte Johanssen, my babysitting charge. Charlotte is eight years old.

She was reading *The New York Times*.

She had just finished going through the *Stoneybrook News*.

"Wow," said Charlotte.

"What?" I asked her.

"It says here that in New York this woman had a gun and she—"

"Stop!" I cried. "I don't want to hear about it! And why are you reading that story, anyway?"

"I don't know. It's just here in the paper."

I suppose I couldn't fault Charlotte for reading something great (and grown-up) like the *Times*. But did she have to read the grisly stuff? And did she have to read it out loud?

"Gosh," said Charlotte. "*Here* it says that there was a huge fire in a big, posh hotel one night and—"

"Char! I really don't want to hear about it. . . Okay?"

"Okay. Actually, I was looking for science articles. Oh, here's one! Hey, Stacey! There's a whole article about diabetes."

"Really?" Now I was interested. That's because I have diabetes myself. Diabetes is an illness. If your blood sugar level gets too high, you can become really ill. There are different kinds of diabetes and different ways to treat the illness. Some people just stick to a low sugar diet. Other people have to have injections every day. (I'm one of those people. I know giving yourself injections sounds gross, but the injections save my life.) The injections are of insulin, which is what the pancreas (that's a gland in your body) produces to break down sugar. When your body's natural insulin isn't working properly, then sometimes you have to give *yourself* insulin. From outside your body. But that doesn't always work. Natural insulin is more effective.

I am lucky in one way because I *can* give myself insulin. Before doctors knew how to do that, I think people with diabetes suffered a lot. But I am unlucky in another way: I have a severe form of diabetes. My mum told me recently that I'm called a brittle diabetic. That means that my illness is hard to control. I have to have insulin injections *and* stay on a strict diet. And I mean strict. My mum helps me count calories. This is complicated. We don't simply count calories. We count different *kinds* of calories, like proteins and fats, and we have to balance them. Plus, I have to test my blood. And I have to do it several times each day. How do I test my blood? I prick my finger (I know – you're thinking that diabetes is all injections and finger sticks), then I squeeze out a drop of blood, wipe it on this thing called a test strip, and put the test strip into a machine. A number comes up on the machine, and the number tells me if the level of sugar in my blood is too high (either because I've misjudged and eaten something that has a lot of natural sugar in it, like fruit, or because I have too little insulin in my body), too low (not *enough* sugar in my blood; everybody needs some), or just right.

A few times recently I've seen some numbers that haven't been what they should be. Also, lately, I've been hungrier and thirstier than usual – and also tired. (I've had some sore throats and things, too.) I haven't told Mum about the blood tests, though. She's been through a lot in the past few months. (My parents have just got divorced, but I'll explain about that later.) I don't want Mum to have to worry about me as well as everything else.

Anyway, I'm thirteen years old, and I know my body is going through lots of chemical changes. (Everyone's does when they reach puberty.) So maybe the insulin was just another chemical in my body that was changing – reacting differently to my diet and injections. That's what I *wanted* to believe, but it was my own theory. To tell you the truth, I didn't want to worry Mum because *I* was already worried.

"What does the article say, Char?" I asked her.

"Oh, it's a bit boring, really." Charlotte skimmed down the page. "It's nothing about treating diabetes. It's about how scientists need more money for research so they can study the illness." Charlotte folded up the paper. Then she opened it again and began looking at the headlines.

Charlotte Johanssen is really clever. She's an only child, and her parents spend as much time with her as possible – but that isn't a lot. They both work hard, especially Charlotte's mother, who's a doctor. Charlotte's teachers once asked the Johanssens if they'd let Char skip a year – which Dr and Mr Johanssen finally said yes to. It was a big decision. Charlotte may be clever, but she's shy and clingy (although not as bad as she used to be) and has a bit of trouble making friends.

Sometimes she can be awfully serious, too, which is why I said then, "Hey, Char, let's read something more fun than the paper."

"Okay," she agreed. "Can I see what's in your Kid-Kit?"

A Kid-Kit is a box full of my old toys, books and games, as well as some new things, such as art materials. I bring the Kid-Kit with me on sitting jobs. I wish I could take credit for this great idea, but it wasn't mine. Kristy Thomas, the chairman and founder of the Babysitters Club (which I belong to), thought up Kid-Kits – and a lot of other things as well. But I'll tell you about Kristy and the BSC later, along with my parents' divorce.

Charlotte poked through the Kid-Kit. She pulled out the first book she saw. "Oh, Paddington," she said, sounding disappointed. "We've already read this one."

"Keep looking," I told her.

Char did. Finally she emerged with *The Dancing Cats of Applesap*. "This is a new book, Stacey! Cool!"

"Do you want me to read to you?" (Of course, Charlotte could read the book perfectly well by herself, but there's nothing like being read *to*, no matter how old you are.)

"Yes!" said Charlotte, jumping to her feet.

We both moved to the sofa, and Char snuggled up next to me while I began

7

reading. I glanced at her a couple of times, because she was *so* engrossed.

Charlotte and I could practically be sisters. Not because we look alike (we don't), but because that's how close we are. Charlotte even stayed at my house once when her parents suddenly had to go out of town for a few days. Maybe I shouldn't say this, but Char is my favourite sitting charge – and I'm her favourite sitter. We mean more to each other than that, though, which is why I think of us as sisters.

Also, I wish I really did have a sister or a brother. But, like Charlotte, I'm an only child. And since my parents' divorce, I live mostly with my mother.

Maybe this would be a good time to tell you about the divorce. But beware, it's complicated! Oh, well. Here goes. I grew up in New York City. My dad has a really good job there. But just before I began the seventh grade, the company he works for transferred him to Stamford, Connecticut, so my parents went house-hunting, and found a place for us here in Stoneybrook, which is not far from Stamford. Then, in the middle of this school year (eighth grade), the company transferred Dad *back* to New York. (I didn't mind much. I had joined the BSC and made friends in Connecticut, but I also wanted to return to New York and live in the city that felt like home to me.) However, we hadn't been back in New York for more than a few months when my parents began to have problems with each other. They were always fighting. And the next thing I knew, they were getting a divorce. Worse, my father was staying in New York, my mother wanted to return to Connecticut (she *loves* Stoneybrook), and I was given the choice of where I wanted to live. (In other words, with which parent I wanted to live.) It was an awful decision, but finally I chose Connecticut, promising my dad I would visit him at weekends and holidays whenever I could. I've been *pretty* good about that, but lately, what with feeling tired and irritable and just not *well*, I haven't gone to New York as often as Dad would like. All my energy goes into babysitting, school and homework. I can't think about travelling. It wears me out.

I also feel as though Mum and Dad have been using me a bit. I know that's a terrible thing to say about your own parents, but it's true. And it makes me resent the divorce even more, which makes me want to stay put in Connecticut. I'm not trying to punish my dad, I'm just trying to feel like a normal kid with one home. Each time I have to get on the train and *travel* to see my father, I'm reminded of the divorce. I don't like to think of myself as a divorced kid, even though the parents of half of my friends are divorced, too.

Oh. I'm getting sidetracked. I started to say that I feel as if Mum and Dad are using me. By that I mean that they're putting me in the middle. In the middle of them. For instance, when I come home from New York, Mum usually wants to know what Dad's "up to". After a few more questions, I can tell that what she really wants to know is whether Dad is dating someone. Dad does the same thing to me on my weekend visits. What am I supposed to do? In the first place, I usually don't know the answers to their questions. In the second place, when I do know, if I tell, am I being an informant? Is one parent going to call the other and say, "Stacey told me you went out with so-and-so the other night"? And then will I be in trouble?

"Stacey?" asked Charlotte. "Are you okay? You've stopped reading."

"Oh, Char, I'm sorry," I told her. "My mind was wandering. Let's see. Where was I?" I'd been reading without paying any attention.

"Right here," said Charlotte, pointing to a spot on page nine.

"Okay." I began reading again. This time I kept my mind on the book. In fact, Charlotte and I both became so caught up in the story that when Dr Johanssen returned, she startled us!

After I'd been paid (and also after I'd lent Charlotte *The Dancing Cats of Applesap* because she couldn't bear not knowing the end of the story), I asked Dr Johanssen if I could talk to her in private.

"Of course," said Charlotte's mother, and we sat down in the kitchen.

"It's my diabetes," I blurted out. "I'm tired all the time, hungrier and thirstier than I should be and . . . and. . ." I finally managed to admit to her that I'd been getting funny blood sugar readings.

I was afraid Dr Johanssen might blow up at me for ignoring all this stuff. She's not my doctor, but she's *a* doctor, and she's told me I can always go to her when I have questions. But Dr Johanssen didn't blow up. (I should have known she wouldn't. She's not an explosive person.)

However, she did say, "I think you should have this checked out *soon,* Stacey. You're awfully busy, you're under a lot of stress, and you do have a tricky form of diabetes. Why don't you ask your mum to call your doctor in New York? Or make an appointment to see your doctor, since you're going to visit your dad in a few days."

"Okay," I replied. "Thanks, Doctor Johanssen."

"Any time, sweetheart."

I called goodbye to Charlotte then and left the Johanssens' house. I had intended to go home and catch up on some of my homework. Besides, I was *ravenous*. I could have eaten a horse. Maybe two. Even so, I suddenly didn't feel like going home. I wanted to be with someone – in particular with my best friend, Claudia Kishi. I needed to talk to her.

I needed an escape.

2nd CHAPTER

Claudia and I have been best friends since that day at the beginning of the seventh grade when we ran into each other. (I mean, actually *ran* into each other.) We realized we were dressed alike – in *very* trendy clothes – and somehow we hit it off. Then when Kristy Thomas, one of Claudia's friends, wanted to start a babysitting club, I was asked to join. So I became friends with Kristy and *her* best friend, Mary Anne Spier, as well. But Claudia is my best friend. (Well, she's my best Connecticut friend. My best New York friend is Laine Cummings. I usually see her when I visit my father.) Anyway, like most best friends, Claudia and I are similar in some ways and different in other ways. We're similar in that (I hope this doesn't sound stuck-up; I just think it's true) we're both pretty sophisticated for thirteen. We wear really trendy clothes – leggings, cowboy boots, oversized shirts, hats (Claud wears hats more than I do), and wild jewellery. Claudia, who is an excellent artist, makes some of our jewellery herself. Both Claud and I are pretty interested in boys (I've been described as "boy-crazy"), and we like *action*! But that's where the similarities end.

We look as different as different can be. I have blue eyes and blonde hair, and my mother allows me to get perms, so my hair is usually fluffy or curly. Claudia, on the other hand, is Japanese-American. She's got these beautiful, very dark, almond-shaped eyes; creamy, flawless skin; and long, black, silky hair. While I wear my hair pretty much the same way each day, Claud is always experimenting with hers. She plaits it, puts it in clips, swoops it over to one side of her head in a big ponytail, etc. And she loves weaving ribbons in her hair, buying or making fancy hairslides, and trying out scarves, headbands, you name it. Then, while I'm an only child in a family that seems pretty mixed up at the moment, Claud comes from an ordinary family. She grew up here in Stoneybrook, and she lives with her parents and her older sister, Janine. Janine is a genius. I mean, a real one with an IQ that's way over 150, which is the genius mark. She goes to Stoneybrook High School, but she also goes to classes at our local college. Can you imagine? Sixteen and doing college courses? I don't know why she doesn't just go off to college right now and forget the rest of high school. If she did, she'd certainly make life easier for Claudia. That's because although Claud is clever, she's a terrible pupil – and an even worse speller. I think that school just doesn't interest her. What does interest her is art. Claud's very talented. As I mentioned earlier, she makes jewellery. She also paints, draws, sculpts and sometimes experiments with pottery. Her work has even won some local awards. Another thing Claud likes is reading Nancy Drew mysteries. Her parents, however, think she should be reading classics or something. (Mrs Kishi is a librarian.) But Claud loves mysteries, so she buys the books anyway and hides them around her room. Along with junk food, which she's addicted to. Her room can be pretty interesting. You reach into a container labelled PAPERCLIPS and pull out a handful of wine gums. You open a desk drawer, looking for a pencil, and find a bag of M&M's. You ask Claud about the latest book she's read – and she retrieves it from the folds of a quilt at the end of her bed. Claudia is fun, funny, generous and talented. I just wish she had higher self-esteem.

Talk about self-esteem, Kristy Thomas has it, despite what *she's* been through in the last year or so. You think my family's mixed up? Wait until you hear about Kristy's. Kristy, the chairman of the Babysitters Club, used to live opposite Claud. She lived there with her mother and her three brothers – Charlie and Sam, who are at high school, and David Michael, who's seven. Mr Thomas had walked out on the family when Kristy was six or seven (I think). He just walked out, leaving Kristy's mum to raise four kids. Which she did. She got herself together and found a good job with a company in Stamford. Then, a few months before Kristy began the seventh grade, her mother started going out with this millionaire, Watson Brewer. He was the first man Mrs Thomas had been serious about since her husband left. And he was the first man that Kristy said she didn't like. Watson had been married once before, and he's got two children, Andrew and Karen, who are four and seven now. During the summer between the seventh and eighth grade, Mrs Thomas married Watson. (That's how I always think of him, because that's what Kristy calls him.) After the wedding, Watson moved Kristy and her family from their small house into his mansion across town. Naturally, Kristy resented this, even though everyone in the family has a room to himself or herself, including Karen and Andrew, who only live with their father every other weekend.

Guess what? Not long ago, Watson and Mrs Thomas adopted a little girl. They called her Emily Michelle. She's two and a half, and she comes from Vietnam. She's adorable. With such a little kid around, though, arrangements had to be made for someone to be at home while the adults were at work and everyone else was at school. So Nannie, Kristy's grandmother, joined the household. What with Kristy, her mum, her brothers, her stepfather, her stepsister and stepbrother, her adopted sister, her grandmother and the pets (a cat, a dog and two goldfish), the Brewer/Thomas house is wild, crazy . . . and wonderful! (Even Kristy admits that now.)

Kristy herself is outgoing (she's noted for her big mouth), a tomboy, and just a little bit immature compared to the rest of us in the BSC. She couldn't care less about clothes and almost always wears jeans, a poloneck, a sweater or sweat shirt, and running shoes. Sometimes she wears her baseball cap with the collie on it. She's pretty, although I don't think she knows it. Best of all, when you dig below the loud-mouthed exterior, you find a caring, concerned, organized person, full of good ideas and creativity. (Needless to say, Kristy – like the rest of us – *loves* kids.)

Kristy's best friend, Mary Anne Spier, actually looks a little bit like Kristy. They're both short for their age (Kristy is shorter) and have brown hair and brown eyes. Their features are even similar. But beyond looks, they are two extremely different people. While Kristy is outgoing, Mary Anne is shy. She has trouble speaking up for herself or voicing her opinions, although she's better about that than she was when I first met her. She's a romantic and cries easily. (Never see a sad film with her.) She even had a steady boyfriend for a long time.

Mary Anne grew up next door to Kristy. (She's moved, too, though. I'll explain in a minute.) But her home life was certainly different from Kristy's. It was quiet (no brothers leaping around), just Mary Anne and her dad. Mary Anne's mum died when Mary Anne was quite little. She hardly remembers her mother. Mary Anne was brought up by Mr Spier, who was awfully strict with her. Not that he's nasty, but he does have this thing about orderliness and neatness and organization. Also, I think he wanted to prove to everyone that he could bring up a little girl all by himself perfectly OK. So he invented these rules for Mary Anne and practically took over her life. When I first met Mary Anne she seemed like such a little girl, even though she's my age. That changed when Mary Anne was able to show her father that she was as grown up as the rest of her friends. Then he relaxed a little, and Mary Anne loosened up, too.

Halfway through the seventh grade, a new girl, Dawn Schafer, moved to Stoneybrook – all the way from California. Dawn, a member of the BSC now, had moved here with her mother and younger brother, Jeff, after her parents had got divorced. (Sound familiar?) Her mum had chosen Stoneybrook because she grew up here and Dawn's grandparents still live here. Our California girl has the most amazingly blonde hair I've ever seen. And it's *long*. Her eyes are a sparkly blue, and, well, she's striking-looking. Dawn hates the cold Connecticut winters, loves the warm summers and health food, and is into exercising. Also, she's always liked ghost stories. This is interesting, considering that Dawn's mother bought an *old* (colonial) farmhouse, which has a secret passage that just may be haunted. (We're not sure.) Dawn is self-assured and an individualist. She doesn't care much about what other people think of her. And she dresses in her own casual-trendy, one-of-a-kind style.

Anyway, shortly after Dawn moved here, she and Mary Anne became friends. Now they're stepsisters. How did that happen? Well, Dawn and Mary Anne are partially responsible. They were looking through some old Stoneybrook High yearbooks and discovered that Mary Anne's father and Dawn's mother had been high-school sweethearts. But after graduation, they went in different directions. So Dawn and Mary Anne found a way for their parents to meet again, Mrs Schafer and Mr Spier began going out together and after what seemed like for ever, they got married! Then Mary Anne, her father, and her kitten, Tigger, moved into Dawn's house. (Jeff wasn't there, though. He had never adjusted to his new life and had returned to California to live with his dad.) Now Dawn and Mary Anne are living under the same roof, which has been difficult sometimes, but mostly okay.

While Claudia, Kristy, Mary Anne, Dawn and I are all thirteen and in the seventh grade, the two other BSC members are eleven and in the sixth grade. Their names are Jessi (short for Jessica) Ramsey and Mallory (usually known as Mal) Pike. And *they* are best friends, too. (I think it's interesting that there are so many pairs of best friends in the BSC, yet we get along really well as a group.) Anyway, Jessi and Mal are both the oldest kids in their families, they *love* reading (especially horse stories, and especially the ones by Marguerite Henry), they also like writing (Mallory more so than Jessi), and they both feel that their parents treat them like infants, even though they are old enough to babysit, and old enough for plenty of other things. I remember being eleven. It wasn't a great age.

Jessi comes from a pretty average family. She lives with her parents, her Aunt Cecelia, her eight-year-old sister, Becca (Charlotte Jonanssen's best friend), and her baby brother, Squirt. Guess where her family lives? In *my* old house! The one I lived in before we went back to New York and my parents got divorced. (Jessi's family moved here from New Jersey.) Jessi is a really talented ballet dancer. I've seen her perform. She's used to dancing onstage in front of big audiences, and she takes lessons at a school in Stamford that she had to audition for just to be allowed to enroll. Jessi has long dark eyelashes, big brown eyes, legs that go on for ever, and chocolatey brown skin.

Mal, on the other hand, comes from a huge family. She's got *seven* younger brothers and sisters, three of whom are identical triplets (boys). Mal's passion is writing. Also drawing. She'd like to write and illustrate children's books one day. Mal is not feeling very pretty at the moment. She's got wavy red hair (her hair and face *are* pretty), but she's also got glasses and a brace. Her brace, at least, is the clear plastic kind, so it doesn't show too much. Mal's parents will *not* let her wear contact lenses instead of glasses. They did, however, finally let her get her ears pierced (the Ramseys let Jessi do the same), so there's hope. Besides, the brace will come off eventually.

So there you are. Those are my friends: Kristy, Dawn, Mallory, Jessi, Mary Anne and Claudia, my best friend, with whom I needed to talk to pretty desperately. She lives not far from Charlotte, and I was hoping she'd be at home.

3rd CHAPTER

Claudia was at home and we had a nice talk. There's something comforting about Claud's room, as well as about Claudia herself. Maybe that's one reason the Babysitters Club meets there.

I suppose now I ought to tell you just what the BSC is, since I've mentioned it several times. The club was Kristy's idea. She got it back at the beginning of the seventh grade, when her mum was first dating Watson, and just after I'd moved to Stoneybrook (for the first time). In those days (they seem so long ago, but they really weren't), Kristy and Mary Anne still lived next door to each other and across the street from Claud. And Kristy and her older brothers were responsible for taking turns watching David Michael after school. That was a good arrangement – as long as one of them was free each afternoon. Of course, they weren't always free. And one evening, when Kristy, Sam and Charlie had realized that they were all busy the next day, Kristy sat eating pizza and watching her mum make one phone call after another, trying to arrange a babysitter for David Michael. Unfortunately, David Michael was watching, too, and Kristy felt sorry for him. (David Michael knew he was the source of some sort of trouble.) Too bad, thought Kristy, that her mum couldn't make just one phone call and reach a whole lot of sitters at once. And that was when she got one of the great ideas she's famous for. She and her friends could start a babysitting business! If they met somewhere a few times a week, parents could phone them and, just as Kristy had imagined, reach several sitters at the same time. Somebody was bound to be free (and get a job), and the parent would be satisfied. So Kristy phoned Claud and Mary Anne, and they decided to start the Babysitters Club.

Straight away, the girls realized that a fourth member would be a good idea. Claud suggested me, since she and I were already getting to know each other and I'd done a lot of sitting in New York. And so the BSC was up and running. Well, almost. We had to do a lot of work in the beginning. First, we planned to meet three afternoons each week in Claud's room (she has her own phone); on Mondays,

Wednesdays and Fridays, from five-thirty until six. Parents could phone us on Claud's line during those times and reach four experienced babysitters. But how would they know about our meetings?

"We'll advertise," said Kristy.

So we advertised. We told practically everyone about the BSC. We sent out leaflets. We even placed an advert in the *Stoneybrook News*. And when we held our first official meeting, we actually got job calls. After that, the calls kept coming, and they haven't stopped. In fact, we started getting so many that the club had to expand. Dawn joined us after she moved to Connecticut. Then, when I had to go back to New York, Kristy asked both Jessi and Mal to join. And then I returned. I was allowed back into the club. I became the seventh member, and I think I'll be the last. (Unless someone else has to leave.) Claudia's bedroom can't hold more than seven people. Well, comfortably. We'd have to work out how to drape new people around the ceiling.

The BSC is run very efficiently. Kristy makes sure of that. She's our chairman. The rest of us are officers, too, and we each have our own job or function. Kristy is chairman because the club was her idea. That makes sense. Also, Kristy is the kind of person who's good at running things. And with the great ideas she's always

25

getting, she keeps coming up with new ways to promote the club, to attract more clients, or to run the club even *more* efficiently. (Sometimes she gets carried away, but the rest of us let her know straight away when she's gone too far.)

Claudia is the vice-chairman. She should be, since the members of the club swarm into her bedroom three times a week, eat her junk food, and use her phone. Also, parents sometimes call Claud's line during non-meeting times, and Claudia has to deal with those job appointments on her own.

The secretary of the club is Mary Anne. She's neat and organized – thank goodness. Sometimes I think she works harder than anyone else at a meeting. Her job is to keep the record book up-to-date and in order. The record book was one of Kristy's ideas. In it, Mary Anne keeps track of our clients – their names, addresses, phone numbers, rates paid and special information about their children. More importantly, she schedules every babysitting job that comes in. That means that she has to know all our schedules – when Jessi has ballet lessons or Claud has an art class or Mal has a dental appointment. I don't think Mary Anne has ever made a scheduling mistake.

I am the club treasurer. Not to brag, but I happen to be very good at maths. It just comes naturally to me. I can add up numbers in a flash – in my head. My job is to collect the club subs from every member each Monday, to put the money in our treasury (a manila envelope), and then to dole out the money as it's needed. What do we use the money for? Lots of things. To help Claud pay her monthly phone bill, to pay Charlie Thomas to drive Kristy back and forth to meetings now that she lives too far away to get to Claud's on her own, to fund an occasional club party, and to restock the Kid-Kits when we run out of things such as crayons or stickers. Remember my Kid-Kit? Well, we've each got one. They're great babysitting aids. We don't bring them along *every* time we sit, but pretty often. The kids love them, so their parents see happy faces when they come home – and then they're more apt to turn to the BSC the next time they need a sitter.

Dawn's position is alternate officer of the BSC. That means that she can take over the job of anyone who misses a meeting. And *that* means that Dawn has to be familiar with the duties of each officer. I know that sounds difficult, but it isn't really that bad. Anyway, the BSC members don't miss meetings very often. So Dawn answers the telephone a lot.

Jessi and Mallory are junior officers. This is because they're eleven and not allowed to sit at night unless they're looking after their own brothers and sisters.

They're a huge help, though. By taking over a lot of the afternoon jobs they free us older members for the evening jobs.

Hmm. Let me see. A couple of other things about the workings of the BSC...

Just in case a call should come in that *none* of us can take (and that does happen every now and then), Kristy signed up two associate members of the club. These are reliable sitters who don't go to meetings, but whom we can call on in a pinch so that we won't have to disappoint our clients. Our associate members are Shannon Kilbourne, a friend of Kristy's in her new neighbourhood, and Logan Bruno. He's the boy Mary Anne used to go steady with!

Finally, *another* of Kristy's ideas was to keep a club notebook. The notebook is more like a diary. In it, each member is responsible for writing up about every job she goes on. Then we're supposed to read the notebook once a week to catch up on what's happening with our clients, and also to see how our friends have handled sticky sitting situations. No one likes writing in the notebook much (except Mallory), but we have to agree that it's pretty helpful.

"Ahem!"

It was later in the afternoon. Claud and I had finished our talk, and now all of my friends and I had gathered together. Kristy was sitting up straight and tall (well, as tall as she could make herself) in Claudia's director's chair. She was wearing her chairman's visor and, as usual, a pencil was stuck behind one ear.

"Ahem!" Kristy cleared her throat again loudly. She didn't have a cold. She was signalling to the rest of us that it was 5:31 according to Claud's digital alarm clock, the official BSC timekeeper, and reminding us that she'd called the day's meeting to order a full minute earlier.

What were the rest of us doing? Jessi and Mal were sitting on the floor, leaning against the bed and playing with these paper fortune-telling things they'd made (that, for some reason, they called Cootie Catchers). They kept opening and closing them and reciting, "Eenie, meenie, minie, moe. Catch a tiger by the toe. If he roars then let him go. Eenie, meenie, minie, moe. My mother said to pick just one, and this . . . is . . . it!" Then they'd read a fortune written under a flap of paper. (Cootie Catchers are hard to explain.) Claudia, Mary Anne and I were lined up on Claud's bed, leaning against the wall. And Dawn was straddling Claud's desk chair, sitting in it backwards, her chin resting on the top rung.

Claud had unearthed some packets of Maltesers and was passing them round. The smell of chocolate was driving me crazy. At least I wasn't the only one not eating them, though. Dawn wouldn't touch them. She nibbled at some crackers instead. I did, too, but the crackers didn't begin to quiet the rumbling in my *very* hungry stomach – too hungry for that time of day. A Malteser or two might have taken care of things.

Anyway, when Kristy began her throat clearing, we sat to attention. And just in time. The phone rang. Dawn answered it.

"Hello, Babysitters Club. . . Hi, Dr Johanssen. . . Next Tuesday? I'll ask Mary Anne to check. I'll get right back to you. . . Okay. Bye." Dawn hung up and faced the rest of us. "Sitter for Charlotte next Tuesday night from seven till ten."

While Mary Anne looked at the appointment pages in the record book, Jessi and Mal let out groans. An evening sitting job. Neither of them could take it. They were disappointed.

"Okay," said Mary Anne, glancing up. "Stacey, Kristy and Dawn are free."

"I've got a history test the next day," said Dawn. "I'd better stay at home where I can really concentrate while I'm studying."

"You take the job then, Stace," said Kristy. "You live much closer to Char."

So I got the job. Mary Anne pencilled it into the record book, and Dawn phoned Dr Johanssen to tell her who the sitter would be. That's how we always schedule jobs. Diplomatically. (Okay, *usually*. But we hardly ever argue at meetings.)

The rest of the half-hour passed busily. The phone rang a lot. (Twice, though, the calls were joke-calls from Sam Thomas.) At six o'clock, Kristy jumped to her feet, announcing, "Meeting adjourned!"

We all stood up. Mal and Jessi took out their Cootie Catchers again. Kristy looked out of the window to see if Charlie had arrived to pick her up. Dawn and Mary Anne hurried towards the door, and Claudia followed them. It was her turn to help with dinner that night.

Since no one was watching, I stuck my hand in the dressing table drawer where I'd seen Claudia hide the Maltesers.

I pulled out a packet and stuffed it into my bag.

4th CHAPTER

Ring, ring.

I could hear the telephone in my mother's room. Why doesn't she answer it? I wondered, feeling grumpy. Then I remembered that Mum had run over to the Pikes'. (Mallory's house is behind ours. Her back windows face our back windows.) Mum had said she'd be home in fifteen or twenty minutes.

So I would have to get the phone.

"Yuck," I said as I sat up. It was a Wednesday evening. I was lying on my bed, trying to find the energy to start my homework. I hadn't found it yet.

Ring, ring!

The telephone actually sounded impatient. I struggled to my feet and hurried into Mum's room.

"Hello?" I said, placing the receiver to my ear.

"Hi, Boontsie." It was Dad, using his awful baby name for me.

"Hi, Dad!" I tried to sound perky rather than dead tired.

"How are you doing? Are you ready for the weekend?"

"Of course," I replied. The coming weekend was a Dad Weekend. (I had conveniently forgotten to phone my doctor.) I would leave for New York on Friday afternoon, missing a BSC meeting. (Dawn would get to be the treasurer that day.)

"What train are you taking?" asked Dad.

"The one that gets in at six-oh-four," I replied.

"Great. I'll meet you at the Information Booth at Grand Central then."

"Oh, Dad. You don't have to meet me," I said. (We have this discussion practically every time I go to New York.) "I can get a taxi to your flat."

"You won't have time. I've booked dinner for six-thirty."

"But I'll have all my stuff with me," I pointed out, trying not to whine. "I don't want to lug it around some restaurant."

"Don't worry. You can put your things with our coats. Then we'll have a nice leisurely dinner before we go home."

"Okay." Inwardly I sighed. I had a feeling that Dad had made lots of plans for the weekend. Sometimes that's okay. But not when I'm so tired. And not when I have a mountain of homework to catch up on. I'd been planning to do some of it in New York. Oh, well. I could work on the train. (I'd be spending three and a half or four hours on the train that weekend.)

Dad *did* have a lot of plans. It turned out that he'd bought tickets to a Broadway musical for Saturday night. He knew about special exhibitions at practically every museum in New York. And he'd made reservations for about sixteen hundred meals. (I don't think my father ever cooks for himself. His fridge looks like a hole: empty.)

"Will I get to see Laine sometime?" I asked.

"Of course. She can come to the MOMA with us." (The MOMA is the Museum of Modern Art. It isn't Laine's favourite place.)

"Dad? Maybe we could skip the MOMA on Saturday afternoon? Then Laine could come over and we could just talk."

"Is that really how you want to spend Saturday?" asked Dad.

"Just the afternoon." I yawned.

"You sound awfully tired, sweetheart."

"I suppose I am, a little. I've got a lot of homework." I almost said to Dad then, "Couldn't we cancel this weekened so I could stay at home and rest and catch up on things?" But I knew I'd hurt his feelings if I did that.

"Well, try to get some extra sleep," said Dad matter-of-factly. "we've got a big weekend ahead of us."

Tell me about it, I thought. "Okay," I said.

"So I'll meet you at Grand Central just after six."

"Right." I stifled another yawn.

There was a pause. Then Dad said, "Is your mother there?"

"No." I didn't mean to sound evasive. I was thinking about the weekend that lay ahead, mentally trying to conjure up some energy.

"Where is she?" asked Dad suspiciously.

Uh-oh. He was going to do it again.

"She's at the Pikes'."

"At this hour?"

"Dad, it's eight-thirty."

"Well, what's she doing over there? And why are you at home alone?"

Oh, brother. I tried to sidestep what was coming by saying, "I've been able to stay at home alone for several years now. Sometimes I even babysit."

"Anastasia," said Dad. (Yikes, my full name.) "You know what I mean. Why is your mother at the Pikes' on a weekday night without you?"

"Because she and Mrs Pike are friends." Why did I always end up defending my parents to each other? And what if Mum *was* out on a date? She's allowed to go out.

She and my father are divorced, for heaven's sake.

"What does that mean?" asked Dad.

"It means that Mrs Pike's got a new dress and she wants Mum's opinion."

"Why?"

"Because she wants to get a hat to go with it or something. I don't know." I felt extremely exasperated.

"You're sure she's at the Pikes'?"

"*Da-ad.*"

"Okay. Just wondering."

And *I* was wondering what would happen if one day I said to my father, "Mum's out with someone. A *man*. He's taking her out to dinner. He's *really* handsome, he has a very important job and he's never been married. He's saving himself for the perfect woman, and that perfect woman is Mum." Or what would happen if I said to my mother one Sunday night when she was grilling me about my weekend in New York with Dad, "Mum, you should *see* who Dad's going out with. She's a really sophisticated, beautiful, *younger* woman. She's terribly wealthy, she has a penthouse flat in the city and a cottage in the country. She can cook *and* she's great at DIY."

If I ever said anything like that, would my parents be angry with *me*? I didn't want to find out.

"Stacey?" Dad was saying.

"Yeah?"

"You didn't answer me. I asked how school was going."

"Oh, it's fine."

"And the Babysitters Club?"

"Fine." I heard a door downstairs open and close. "Hey, Mum's home!" I exclaimed. Now I could show Dad that I'd been telling the truth.

"Can you put her on a for a minute?" he asked.

"Of course. Oh, and I'll see you on Friday. Bye, Dad. Hold on for Mum." I went to the top of the stairs and yelled, "Hey, Mum! Dad's on the phone. He wants to talk to you!" Then I dashed back to her bedroom. I didn't give my mother a chance to whisper frantically to me that she didn't want to talk to my father. If I had to get back on the phone and make an excuse for her, Dad would be *sure* something was going on.

In Mum's bedroom, I did the first of the two things that I really shouldn't have done that night. I listened to my parents' conversation.

When Mum picked up the phone in the kitchen, Dad greeted her with, "Did you decide on a hat?" He thought he was being crafty. If Mum didn't know what he was talking about, then Dad could assume she'd been out somewhere with 'Wonder Date'.

"A hat?" Mum repeated. "For Mrs Pike? Yes. Why?"

"Oh, never mind." Dad didn't really have anything to say after that, so he and Mum just went over the plans for my weekend in the city. I waited until they'd said goodbye. After each of them had hung up, I hung up the extension I'd been listening in on. Then I crept back to my room.

I lay down on my bed. My stomach was growling, and I desperately wanted something to drink – even though Mum and I had finished our dinner not very much earlier. I didn't want to go to the kitchen, though. I had a feeling Mum would be annoyed with me for having called her to the phone. Besides, did she know, somehow, that I'd eavesdropped?

I had to give her time to cool off.

I also had to eat something . . . anything. So I tiptoed across the room, gently closed the door, and then tiptoed to my desk. Feeling like Claudia, I pulled out a drawer, lifted up a pile of papers, opened an old pencil box, and removed – a large chocolate bar.

Ah, sugar, I thought.

I peeled back the top of the paper and, for a second, just breathed in the incredible smell of chocolate.

I was tired. *Sick* and tired, I reminded myself. And I was sick and tired of being sick and tired. Nobody else I knew had to stick to a diet like mine. Dawn didn't touch junk food, but that was her decision. My diet was *not my* decision.

Oh, I had longed for the taste of chocolate again. I had not had *any* since the doctors first discovered that I was diabetic. Claudia's Maltesers had tasted out of this world. When I'd eaten them, I'd felt as if I was tasting chocolate for the first time.

So I ate the whole bar of chocolate.

Then I felt really guilty.

I just couldn't win.

5th CHAPTER

The next day, after school, I sat for Charlotte again. Charlotte wasn't her usual quiet self. She wanted to *do* something, to *create* something.

"Like what?" I asked, thinking of arts and crafts and wishing I'd brought along my Kid-Kit that afternoon. "A painting?"

"No. Something more complicated."

Char and I were sitting opposite each other at the Johanssens' kitchen table. Charlotte grew thoughtful.

"More complicated? How about a paper sculpture?" I suggested.

Charlotte considered. Finally, she shook her head slowly and said, "I think I want to make fudge."

Fudge? Really? Of all things, why did Charlotte want to make fudge? I didn't think I could stand being within a mile of something chocolate and not eating it. Fudge making would be torture.

"Not paper sculpture?" I asked lamely.

"No, fudge. Please, Stacey? Puh-*lease*? We've got all the ingredients. And Becca could come over and help me. We would have so much fun. We could pretend we were chefs in a famous restaurant and that people came from miles around for our special fudge."

How could I ignore that? "Okay. Phone Becca," I said, hiding my disappointment.

"Thank you, thank you, thank you!" Charlotte cried. She was on the phone in an instant. "Hi, Becca, it's me," she said. (I smiled, thinking that only really good friends can do that.) "Stacey's here. She's babysitting for me. She said I could make fudge. Do you want to come over and help. . .? Okay, I'll see you in a few minutes."

By the time Becca arrived, Charlotte was already assembling ingredients on the kitchen table. Sugar, chocolate . . . *Ohhh*.

"Hi!" said Charlotte excitedly, as Becca entered the kitchen. "I'm Chef Charlotte and you're Chef Becca. We work at the Grand Sparkle-Glitter Hotel. We are famous chefs."

"World famous?" asked Becca, tying on the apron I had handed her.

"Galaxy famous," replied Charlotte. "Known on planets everywhere."

"Boy. . ." said Becca.

"Fudge is our speciality," Charlotte went on. "Isn't it, Stacey?"

I smiled. "Yup. And it's a *special* speciality on Saturn."

"No, make it Mars!" cried Becca.

"Okay, on Mars. But why?" I asked.

"Because we could pretend to travel there and be Martian fudge makers. Or we could make Milky Ways."

Charlotte giggled. Then she said, "Wait! I know! Don't start the fudge yet, anybody. I'll be right back!"

Char darted off. Becca and I looked at each other. What could Charlotte possibly be doing? our eyes asked.

We found out in less than a minute. Charlotte scampered back into the kitchen, wearing a pair of waving, bobbing antennae on her head. She handed another set to Becca.

"Put them on!" said Charlotte. "Now we'll really look like Martian fudge makers. Isn't this great?"

"Yeah!" agreed Becca.

So the two Martians set to work. At first I wished I had my camera. I'd never seen anything like Becca and Char, wearing antennae on their heads and oversized aprons around their middles, up to their elbows in chocolate goo. But soon my amusement faded.

It was the chocolate smell. I could barely concentrate on anything except that delicious, sweet odour. (Torture, torture.) I hoped I didn't look as upset as I felt. And soon I decided I didn't. The girls weren't paying attention to me.

"Look! We're flying past the moon," said Becca.

"Yeah. We should stop there. Did you know that moon dust is a good substitute for sugar? Let's stock up."

"Oh, no! We've gone too far!" cried Becca.

"Stop the rocket ship!" added Charlotte.

This conversation was being held while the girls stood quietly at the table, stirring the fudge in a plastic bowl with wooden spoons. Then:

"Eeetch!" screeched Becca, imitating the sound of skidding brakes. As she did so, she flung one arm up to her head, as if to protect herself from a crash. Unfortunately, it was the arm that was stirring the fudge, so she flung the spoon up, too. The fudge mixture flew behind her and sprayed the wall over the sink.

"Uh-oh," said Becca. "I didn't mean to do that. Honest."

"I know you didn't. It's okay," I told her. I stood up wearily and headed for the sink. "You two keep working," I went on. "I'll clear up."

"Thanks," said Becca with a sigh of relief.

While I dampened a sponge and began to wipe down the wall, Charlotte and

Becca continued their imaginary space game.

"The famous Martian fudge makers!" cried Charlotte.

"Have we reached Mars yet?" asked Becca.

"Not quite. Our spaceship feels. . . Oh, no! We're flying straight towards a huge meteor shower! We're going to crash!"

I turned round. My usually quiet Charlotte was becoming raucous. I almost told her to calm down but decided not to. Char hardly ever let go like this. Maybe it was good for her. So I kept my mouth shut, turned back to the wall, and continued scrubbing.

"A meteor shower!" Becca exclaimed. "What's that?"

"It's a – Wait a sec! We've hit it! . . . *Bam bam, bam!* Our ship is being bombarded by meteors. One is heading for our windscreen. Duck!"

At that moment, I heard the thump. In their excitement, their imaginations completely runaway, the girls had dropped to the floor. And somehow their bowl of fudge had come with them.

Chocolate, chocolate everywhere.

"Oops," said Charlotte.

The girls had stood up and were looking at me. I had turned round and was looking at them. I sighed.

"Can we start again?" asked Charlotte in a very small voice.

"If you two clear up this mess," I replied. "And if, when you start the next batch, you promise to be earthling girls, cooking in a nice kitchen in Connecticut. Without antennae."

"We promise," said Charlotte and Becca in unison.

They removed their antennae. I handed them a roll of paper towels and the sponge I'd been using, and they set to work. When the kitchen was clean, they began their project again. Calmly.

At last the fudge was finished.

"Can we taste it?" asked Char. "I know it's too close to dinner to have a whole piece, but can we each have a little sample?"

I smiled. "Okay." I cut each of the girls a tiny square of fudge.

"Yummm," they said, their eyes closed.

Yummmm, I thought. What I wouldn't give for—

"Hey!" cried Becca. "Guess what's on TV *right now*?"

"What?" asked Charlotte.

"That special. The one about the boy and his horse."

"Oh, I want to see that!" exclaimed Char. Then she added, "But we should help Stacey cut up the fudge."

She sounded completely unenthusiastic. And no wonder. Cutting up something

45

you've just made is the boring part. So I said, "You two go on and watch the special. I'll cut up the fudge." (I wouldn't have let them cut it up anyway, since you need a sharp knife.)

The girls ran off. I sliced the fudge into small, neat squares.

I put aside a pile for Becca to take home with her.

And then I wrapped two pieces in a serviette and stashed the bundle in my bag.

In my bedroom that night, I tried to concentrate on my homework. How had I got so far behind? My teachers were on my back, but at least they hadn't told my mother yet. If I could catch up, she'd probably never have to know.

But I was having trouble keeping my mind on my work. For one thing, I was hungry – again. I thought of the fudge in my bag. Do you know the phrase "money burning a hole in your pocket"? Well, the fudge was burning a hole in my bag. I couldn't stop thinking about it. At last, I reached into my bag, found the fudge, and ate both pieces. Oh, yum. I *craved* chocolate now. I'd bought a bar of chocolate at school and eaten it secretly in the girls' toilets that afternoon. And then there was that other bar of chocolate . . . and the Maltesers. . .

What was I doing to myself? I wondered. And just then, I realized that I hadn't yet packed to go to Dad's. I was supposed to leave after school the next day. So I would have to pack now. What a drag. I stood up slowly, went to my wardrobe, and pulled out my overnight bag. I could hear the phone ringing, but Mum was at home and she picked it up in her bedroom. When she didn't shout to me that I had a call, I began packing.

I forgot about the telephone completely until I heard Mum's raised voice say, "You are *spoil*ing her! I'm serious."

Dad must be on the phone. (I couldn't imagine Mum talking like that to anyone else.) And the "her" who was getting spoiled must be me.

I crept into the hall and tiptoed as close to Mum's room as I dared. I could hear her end of the conversation as clearly as a bell ringing on a quiet night. But her voice didn't sound pleasant and magical the way I thought an evening bell might. In a forced whisper (Mum must have realized how loudly she'd been speaking) she said, "Don't *buy* Stacey so many things this weekend. And give her a break. She's been pretty tired recently. She could do with a nice, quiet weekend. . . What. . .? Well, that's what I'm *say*ing. She doesn't need to eat out four or five times *and* go to the theatre *and* to museums." There was a long pause. Then Mum said harshly, "I am *not* jealous of what you can do for Stacey. Just give her some time off... All ri-ight," she went on, as if to say, "I know you're going to do everything anyway – and it will be a bad idea." After another, shorter pause, Mum said, "I'll be checking with Stacey on Sunday."

And Dad will be grilling me about Mum, her job and the non-existent Wonder Date. That was just great. I couldn't wait to be Stacey-in-the-middle again.

I tiptoed back to my bedroom. There was my half-packed overnight bag. There was my unfinished homework.

I finished packing. Then I put my books away. I stretched out on my bed, even though I was still dressed.

I had a horrible headache.

6th CHAPTER

I was all packed and ready to go. But leaving for New York was the last thing I wanted to do. It wasn't just Mum and Dad and the divorce. It was everything rolled into one: those things, plus school, plus not feeling well. To be honest, I was more concerned about my schoolwork that day than about anything else. I was *so* far behind. I was surprised that someone at school – for instance, my form teacher, who preferred to think of herself as my "friend" – hadn't phoned Mum yet. The only grade I was keeping up was in maths. The others were slipping, and I was in danger of failing French.

Late the night before, when something had been keeping me awake, I'd thought: Oh, no! What if someone at school *has* phoned my mother, and Mum just hasn't mentioned it because she doesn't want to worry me? What if I'm very ill and everyone knows but me. . .? That's paranoid, isn't it? I'm just thinking that way because I'm not feeling well and I haven't told Mum, so I have a guilty conscience.

At the end of school on Friday, I'd said to my friends when we gathered in the hall, "I'm sorry I have to miss today's club meeting."

"That's okay," said Kristy. "We understand."

"Boy, I wish *I* was going to New York with you," spoke up Mary Anne wistfully. "Do you think you'll go to the Hard Rock Cafe?"

"With *Dad*?" I replied. "No. We're eating at the Sign of the Dove tonight. And at the Russian Tea Room tomorrow night."

"Sign of the Dove *and* the Russian Tea Room?" squealed Mary Anne. "You're kidding . . . aren't you?"

"Nope."

"What are the Sign of the Dove and the Russian Tea Room?" asked Mallory.

"Only two of the finest dining establishments in New York City," Mary Anne answered. (If she sounded like a guidebook on New York, it's probably because she's read about a million of them. Mary Anne's dream is to live in New York City one day.) She went on, "You're so lucky, Stacey!"

"Dining establishments?" Mallory repeated. "You mean places to eat?"

"Awesome, fresh, *distant* places to eat," replied Mary Anne.

"I doubt if the owners of those restaurants would describe them like that, though," said Dawn.

"No, of course not," agreed Mary Anne, aghast at what she'd said. "They'd use phrases like, 'culinary delights' or . . . 'splendiferous spreads'."

"Spen*di*ferous *spreads*?" I laughed. I couldn't help it.

"Oh, okay. Then they're just four-star restaurants, at least in my book."

"Hey, Stace! There's your mum!" cried Claudia. "Listen, have a *great* weekend. Phone me on Sunday night when you get back and tell me everything."

"No, wait until Monday!" exclaimed Mary Anne. "Tell all of us about your weekend while we're holding our meeting. We'll want every detail."

"No, *you* will," whispered Kristy, but Mary Anne didn't hear her.

"What you ate, how it was prepared, who you saw in the restaurants. You're bound to spot celebrities," Mary Anne continued excitedly. "If you see anyone *really* famous, try to bring me back a personal souvenir, like a table scrap."

"You mean like a half-eaten piece of bread?"

"Yeah!"

"Mary Anne, that's *so* disgusting," said Jessi.

And Kristy added, "If, for whatever strange reason, I ever end up as a celebrity, don't let Mary Anne anywhere near me."

Mum honked the horn twice then. "I'd better go," I said. "We're going to be early for the train, but I hate to keep Mum waiting. I'll see you all on Monday."

We called goodbye to each other and, as my friends walked off, I headed towards Mum and our car. I was carrying a pile of books, hoping to catch up over the weekend.

"Hi!" I said to Mum as I opened the front door. "Did you bring my bag?"

"It's right there on the back seat," Mum answered. "Are you ready for the weekend?" She glanced sideways at me. "You look a bit pale."

"Just tired I suppose. I didn't sleep much last night. How are you? You didn't have any trouble getting off work early today?"

"Not a bit." Mum smiled.

A half-hour or so later, the train pulled into Stoneybrook station, where Mum and I had been waiting. She was sipping coffee, and I was finishing a diet coke.

"Have fun, sweetie!" called Mum, after I'd kissed her goodbye and was stepping into the train.

"I will," I answered. I found a seat by a

window and waved to Mum as the train ground into motion and my mother and the platform slipped away from me. I looked around. The train wasn't too crowded. In fact, my car was only about half full. Good. Things would be quiet. Maybe I could actually get some work done. I stowed my overnight bag on the floor by my feet, stuck my bag protectively between me and the side of the train, and put my book bag on the empty seat next to me. I reached inside, pulled out my French textbook, and turned to the chapter in which I'd been having trouble. (That was a number of chapters before the one we were already working on.) "The *pluperfect*," I muttered, and began to read.

The next thing I knew, an announcement was coming over the loudspeaker. "Station stop, Pennington. This is Pennington!"

Pennington! That was more than halfway to New York! I'd fallen asleep and had just wasted over an hour's worth of studying time.

I yawned and stretched. Yechh. I felt *awful*. No wonder I'd fallen asleep. Maybe I was coming down with something again. Boy, was I thirsty. Did I have a temperature? I didn't care. All I knew was that I needed something to drink – desperately. I was opening my bag when I remembered that the train didn't have a buffet car. *Now* what was I going to do? Well, I don't need to have a lemonade, I told myself. Water will be okay.

I looked behind me. Thank goodness there was a toilet in my carriage. A toilet would have running water and little paper cups, wouldn't it?

Sort of. I mean, I was half right. The toilet, which, by the way, didn't smell too nice, had a basin with nice, cold running water. It even had a bar of dirty pink soap and a stack of paper towels. But there were no cups.

I thought of this silly fold-up plastic cup that Mum used to bring along on holidays – for situations just like this. I used to tease her about that cup. Now I would have *paid* her for it.

I stood in the toilet and thought. The idea of *not* drinking some water didn't even occur to me. It was just a question of *how* to drink it. Finally I decided that there was only one thing to do. Wrinkling my nose, I washed my hands with the dirty soap. I decided that washing my hands with dirty soap was cleaner than not washing them at all. When I'd finished, I turned off the hot water, cupped my hands under the cold water, and drank . . . and drank . . . and drank. Ooh. At that moment, nothing – not even chocolate – would have tasted as good as that water did.

I went back to my seat.

Five minutes later I was thirsty again.

By the time I reached Grand Central Station, I had got up for drinks of water six more times. (And I'd been to the toilet twice.) When I saw Dad at the information booth, the first thing I said to him was, "Can I buy a lemonade?" My thirst was raging. I couldn't make it go away.

Dad looked closely at me as he took my bag. "Darling," he said. "Are you feeling all right?"

"Not really," I had to admit. I didn't think I could hide it any longer.

"What about dinner?" asked Dad.

"I'm *star*ving," I replied. "I've been starving all day—"

"Have you eaten?" Dad interrupted.

"Yes. Breakfast and lunch." (I didn't mention the packet of M&M's that I'd sneaked while I was hiding in the toilets.) "But I'm still hungry. The only thing is, I'm tired, too. I'd *like* to go out to dinner. I love the Sign of the Dove, but I'm just not sure – I mean, I don't know—"

Dad interrupted me again. "We'll eat at home. We'll order something in. Let's get a taxi straight away." He began hurrying towards the doors.

"Can I get a lemonade first?" I asked.

"Can't you wait until we get home?"

I shook my head.

"All right." Dad looked even more

concerned as he glanced around for the nearest drinks kiosk. He bought me a large diet lemonade. I'd finished it before we reached his flat.

That evening Dad ordered two kinds of salad and some sandwiches from a nearby delicatessen. We ate dinner in the kitchen, which was much more relaxing than eating out, even at the Sign of the Dove. I changed into jeans, and Dad and I just sat around and talked and ate.

I considered phoning Laine, but by nine o'clock I was *so* relaxed that I yawned and said, "I think I'll go to bed now."

"Now?" Dad looked surprised.

"Yeah, I'm really zonked." Thirsty, too, but I didn't say so.

It was hard to hide this from Dad, though. His flat is not all that big. There's only one bathroom, and it's closer to his bedroom than to mine. So he heard me when I kept getting up all night for drinks of water. (At least Dad's bathroom has clean soap and my own personal glass.)

Once during the night, Dad was waiting for me when I came out of the bathroom. "Are you okay?" he asked. "I knew we shouldn't have ordered from the deli."

"Oh, my stomach's fine," I answered. "It's just that I'm still so thirsty. I keep drinking water and then I have to go to the toilet all the time."

Dad frowned. "We should check your blood sugar level."

"*Now*?" It was three-thirty. "No way. I'm falling asleep. Tomorrow." I made my getaway as quickly as I could.

But by the next morning, when I was still drinking like mad, Dad didn't even suggest checking my blood sugar level again. He just said, "I think it's time to call the doctor, don't you?"

I nodded. Something was very wrong. I couldn't deny it any longer.

Dad ran for the phone. When he couldn't reach my doctor immediately, he put me in a taxi and we went to the nearest hospital.

7th CHAPTER

Sunday

Last night I babysat for Charlot Johansin. At first I was worreid that she midgt whant to play martins again but I didn't need to worry about that she never mention martins she whanted to play pairs. That was OK whith me. Beleive it or not I'm am a good pairs player so is Charlote so we were evenly matched. It turned out that I shold have been worreid about something else I shold have been worreid about Stacey. But I wasn't so I was pretty surprized to get the phone call form Mrs. McGill.

58

Saturday had been a good day for Claud. At least that's what she said the first time we had a chance to talk after I was admitted to the hospital. The taxi had taken Dad and me to one of New York's finest. However, having been in a number of hospitals, I can tell you that no matter what . . . the food *stinks*. It makes the food in our school cafeteria look – and taste – like gourmet dishes prepared by a great chef of the world. In a hospital nowadays, everthing that can be is individually wrapped – a slice of bread in a plastic wrapper, juice in a disposable plastic cup with a foil lid, etc. I would look at my plate after a meal, and it would practically be hidden by a pile of plastic and foil and paper.

What a waste.

If one person in one hospital generates this much rubbish, I thought, after my first "factory-fresh" meal, how can our environment possibly deal with it? How can – Oops. I am *way* off the track. I'll tell you about the hospital later. What I started to tell you about was Claudia and her good day. It began with a pottery class. At the end of the class, Miss Baehr, the teacher, chose Claudia's piece (I think Claud said she was working on a vase) as "exemplary" and asked the rest of the class to look at it before they went home. What a boost to Claudia's ego!

That afternoon, Claud studied for a spelling test. When Janine tested her on the words, Claud spelled seventeen out of twenty correctly (although you'd never know it from her notebook entry).

And then Claudia headed for the Johanssens'. After such a good day, she wasn't *too* worried that Charlotte would want to be a Martian chef again, but it had crossed her mind after reading my last notebook entry. However, the first thing Charlotte said when her parents left was, "Let's play Memory, Claudia, okay? I've got a new Memory game!"

"Have you?" said Claudia.

"Yup." Charlotte pulled Claud into the living room. "Here. Sit on the floor," she said. "The game's in my room. I'll go and get it."

Charlotte dashed up the stairs and a few moments later reappeared with a box of square cards, which she dumped on to the floor between her and Claudia.

Claud glanced at one of the upturned cards. "This looks different," she commented.

"I told you it was a new game." Charlotte grinned. "See, instead of matching up pairs of things, like two beach balls, you match animal mothers with their babies. A cat with her kitten, a goose with her gosling. Get it?"

"Yup," replied Claud. "This should be fun."

"It is," Char exclaimed. "I beat Mummy twice today."

"Really? That's terrific."

"Thanks. Now let's spread out the cards."

Charlotte and Claudia needed several minutes to shuffle the cards, turn them all face-down, and then arranging them on the carpet in a neat square of rows.

When that was done, Charlotte said grandly, "You may go first, Claudia. You're a new player, and I've already won some games."

"Okay." Claudia randomly turned over two cards.

"A puppy and a chick. No match!" cried Char.

Claudia turned the two cards face down again, and then Charlotte took her turn at trying to find a pair. No match.

The game continued. It was very close. Charlotte is very intelligent, and Claudia has a good visual memory. (Maybe that's why art is so appealing to her.)

The game was tied nine to nine when the telephone rang.

"I'll get it," said Char.

"Okay," replied Claudia. "But remember, don't say that your mummy and daddy aren't at home. Just say—"

"I know," Charlotte interrupted. "Say they can't come to the phone right now. Then take a message."

"Right." Claudia smiled.

"Oh, and no peeping at the cards while I'm gone," said Char.

61

"Promise," Claud answered. "No peeping. Cross my heart."

Charlotte ran into the kitchen. A few moments later she returned to the living room. "Claudia?" she said, with a catch in her voice. "It's Mrs McGill. She wants to talk to you. She sounds as if she's been crying or something."

"Are you sure?" said Claud, not even bothering to wait for an answer. She dashed into the kitchen and picked up the phone. "Mrs McGill?" she said.

My mother *did* sound as if she'd been crying. That was because she had been. My father had phoned her an hour or two earlier, to tell her what had happened. And as soon as they'd hung up, Mum had freaked out completely. Then she began packing two suitcases – one for her and one for me.

Mum thought about driving straight to New York that very moment, but Dad discouraged her. This was not because he didn't want to see her. It was because she wouldn't have enough time to pack before the last train of the night left for New York, and Dad could tell that Mum was much too worried to drive the car for two hours in the pitch-black. So Mum decided to drive to New York the next morning. (I know all this because Dad was sitting in a chair in my private room at the hospital when he phoned Mum. I couldn't help but hear his end of the conversation.)

Maybe it was no wonder that Mum had freaked out. She and Dad and I know that with the kind of diabetes I have, I can get ill no matter how strictly I stick to my diet and no matter how careful I am about giving myself the insulin injections. I suppose none of us wanted to think about that, though.

Anyway, Mum felt better (she said) if she kept herself busy. So first she packed the suitcases. She knew I'd brought only enough things for the weekend, so she put some extra underwear, some nightdresses, my bathrobe and a few other things into a bag for me.

Then she reorganized the wardrobe.

And then she phoned Claudia.

She knew that Claud and the rest of my friends should be told what had happened. *They* would freak out if they thought my mum and I had disappeared off the face of the earth. Anyway, a best friend should know when *her* best friend is in hospital.

"Hi, Claudia?" said my mother when Claud picked up the phone in the Johanssens' kitchen. Mum wasn't sure how to break the news.

"This is Claudia. Um . . . is everything all right?"

"Well, not exactly. I suppose I might as well come right out and tell you. Stacey went into hospital today. In New York."

"Oh, my lord," Claud whispered. "What happened?" (Claud told me later that the

63

first thing she thought of was *not* my diabetes but the horrible news reports she hears on TV every night. All the murders and attacks and muggings in New York. I don't think this is quite fair, because people can get mugged or murdered anywhere, but I suppose New York City *does* have a bad reputation.)

"Stacey's blood sugar has shot right up," my mum told Claud.

At this point, Claud actually sighed with relief. She'd been picturing me lying in bed with stab wounds or something. But then Mum went on to say, "She's pretty ill. The doctors aren't yet sure *why* her blood sugar level is so high. At the moment, they're just trying to stabilize it. Then they'll begin doing tests. A lot of them, apparently. She may be in hospital for a while. . . I just thought you'd want to know."

"Oh . . . oh, yes. I – I'm glad you phoned. I mean – I mean, I'm sorry Stacey's ill," Claudia stammered, "but I do want to know. . . Can I phone her?"

"Of course. Not tonight, because she needs her rest, but I know she'd be delighted to hear from her friends tomorrow. And if she's still in hospital next weekend – and I'm not saying she will be – but if she is, you can come and visit her on Saturday or Sunday, if your parents give you permission."

"Okay," said Claud, her voice shaking slightly. She took down the phone number that my mum gave her. Then Mum said she was leaving for New York the next day, asked Claud to get my homework assignments from my teachers (why did Mum have to think of *that*?), and told Claud not to worry and that she'd keep in touch.

When Claudia had put the phone down, she knew what she had to do first. Tell Charlotte the news. And she would have to do that carefully, since Charlotte is pretty attached to me.

"Char?" said Claudia, not wasting a moment.

"Yes?" Charlotte had been standing in the doorway to the kitchen all that time. She knew something was wrong.

"Char, um, let's go into the living room and talk." Claudia led Charlotte to the sofa and sat down next to her. "I suppose the easiest way to tell you this is just to say it. Stacey's in hospital in New York."

Charlotte looked horrified. "Did the Stalker get her?" she asked shrilly.

"What?" said Claud.

"The Stalker. I've been reading about him in the paper. He stalks girls and then he—"

"Oh, no!" interrupted Claud. "It's not that. Stacey's ill. Her diabetes."

"Oooh."

And in a flash, pretty much as Claudia had expected, Charlotte fell apart. She began to sob. All Claudia could do was hold her. She couldn't tell her it would be all right, because she didn't know that for sure. However, when Char had calmed down, she and Claud put together some things for me: a crossword puzzle book, a drawing by Charlotte and a few other things. Claud promised to post them to me on Monday. During the rest of the evening, Charlotte asked questions such as, "Is Stacey going to die? What if she has to stay in New York where her doctors are and she can never come back here?"

Poor Claudia was stuck with the job of trying to answer those questions – and later with phoning the other BSC members to spread the bad news.

8th CHAPTER

On Sunday at midday, Mum walked into my room in the hospital. I had been in there for almost twenty-four hours. Dad had stayed with me the whole time, except for a few hours very early in the morning when he'd gone back to his flat to try to catch up on some sleep and change his clothes. I had told Dad that he didn't *have* to stay with me, but when he said that he wanted to, I was secretly glad. You won't understand why unless you've been in hospital yourself. (I mean, apart from the time you were born. That doesn't count, because you don't remember it.) The thing is that no matter how hard the doctors and nurses and other staff members try, most hospitals are very impersonal places. They feel impersonal, anyway. At least to me. I don't care how many clowns come to visit or how many pretty posters and balloons decorate the walls of the ward. A hospital is still a hospital, and that means:

—There are so many nurses and doctors you can't keep track of them all. (I wished my specialist was there, but he was on holiday for two weeks. He wasn't even in New York.)

—You wonder how the nurses and doctors know who *you* are. (Are you really Stacey McGill – a person – or are you just "that patient in Room 322"?)

—You have hardly any privacy. All day long, you are poked and prodded, sometimes by people you've never seen before. All night long, the nurses check on you. This happens about once an hour. Since the door to your room is left open, there is always light flooding in on you. On top of that, squeaky, rubbery nurses' shoes constantly step into your room. Sometimes they approach your bed, and then you know that the night nurse is going to take your temperature or something.

For these reasons and plenty more, I was glad that Dad stayed with me. *Dad* knew I was Stacey McGill, his daughter, a person – and not just "that patient in Room 322". He could be my advocate. Oh, well. I'm going off the subject again.

As I started to say before, Mum turned up on Sunday around midday.

"Mum!" I cried when I saw her. (I don't know why I sounded so surprised. She had told Dad, and he had told me, that she was going to come to New York that day and stay until I was out of hospital.)

"Hi, sweetie," Mum replied. Her eyes were bright with tears, but she didn't cry. Instead, she leaned over, kissed me, and placed a big, fuzzy, pink pig next to me. "I tried to find Porky Pig," she said apologetically, "but that's hard to do at such short notice." (Porky Pig is a favourite of mine. I can even imitate his voice.)

"That's okay," I said. "I don't think I've ever had a stuffed pig before."

Mum's eyes cleared and she smiled at me.

I smiled back, looking from my mum to my dad and back to my mum again. When was the last time all three of us had been in the same room at the same time? I wasn't sure, but it definitely felt nice. My family was together again.

But not for long.

As soon as Mum had taken off her coat and found a place to sit down, Dad jumped up from his chair. "I could do with some coffee," he said. (Or, I *think* that's what he said. He left the room so fast I wasn't sure.)

Mum and I were alone. Before Mum could ask how I was feeling or what the doctors were doing, I said, "I hope my room isn't too messy for you."

Mum looked puzzled. She glanced around her. "You've just got here, Stacey," she said. "You haven't had time to make a mess."

I laughed. "No, I mean my room at Dad's flat. You probably couldn't even find the bed. I left clothes everywhere. Your suitcase—"

"Darling," Mum interrupted me, "I'm not staying in your room. I'm staying at Laine's flat, in the spare bedroom."

"You're staying at the Cummingses'?" I exclaimed. "*Why?*"

"Because," Mum said calmly, "your aunt and uncle are away." (I have some relatives in New York, but I don't see them very often.)

"Why aren't you staying at *Dad's* though?" I asked.

"Stacey, your father and I are divorced."

"I know you're divorced," I said grumpily. "Does that mean you can't stay under the same roof together?"

"In our case, yes," Mum answered.

I think she was going to say something else, but she changed her mind and stopped speaking. So I changed the subject.

"Look at my arm," I said. I held it out. In the crook of my right elbow were two plasters. "They keep taking blood to do tests on it. And every time I go to the toilet, I have to go in a plastic cup. They keep testing my urine. It is *so* embarrassing... Have you talked to any of the doctors yet?"

"Not yet," replied Mum. "Your father has, though. And no one knows much more than they did yesterday."

I suppose that was why doctors and nurses were bustling in and out of my room more than usual. Not only did they continue to take blood and check my urine, but they tested my kidney function. They also raised my insulin. But that didn't seem to make a difference.

"It hasn't made a difference *yet*," Mum reminded me. "But it might."

I nodded. I was worried, though.

When Dad returned an hour and a half later (that was a *long* coffee break), Mum rushed out as quickly as my father had, earlier, saying that now *she* needed coffee.

"Dad," I said when Mum had left, "you don't have to stay with me."

"I know I don't—" Dad started to say.

"No, really. It's okay," I told him. "I think I need some sleep. I'm pretty tired. Why don't you go home for a while?"

"We-ell." Dad was hedging.

"I need my address book and some more toothpaste," I told him.

"All right," said Dad.

I was alone. I didn't really need the address book or the toothpaste, but I did need some time alone to think (despite what I'd said earlier about wanting people with me, and hospitals being impersonal and everything). I turned my pillow over, eased myself against it, and started to think about Mum and Dad.

Before I had got too far, though, I found myself just gazing round my room. It was like every hospital room I'd ever been in, except that it was private. Sometimes I have stayed in double rooms, or even in rooms with three other kids. Private rooms are much smaller, of course, but then you do have a sense of privacy. (Duh. That's why they're called "private" rooms.) Well, you don't *really* have privacy because of the constant stream of doctors, nurses, porters, maintenance people and anyone else who feels that he or she has a job to do in your room. But at least you don't have to put up with other patients and their visitors.

In my room was my bed. (Of course. That's the most important feature of any hospital room.) It was one of those beds that can change position. During the day, I raised the part that's under my top half so that I could sit up. On the bed were sheets and two thin white blankets. I think the same company must provide blankets to every hospital in the world. The sheets, by the way, were stamped with the name of the hospital. I can't imagine why. Did anyone think that a patient would actually want to be reminded of her hospital stay by stashing a set of the sheets in a wardrobe at home? Anyway, apart from my bed were two chairs for visitors, a bed table so that I could eat meals comfortably upright in bed, a chest of drawers, and a TV. The TV was bolted into a corner of the room, up near the ceiling. Now why was it bolted? It would be awfully hard to smuggle a television set out of the hospital. I mean, a TV isn't exactly something you can slip into your pocket or hide under your coat. Oh, well. I was glad there was a TV at all, even if it was bolted to the wall at such an angle that I got a stiff neck if I watched it for too long.

I looked out of the window. The view was of a grey building across the street. I couldn't tell whether it was an office building or some kind of warehouse. Whatever it was, it was boring. But a room with a bad view was better than a room with no view at all. I watched two pigeons swoop by. And, for the first time, began to worry (and I mean *really* worry) about why I was in the hospital. Was it all the chocolate and sugar I'd eaten recently? Maybe. But I hadn't been feeling well before I'd gone off my diet. I suppose the sugar hadn't helped things, though. How ill was I? Why did I need a change in my insulin? Learning that I'm a brittle diabetic hadn't concerned me too much. As long as the insulin was doing its job, I was okay. But now the insulin wasn't working. What if the doctors raised the level and I got better for a while, but then needed even *more* insulin? What if no one could find a way to give me *enough* insulin? What if . . . I died? I'd read a book once about a girl with diabetes who couldn't get enough insulin and she *did* die. I also knew that was extremely rare. But what if it happened to me?

Stop playing "what if", I told myself.

I couldn't, though. I felt trapped in my room. Four stark white walls, the dreary building across the street, not even my pigeons now. What if the doctors couldn't find—

"Hey, Stace," said a familiar voice.

I turned my gaze from the window to the doorway. There stood Laine Cummings.

"Hi!" I exclaimed. "Come on in. Have an uncomfortable seat." (The two chairs for visitors were made of hard, moulded plastic.)

Laine grinned. She slumped into one of the chairs. "Ah. Restful," she said.

I laughed. "So how did you get in here?"

"Hey, I'm over twelve," replied Laine. "Anyway, at the visitors' desk downstairs I just pretended I was part of this crowd who was going to visit other people. Then I got off on your floor. . . So how are you feeling?"

"Relieved, I suppose," I told her. "Well, not completely relieved. I'm really worried about whatever is wrong with me. But I have to admit that now that I'm in the hospital, awful as it is, I'm glad to know there are all these doctors around. I feel taken care of."

"That's good," said Laine slowly. She frowned slightly. Then her face brightened. "Wait till you see what I've brought you!" she cried.

"What?" I asked suspiciously. Laine's taste can sometimes be strange. Once, she had given me a key ring that looked like a cicada (a really ugly, *big*, green, winged insect). That was bad enough. But when you pressed a button on the underside of the insect, its green eyes flashed on and off, and it made this weird high-pitched humming sound. (I scared people with it until the battery wore out.)

"Okay," said Laine. "First" (she reached into a plastic bag that she'd put on the floor beside her chair), "these beautiful flowers. Anyone who's in hospital should receive flowers. So here you are." Laine handed me a bouquet of electric-blue plastic tulips. They were wrapped beautifully in cellophane.

"Charming," I said. I stuck them in an empty water jug.

"And they're easy to look after," Laine went on. "No watering, and they don't need any light. Just dust them once in a while."

I giggled. "Okay."

"Next," said Laine, reaching into the bag again, "is this." She handed me a small box. "It came from the Last Wound-Up."

"Oh, great!" I cried. (The Last Wound-Up is this shop near Laine's flat that sells all sorts of funny wind-up toys.) I lifted the lid. Inside the box lay a huge brown plastic spider – wearing a pair of red glasses. Laine wound him up and let him wiggle across my bed table.

"Gross!" I exclaimed. But I couldn't help laughing.

"Can you believe it?" Laine said. "I got the red glasses somewhere else. They just happened to fit the spider."

"He looks very scholarly," I told Laine.

Laine and I watched the spider crawl across the table and fall to the floor.

"Two more things," Laine continued. She handed me a big, gaudy get-well card.

"Thanks!" I said.

"And last," began Laine, "I've talked with the members of the BSC. I phoned Claudia this morning, and it turned out that your friends were holding an emergency club meeting. I have messages from everybody. Mal says she's thinking about you. Mary Anne and Dawn say they miss you. Kristy says to get back on your feet because Dawn isn't all that good at handling the money in the treasury. Jessi promises to write to you so you'll be sure to get post in the hospital. And Claud says she's getting your homework assignments – and that she misses you an awful lot."

By the time Laine left, I felt loads better.

9th CHAPTER

Wednesday morning.

I was beginning my fourth full day of hospital life. My blood sugar level had been lowered, but the doctors still weren't satisfied. They were giving me an awful lot of insulin just to keep the blood sugar *down* — but not where it should be. However, I was feeling better. I was much less tired. Mum encouraged me to make my days as normal as possible.

That meant getting dressed, doing homework assignments (plus *still* trying to catch up in most of my subjects), and waking up fairly early. No sleeping late. (Drat.) Of course, it would have been difficult to sleep late anyway, considering the bustle of hospital life. What was a typical day like for me? Well, I'll tell you.

Wednesday began at seven o'clock when my alarm clock (yes, my alarm clock) went off. I got up, changed out of my nightgown and into ordinary old clothes (jeans and things), and washed as well as I could in my bathroom. (The bathroom had a basin and a toilet, but no shower or bath.)

At seven-thirty I flopped on to my bed and began doing schoolwork. My mum had said that getting dressed and leading a "normal" life would make my hospital stay more manageable. And it did, I suppose. Even so, the hospital was still a foreign place, with lots of intrusions on my "normality".

For instance, by eight o'clock, I was deeply engrossed in writing an overdue essay for social studies, when I heard trolleys and machinery being rolled down the hall. "Yuck," I said to myself. "It's—"

"Time for vital signs," said a nurse cheerfully as he wheeled a blood pressure instrument into my room. (I happen to know that the blood pressure instrument is called a sphygmomanometer. This is the kind of information you pick up when you spend a lot of time in hospitals and doctors' surgeries.)

"Okay," I replied. I put my books aside. Then I sat in one of the visitor's chairs and, without being told, opened my mouth and extended my arm.

The nurse grinned. "I suppose you're an old pro now," he said.

"Unfortunately," I agreed.

The nurse put a thermometer in my mouth and wrapped the black cuff of the sphygmomanometer around my upper arm. He listened to the pulse in the crook of my elbow with a stethoscope for a few moments, made a note on a chart, and then said, "Stand, please." I stood. I don't know why they take your blood pressure when you're both sitting and standing, but they do.

I sat down again. The nurse removed the cuff from my arm. Then he took my pulse. Just as he was finishing, the thermometer beeped. I should add here that the thermometer wasn't a normal glass one. It was plastic and wired to a box. A tone sounded when the thermometer had taken your temperature, and then your temperature flashed up digitally on the box, like the time on a clock radio. Another miracle of modern medicine.

"All systems go," said the nurse.

"Good," I replied. Then I added, "Thank you."

The nurse's name was Rufus. (That's what was printed across the front of his uniform.) But I didn't bother to remember it. A different nurse had taken my vital signs every morning.

I returned to my social studies essay, only to be interrupted by a trainee bringing breakfast. So I set aside my books and tried to force down the disgusting food.

Before I had finished, Mum appeared in the doorway.

"Hi, lovey," she said, settling into a chair.

"Hi!" I answered.

"How are you feeling today?"

"Not bad," I replied. "But I know the doctors are going to fiddle around with the insulin again."

"Well, that's what you're here for."

"I suppose so."

"Have you been working already?"

I held up the paper with my half-finished essay on it. "I'm trying," I told Mum, "but I keep getting interrupted. Vital signs and breakfast."

"And me."

"No, not you," I said, but I saw that Mum was smiling. She wasn't serious. "Is Dad coming today?" I asked her. (Monday and Tuesday had been somewhat unnerving with Mum and Dad trying to see me but at the same time trying to avoid each other.)

"I don't think so," Mum answered. "I mean, not until later. He has a full day of meetings. I'll stay with you, though."

"Only if you want to," I told her. "Don't feel you have to sit in that chair all day. I've got homework to do, and anyway, I'm much better."

"Okay." Mum actually did leave for a while. She said she was going to have a cup of coffee somewhere and then take a taxi

81

into town (where most of my favourite shops are located). She said she was on a secret mission. I hoped it involved clothes shopping – for me.

Mum left as the trainee nurse came to retrieve my tray. I picked up my essay again, and *again* I was interrupted, this time by a whole group of people in long white coats. I recognized only one of them. He was a doctor who'd examined me several times. He began talking, and the rest of the people took notes on clipboards they were carrying. I suppose that they were medical students or new doctors or something, and that my doctor was their teacher.

The doctor greeted me, then turned back to his class. "This patient," he said, "is a thirteen-year-old girl" (he didn't even use my name!) "with juvenile onset of diabetes. She was hospitalized last Saturday, at which time she was found to have an abnormally high blood sugar level, despite the fact that she's been taking insulin and has been on a strict diet since she was first diagnosed. . ."

The doctor went on and on, and the students scribbled away on their clipboards and sometimes glanced at me. I felt like a goldfish in a glass bowl or an animal in a cage at the zoo. The doctor talked about me as if I wasn't sitting just three feet away from him.

Anyway, the group left my room after five minutes or so. Once *again*, I settled down to work. And this time I was able to accomplish a few things even though a nurse came to check my blood, and even though I knew *Jeopardy* was on TV, followed by a rerun of *The Beverly Hillbillies*. After a bland, tasteless lunch, I worked some more. Then Mum reappeared with a Benetton bag. (Yea!) In it was a beautiful emerald-green sweater and a matching beret.

"Oh, thank you!" I cried. I tried on the new things immediately. Mum stayed with me until about four-thirty. Then she said she had to leave. I think she was afraid she'd run into my father, since she wasn't sure when he was going to turn up that day.

By 4:45, I was alone.

At 5:00, the telephone rang. I reached over to pick it up.

"Hello?" I said. "This is the funny farm. To whom are you speaking?"

There was a pause. Then a giggly voice said, "I'm speaking to you!"

It was Claud. Even so, I said, "Oh. Well, who's this?"

"It's me! Claudia!"

"I know that," I replied. We were both laughing by then.

"How are you doing?" Claud wanted to know.

"Okay," I answered. "I feel a lot better, but I might have to stay here for a while."

I knew Claud wanted to ask, "Why?" I also knew that she could tell I didn't feel like talking about whatever was wrong with me. So after a brief, uncomfortable pause, Claudia said, "The rest of the club is here. Everyone wants to say hi."

"The rest of the club is there?" I repeated. "It's only five o'clock."

"I know. We all wanted to talk to you, so we met early."

"Hey, how are you lot going to pay for this phone call?" I asked suspiciously. "It's going to be an expensive one."

"With treasury money?" Claudia replied.

I sighed. Then I said, "Well, I suppose I'm worth it."

Claud laughed. She put Kristy on the phone. Kristy announced that Emily Michelle had learned a new word: stinky. Only she pronounced it "tinky." *Every*thing was tinky, according to Emily.

I talked to the rest of my friends. When Jessi got on the phone, I asked her how Charlotte Johanssen was doing.

"She's . . . fine," Jessi replied, and quickly handed the phone to Mallory.

By the time we'd hung up, it was nearly five-thirty. We were all talked out, and I was worried that the cost of a few more half-hour, long-distance phone calls would clean out the treasury. Oh, well. I needed my friends. I could tackle the treasury problem when I returned to Stoneybrook.

Just as I was putting the phone back in its cradle, Laine turned up. But we'd hardly had a chance to say hello before a parcel was brought into my room by a hospital porter. (You never know when you are going to get post at the hospital. It seems to appear whenever it pleases.)

"A parcel!" said Laine. "Cool. Who's it from?"

I checked the return address. "Hey, it's from Charlotte!"

I ripped the brown paper off the box, then lifted its lid. The lid was labelled CARE PARCEL. Inside I found the things that Claud and Charlotte had put together on the evening of my first day in the hospital.

"I think I'll call Char," I told Laine. I was remembering Jessi's response when I'd asked her how Charlotte was doing. Was something wrong?

I soon found out. Char was ecstatic to hear from me. At first. But soon her excitement changed to a series of questions, each one more anxious than the first. When was I going to get out of hospital? When would I come back to Stoneybrook? I *was* coming back to Stoneybrook, wasn't I? Why hadn't my insulin injections been working? Did I *really* feel better, or was I just saying so to be polite? Char's last question was, "Do people die from diabetes?" (I'm pretty sure she meant was *I* going to die?) But before

85

I could answer her, she said, "Oh, that's okay. Never mind, Stacey. I'll ask my mum. She'll know the answer."

Gently, I turned the topic of conversation to her parcel. But when I put down the phone, I said to Laine, "I think I've got a problem with Charlotte."

10th CHAPTER

Friday

Stacey was right. Well, she was half right. There was a problem with Charlotte. But it wasn't just Stacey's problem. We all had to deal with it. It was a good thing that the day after her talk with Char, Stacey called Claud to tell her what was going on. This was good because Claudia called me, knowing that I was going to sit for Charlotte last night. I went to the Johanssens' prepared for trouble. It wasn't major trouble -- like sitting at the Rodowskys' for Jackie, the walking disaster. Still, it worried me, so I talked to Dr and Mr Johanssen when *they came home from their meeting. They're worried, too, but they think the only solution is to wait. To wait for Stacey to come home, all well, so that Charlotte can see that everything is okay.*

Dawn hasn't babysat at the Johanssens' as much as some of the other members of the BSC have, but she knows plenty about Charlotte from listening to us (especially me) talk about her, and from reading the club notebook. Also, as she wrote in her own notebook entry, I called Claud after my conversation with Charlotte, and Claudia called Dawn. Dawn, knowing how attached Charlotte is to me, immediately understood that Char might be overly concerned about my health. She might be weepy or clingy.

Dawn was not, however, expecting to find that Char had become such a hypochondriac, even though the Johanssens themselves had warned her about it.

"I actually kept her home from school two days this week," Dr Johanssen told Dawn. Dawn had rung the bell a few moments earlier. She had expected Charlotte to answer the door, but she was nowhere to be seen. Dr Johanssen had answered the door instead, and now she,

Dawn and Charlotte's father were holding a whispered conversation in the front hall.

"But she's not ill?" Dawn said.

"I don't think so. One day she said she had a sore throat. The next day she said her stomach hurt. Now she's complaining of a headache and an earache. She hasn't had a temperature, and her appetite – even on the day she stayed at home with the stomach ache – has been perfectly normal."

"Okay," said Dawn slowly. "In case she *is* ill, I'll keep her quiet tonight."

"That won't be hard,' said Mr Johanssen with a smile. "She's upstairs in bed. I think she plans to stay there." The Johanssens left a few minutes later. Dawn headed upstairs with her Kid-Kit.

"Charlotte?" Dawn ventured, as she reached the doorway to her bedroom.

"Hi, Dawn," replied Char.

It was only seven-thirty, and already Charlotte was wearing her nightdress. However, she was not actually *in* bed. She was sitting on the covers, looking through a book.

"How are you feeling?" asked Dawn.

Charlotte paused. Then she replied, "My neck hurts."

"Your neck? I thought your mum said you have a headache and an earache."

"I do. I mean, I did," Char answered. "But now my neck hurts."

"Have your headache and earache gone, or do you still have them as well as the problem with your neck?" Dawn asked.

"I think they've gone. It's really just my neck. . . I hope I haven't got a pinched nerve in my spine.

"A pinched nerve!" exclaimed Dawn. "How do you know about pinched nerves?"

"I know about a lot of things. Mummy's a doctor," Charlotte reminded Dawn.

"Oh," said Dawn. She sat on the edge of Charlotte's bed. "Well, if you have got a pinched nerve, how do you think it got that way?"

Charlotte shrugged. "I don't know. But I'm pretty sure that's what it is. I should tell Mummy. I should be wearing one of those neck braces. And if the brace doesn't work, then I might need an operation . . . in hospital."

"Well, for now," said Dawn, "why don't you just try to hold your head still."

"Okay," Charlotte answered uncertainly.

"So what do you want to do tonight? Have you finished your homework already?"

"Yes," said Charlotte. "Only I don't think it matters. I probably won't be at school tomorrow. You know."

"Yeah. What with the pinched nerve and all." Dawn hoisted the Kid-Kit on to the bed. "We'll do something quiet tonight."

"Good, I'd better not over exert myself."

"You'd better not *what*?"

"Over exert myself," Charlotte repeated. "That means that I—"

"I know what it means," Dawn interrupted. "I'm just a little surprised that *you* know what it means."

"It's something my mum says sometimes," Char informed Dawn. From the Kid-Kit she had pulled a copy of an old looking book called *The Dachshunds of Mama Island*. "What's this?" she asked.

"Oh. That used to belong to my mother," said Dawn. "She found it and gave it to me. The story is a little old-fashioned, but I think you'd like it."

"Okay. Let's read it," said Charlotte.

Dawn opened the book, being careful of its tattered dust jacket. She began to read to Charlotte, who seemed interested in the story straight away. After about ten minutes, though, Charlotte said, "Dawn? I don't feel very well."

"Your neck?" asked Dawn. "Why don't you lie down then."

Charlotte shook her head. "It isn't my neck. It's my stomach. It's sort of aching and burning. I think maybe I have an ulcer."

Dawn tried to come up with an appropriate response. Finally she said, "People your age hardly ever get ulcers. If you have one, it's pretty rare. What did you eat for dinner tonight?"

"Dawn, this is not indigestion," said Charlotte indignantly.

"All right. How bad is the burning?"

"Why?" asked Charlotte warily.

"Because I'm thinking that maybe I should phone your parents to see if I can give you some medicine or something."

"Oh, no," said Char quickly. "You don't have to do that. But – but now I'm really tired and thirsty. Do you think I've got diabetes . . . like Stacey?"

What *was* this? Dawn asked herself. Sore throats, pinched nerves, ulcers, diabetes. She didn't think Charlotte was ill at all. But how could she convince Charlotte of that?

Then Dawn had an idea. "No, I don't think you have diabetes," she said quickly. "Listen, Char, do you still have your old doctor's kit?"

"Yes. It's in my toy chest."

Dawn located the black plastic bag and set it on Char's bed. "I'd better give you a check up," she said. "I should find out what's wrong with you before I interrupt your parents at their meeting."

"But—" Char started to say.

"No buts," replied Dawn. "Hold still. I have to listen to your heart."

Dawn held the plastic stethoscope to Char's chest. She stuck a fake thermometer under her tongue. She used every instrument that was in the kit. She even wore the pair of red, glassless glasses.

"You're perfectly healthy," she announced several minutes later.

"Can I talk now?" asked Char.

"Yup."

"Dawn, that is *toy* doctor's kit. And anyway, you aren't a doctor."

Dawn sighed. "Shall we read some more?" she asked.

"Okay. Even though I really do think I have diabetes. I may be anaemic, too."

Dawn spent the next hour trying to convince Charlotte that she wasn't ill. Nothing worked. At last she told Char that a patient needs plenty of sleep, so she put her to bed. Dawn tiptoed downstairs with her Kid-Kit and worked on her homework until the Johanssens returned.

"How was Charlotte?" asked Mr Johanssen.

"Fine," Dawn replied, gathering up her books and papers, "except that she now thinks she has a pinched nerve in her spine, an ulcer, diabetes and possibly anaemia."

Dr and Mr Johanssen exchanged a glance. "Hmm," said Char's mother.

"I hope I handled everything all right," said Dawn. She explained what she'd done.

"That sounds fine," Dr Johanssen replied.

"Um . . . can I ask a question?" said Dawn.

"Of course."

"Why do you think Charlotte is acting like this? It must have something to do with Stacey, but I don't know what."

"We're not sure ourselves," said Dr Johanssen. "But I can guess. Charlotte misses Stacey an awful lot. She wants to see her. I have a feeling that somehow Charlotte thinks – although she's probably not aware of it – that if she gets ill enough, she'll end up in hospital with Stacey. Then she can spend time with her, and also reassure herself that Stacey is all right and that she really will come back to Stoneybrook."

"Wow," said Dawn. "What are you going to do?"

"We've been thinking about that," said Mr Johanssen. "We've just decided to be extra patient and understanding with Charlotte. And to let her be in touch with Stacey as often as she likes."

"All right," replied Dawn.

11th CHAPTER

On Friday morning, my first thought as I woke up was, Oh, no. It's back.

What's back? I asked myself, and realized that I didn't have an answer. I just knew that, although I was still lying in bed (I hadn't even sat up yet), and although I'd slept for almost nine hours, I felt incredibly tired – as if I couldn't move a muscle.

Impatiently, I slapped at my alarm clock. When it stopped ringing, I glared at it. "I don't like you this morning," I told the clock. "And I will not obey you. I am not going to get up."

Actually, I thought, I couldn't get up. I didn't want to admit this to myself, but . . . I . . . felt . . . rotten. The idea of getting dressed and doing schoolwork seemed beyond reason.

I rang for a nurse. Five minutes later, one hurried into my room, pausing briefly to check the nameplate outside my door. She didn't even know who I was. And I wished desperately to be with someone who knew me.

I was scared.

I read the nurse's name tag. Darlene Desmond. A film star name.

Okay, so now we each knew each other's name.

"Stacey?" said Darlene Desmond.

I couldn't tell whether that was her way of asking what was wrong, or whether she wanted to make sure that I really was Stacey McGill, as the nameplate said. Oh, well. What did it matter?

"I don't feel too good," I told the nurse. "For the past few days I was feeling a lot better. But now . . . I don't think I can even get out of bed."

That was bad enough. But when Darlene Desmond asked if I needed to go to the toilet and I said yes, she brought me a *bedpan*. A freezing cold, embarrassing bedpan.

And she stayed with me while I used it.

After I had finished, I said, "I'm supposed to get up, get dressed, and start my homework." But even as I said that, my eyelids were drooping.

"Not this morning," replied the nurse. "You can go back to sleep. I'll talk to your doctor as soon as I can."

"I don't have a doctor," I mumbled. "I

have three million of them." But either the nurse had already gone, or I'd just dreamed those words. At any rate, no reply came.

I fell fast asleep. I slept right through Vital Signs.

I didn't wake up until the trolleys carrying the breakfast trays began to rattle up and down the corridor. Usually, I enjoy meals. They're never any good, but at least they're a distraction. That morning, though, I had no appetite. I pushed the bed table away and leaned against my pillows. I wasn't tired enough to go back to sleep, but I didn't have the energy to do anything – even turn on the television.

So when Mum arrived a little bit later, that was how she found me; just lying in bed in a quiet room, my uneaten breakfast sitting on the table.

"Are you okay?" Mum asked before she'd even taken off her coat.

"Not really," I replied. I hate seeming weak with my parents, but just then I was too worried to care.

"You know Mum. I feel almost as bad as I did last Saturday."

"I'll go and find a doctor," said Mum quickly.

"No, don't. I mean, you don't have to. This nurse – her name was Ruby Diamond or something – said she'd get a doctor for me."

"How long ago was that?" Mum wanted to know.

"I'm not sure. I fell asleep. She came in straight after my alarm clock went off. What time is it now?"

"Nine," my mother replied. "The doctor should already have been here."

She stood up, looking furious, just as a man named Dr Motz strode into my room. I tried to remember if I'd seen him before.

I decided that I must have, because he greeted me with, "Good morning, Stacey. Good morning, Mrs McGill. Stacey, one of the nurses said you aren't feeling very well this morning. Can you tell me what's wrong?"

I almost said, "*You're* supposed to tell *me* what's wrong." But I knew what he meant. Besides, Mum was in the room. So I described how I was feeling. The doctor looked slightly concerned, but all he did was raise my insulin dosage (again) and send in a stream of people to draw my blood and perform other tests, some of which had been performed once or twice earlier in the week. Before Dr Motz left he said, "Take it easy, Stacey. I'll look in on you again this afternoon or this evening. And I'll let you know the test results as soon as possible."

"Okay," I replied. "See you later."

And mum called after him, "Thank you!"

Mum and I were alone again. We'd spent a lot of time together that week, just the two of us. Usually, I was working and Mum was reading. But that morning Mum said, "Do you want me to turn on the TV, darling?"

I shook my head. "No. Not now, anyway. . . Mum?"

"Yes?"

"Is Dad going to visit me today?"

Mum couldn't quite look at me. "Maybe after dinner," she said.

"Why doesn't he come during the day?" I wanted to know. "He's hardly been here at all, ever since. . ." I realized that he'd hardly been there at all since my mother had first arrived. But I didn't want to say that. It would hurt her feelings. "Ever since, um, Sunday," I finished up.

"You know your father's a workaholic," said Mum, still not looking directly at me.

"Yeah. But couldn't he visit me during his lunch hour? Or on his way to the office in the morning?"

"I suppose so. Well, maybe something deeper is going on."

"Such as what?" I asked suspiciously.

"Stacey, your father loves you very much—"

"It doesn't feel like it at the moment."

"He loves you so much," Mum went on, "that I think it's been difficult for him to visit you in hospital. He doesn't like seeing you like this."

"Well, I can't help how I look or what happened. If Dad's staying away from me because I'm ill, then he's being very selfish."

At last Mum's gaze met my own. I knew I'd gone one step too far. "That's unfair, Stacey," she said in measured tones. "Listen to me. Do you want to know why your father hasn't been around to see you very often? It's partly because of the things I've just told you, but mostly it's because of me."

"You?"

Mum nodded. "Well, Dad and me. We're having a hard time being together right now. So since I can take time off from my job, and your father can't, we agreed that I would stay with you during the day as much as possible, and he would visit you later."

"Oh." Was that true? Could my parents *really* not be in the same room together for a half-hour or so? Maybe *that* was what was bothering me; not so much that Dad was only spending a little time with me, but that my parents couldn't be together so that the three of us could seem like a family again – at least while I was ill.

"Maybe you should turn on the TV after all," I said to Mum. I didn't want to continue our conversation, but I couldn't just lie in bed while Mum sat next to me, both of us shrouded in silence.

Mum switched the TV on and, after changing channels for a while, we discovered an old Woody Allen film. We began to laugh. By the time the film had finished, our argument was forgotten. Well, maybe not forgotten, but over.

At 3:15 that afternoon, Laine turned up. For the past three days, she'd come in to see me as soon as school had finished.

I know she was surprised to find me in bed in my nightdress, my hair uncombed. She couldn't hide her surprise. But Mum and I tactfully ignored it, and then my mother excused herself to get a cup of coffee so that Laine and I could spend an hour or two alone together.

"So?" Laine said, sitting down.

"So I'm not feeling too great today." I thought I owed her an explanation.

"Maybe you'll feel better tomorrow," Laine replied with that tone of false cheer that I've heard too often whenever I've been in hospital.

"Maybe," I echoed.

Laine leaned down and reached into a shopping bag. "I've brought you something."

"Again?" I couldn't help smiling. Every time Laine came to visit me, she brought one or two weird things. My room was filling up quickly – with a camouflage-print hat that said "Daddy's Little Hunting Buddy" across the top, a pair of light-up sunglasses, glow-in-the-dark jewellery, a pen that looked like a palm tree, and more.

Laine handed me a box. "Open it," she said.

I lifted the top off. Inside lay a hand mirror. An ordinary, plastic mirror. I had mentioned that I wished I had a mirror in my room, but I was surprised to see such an ordinary present from Laine.

"Hold it up," Laine instructed me.

I lifted it in front of my face – and the mirror began to laugh at me!

So did Laine. "Can you believe I found that?" she asked, trying to calm down. "It came from the same place that sells those cicada key rings."

I laughed helplessly, and Laine started up again. We spent the next two hours encouraging anyone who entered my room to look in the mirror.

One nurse practically fainted.

By the time Laine and my mum had left and I was waiting for Dad to arrive, I felt better – emotionally, anyway.

But that didn't last long. Dr Motz came back just as my supper was being placed in front of me.

"Stacey," he said gravely, "tomorrow we plan to start a new procedure with you. I'll need to talk to your parents first, but I'm sure they'll okay it."

"What are you going to do?" I couldn't keep my voice from trembling.

"Just hook you up on an IV drip for a while. I want to see how you do with insulin dripping constantly into your veins."

"Great," I said.

When Dr Motz left, I began to cry.

12th CHAPTER

"There she is!"

"No, that's not her."

"It says 'Stacey McGill' by her door, you dweeb."

Was I dreaming? It was Saturday, I was pretty sure of that. I was also sure that I'd been woken up at around eleven-thirty the night before when a nurse hooked me up to the IV. Then I'd fallen asleep again and had all these weird dreams. Now I could have sworn I heard the voices of my Stoneybrook friends. But that couldn't be true. Why would they be in New York?

"Oh, my lord!" someone cried. "She's got a needle stuck in her arm!"

"SHHH!" said someone else.

"She's sleeping," a whispered voice added.

"No, I'm not." I struggled to open my eyes – and found myself facing Claudia,

Dawn, Mary Anne and Kristy! "Are you really here?" I asked.

"We really are," said Claud.

My head cleared as the four BSC members crowded into my room, hugged me awkwardly (since I was lying down), and dropped presents and cards all over the bed. My friends were beaming.

"We took the train down early this morning," Dawn informed me.

"And we didn't get lost in Grand Central Station," added Mary Anne.

"Jessi and Mal wanted to come, too, but their parents wouldn't let them," said Claudia. "They sent some things for you, though. And Jessi hopes you got the letter she posted."

"Oh, wow! I can't believe this!" I exclaimed. "I thought I was dreaming. But this is a dream come true."

"Boy, the hospital certainly has made you maudlin," said Kristy. She held up one hand and rubbed her index finger back and forth across the top of her thumb.

"What's that?" everyone asked.

"The world's saddest story played on the smallest violin."

I giggled. If I'd had the energy, I would have thrown a pillow at Kristy. Instead, I raised the bed so that I could sit up. I looked at the stuff strewn over my covers.

"You lot are going to spoil me," I said. "What on earth did you bring?"

"Lots of things," replied Claud. "But before you look at them, tell us how you're feeling. You, um, don't sound as good as when I talked to you on Thursday."

"I don't feel as good as I did then." I held up my arm. "They're dripping insulin directly into my veins now. Maybe that will make a difference."

"Gosh," said Mary Anne slowly.

"Let's not talk about it, though," I went on. "I want to know how you're all doing, and everything that's been happening in Stoneybrook."

"Okay," replied Claud. She was perched on my bed, Dawn next to her. Kristy and Mary Anne were sitting in the chairs.

"Wait," said Kristy. "Before you start, Claud, let me try to make myself even more comfortable than I am right now. This chair is really incredible. I've never felt anything quite like it." Kristy tried to adjust herself so that her spine and shoulder blades weren't mashed up against the back of the hard chair. It was impossible. "Ah. I think I'd like a set of these for my bedroom," added Kristy.

The rest of us were laughing, and I said, "Sorry about that. If you want a padded chair, you have to leave the hospital."

"Have you lot finished?" asked Claud. "I want to tell Stacey what's going on."

We tried to compose ourselves. "Okay. Go ahead," I said.

"Well," Claud began. "First of all, *every*one misses you. When you open some of these cards, you'll be surprised to see who they're from. People are always asking about you, wondering when you'll be back home."

"Like who?" I wanted to know.

"Like *every*one. The Newtons, especially Jamie; the Perkinses, especially Myriah and Gabbie; kids at school, including . . . *Ross Brown*; Mr—"

"Ross Brown?" I interrupted. (I had an incredible crush on him.) "Does he know I like him?"

Claudia shrugged. Then she grinned and said, "*He* likes *you*."

Wow. . .

"Mallory's been collecting the post for you and your mum," said Mary Anne. Then she interrupted herself by saying, "My, these chairs *are* comfy." (We laughed.) "Anyway, yesterday she gave me the interesting-looking stuff. That's here along with everything else."

"Great," I replied. "So what's happening at school?"

"Let's see," Dawn answered. "Alan Gray got suspended for setting off a stink bomb in the boys' toilets on the first floor."

"Gross," I said.

"And Cokie's had a nose job."

"What?" I cried. "You're kidding!"

"Nope. That's why she's been away so much."

"So what does she look like?"

"Like she's had a nose job," said Kristy. "You can always tell."

"That's funny. You've never noticed *my* nose job," I said.

Kristy turned pale. "*Your* nose job?" she whispered.

"Just kidding," I said.

There was a moment of silence. Then we all began to laugh again. We laughed so loudly I was afraid a nurse would come in and kick my friends out. But nothing happened.

"Okay, open your things," Claudia finally managed to say. "Open the cards first. Then open the parcels."

"Yes, Mummy," I answered obediently. I picked up the envelope lying nearest to me and slit it open. Inside was a get well card, handmade by five-year-old Claire Pike. GET WELL SON it read, which made us giggle.

"Mallory warned me that the card was a little off. Claire didn't want any help with it," said Dawn.

"I like it the way it is," I announced. "'Get well, son'." (More laughter.)

I opened up card after card. In the middle of this, a nurse came into my room (not Desma Diamond or whoever that other nurse was). She took some blood, and then she left quickly. She didn't say anything about my having four visitors, which isn't

108

allowed. This was because Claud and Dawn were hiding in the bathroom.

"The coast is clear," I called, as soon as the nurse and my blood sample had gone.

Dawn and Claudia returned to the bed. I continued opening cards. I had never seen so many! There were homemade ones from some of the kids I sit for, and shop-bought ones from the kids at school, the parents of some of my babysitting charges and even three of my teachers.

"Now for the presents!" cried Claud.

"No, wait," said Mary Anne. "You're forgetting. Remember what's—" She pointed to the hallway beyond my door.

"Oh, yeah," said Claudia. She dashed out of my room and returned carrying the world's biggest get-well card. It was at least two feet by three feet.

I felt relieved. I was a bit dizzy, and just the thought of opening the presents made me feel more tired than ever. I also felt a bit clammy. And shaky. It was weird. But I tried to hide this. I didn't want to scare my friends.

"Whoa!" I exclaimed, looking at the card that was so big it blocked my view of Claud. "Who's that from?"

"Everybody," answered Kristy.

And it was. The card had been signed by parents, teachers, kids, my friends' brothers and sisters, and of course, my friends themselves.

I was exclaiming over the card when that same nurse burst into my room again. She appeared so quickly that Dawn and Claudia didn't have time to duck into the bathroom.

Uh-oh, I thought. Now I'm in for it. I've broken the sacred two-visitor rule.

But the nurse barely noticed my friends. She bustled to one side of my bed and abruptly turned off the IV drip, although she did not remove the needle from my arm.

"What are you *doing*?" I cried.

"Your blood sugar level is dropping," the nurse replied. "Doctor Motz will be here any second. And your mum's on her way up from the cafeteria."

As the words were coming out of her mouth, I heard a voice on the intercom system paging Dr Motz.

Claud and Dawn stood up. So did Kristy and Mary Anne. They backed away from the bed and huddled near the door.

Nobody, except the nurse, said a word.

Just a few seconds after the IV drip had been stopped, Mum raced into my room. She had beaten Dr Motz. "Hi, girls," said Mum as she whisked by my friends. Then she did a double take. "Where did you come from?" she asked. But she didn't wait for an answer. Instead she began whispering with the nurse.

I felt a cold wave wash over my body and settle in the pit of my stomach, where it sat like a block of ice. I knew something was wrong. Again.

Dr Motz ran into my room then. He took one look at my friends and said, "Okay. Everybody out. Right now."

"Everybody out?" echoed Claudia.

"On the double," said Dr Motz, not bothering to look at Claud. He began examining me and talking to the nurse.

"We'll see you later," called Claudia in a trembly voice.

"Yeah, we'll wait outside until they let us come back," added Kristy.

"Okay. And thanks for all the cards and. . . " My voice trailed off because my friends had disappeared, wanting to escape Dr Motz, I suppose. But I had seen something awful on their faces: fear.

They were afraid for me.

So was I.

By the evening, however, I felt better. Also more optimistic. After a day of testing and consulting, Dr Motz had come up with a new solution to my insulin problem. I was to start injecting myself with a mixture of the kind of insulin I'd been using before plus a second kind of insulin that I hadn't used before.

And now that my blood sugar level was more normal, I had some energy and was hardly dizzy at all. I had even eaten dinner.

"Mum?" I said when the frantic pace of the day had slowed down and just my mother and I were left in my room. "Can my friends come back now?"

"Oh, darling, I'm sorry," Mum replied. "They finally had to go home. Their parents wanted them home by six o'clock."

I didn't answer her. I stared out of the window.

"Claudia said to be sure to tell you to open your cards and presents as soon as you feel like it. She said she's sorry they had to leave, but they'll phone you tomorrow or on Monday before the club meeting."

"Monday. . . I thought I'd be out of here by Monday," I said.

"Well. . ." Mum replied helplessly. And then she began to put on her coat. "Your father will be here any minute."

Was he working today, on a Saturday? I wondered. But what I said was, "Mum, can't you stay here until Dad comes? I want the three of us to be a family again. Even if it's only for five minutes."

"Stacey—" Mum said.

"I'm sorry," I interrupted her. "I understand that this is a bad time for you and Dad, but if we could all be together for a while, then . . . well, it's really important to me. *Really* important."

I knew I wasn't playing fair. I knew that I was pressuring Mum because I was ill and that she would give in because she felt guilty. But she did give in. She removed her coat and sat down again.

"This evening may not be what you're hoping for," she warned me.

"Yes, it will. It'll be wonderful." I couldn't believe Mum was staying! "Maybe we can watch TV together, or—"

I stopped talking. Mum wasn't listening to me. She was looking at the doorway.

My father had arrived.

13th CHAPTER

"Stacey!" Dad exclaimed. He strode across the room to my bed and gave me a big hug. "How are you feeling? I'm glad you're off the IV."

"I'm fine," I replied. "Well, better anyway." Since Dad hadn't spoken to my mother, I added, "Um, Dad, Mum is still here. She's going to stay for a while."

"Well, I could do with some coffee," my father said.

"No, don't go!" I cried. "Stay here with me. I want to see you two together again." (What I meant was, "I want to get you two together again.")

"All right," said Dad. He moved the empty chair as far from Mum as possible – right to the opposite side of my bed.

That's something, I thought. He isn't leaving. It's a start.

But that's all it turned out to be. A start. The rest of the evening was a disaster. Looking back, I don't know whose fault it was. Maybe nobody's. Or everybody's. Anyway, it doesn't matter.

For about ten minutes my parents remained civil by speaking only to me. I was in the middle of two conversations, one with Dad and one with Mum. Dad asked a question about the hospital, and I answered him. Then Mum told me about a phone conversation she'd had with Mrs Pike, and I asked her a question about Mallory. And so on.

Things began to go downhill when Dad said, "So what on earth happened this morning, Boontsie?"

To my surprise, Mum answered him before I could. "If you'd been here you'd know yourself."

"I was *work*ing," said Dad testily. "Besides, I thought we agreed not to visit Stacey together. You said you didn't want to see me."

Mum ignored that last comment. "You were working on Saturday?"

"Yes, I was working on Saturday. If I don't do my job properly, I'll get sacked and then I'll lose my insurance. Do you think we could afford to have such good care for Stacey if I didn't have insurance?"

"What a hero," muttered Mum.

"Excuse me?" said Dad.

"Nothing."

"Nothing worth repeating," I spoke up.

For a moment, Mum and Dad looked at me as if they'd forgotten I was there. Or as if they'd forgotten I was their daughter. Then they picked up the argument again.

"Hospital care is not cheap," said Dad.

"I know that. So why did you put Stacey in a private room?"

"Because I love her."

"Are you saying I don't?"

"All I'm saying is that last weekend Stacey arrived in New York from Stoneybrook looking worse than I've seen her since she was first diagnosed."

I felt my cheeks redden hotly.

"So?" Mum prompted Dad. She was trying to force him into saying something, but I'm not sure what the something was.

Dad remained silent.

"If Stacey's ill, it isn't my fault," Mum finally said. "You know as well as I do that the doctors weren't sure what course this particular kind of diabetes would take. Stacey is a *brittle* diabetic. The doctors have had trouble controlling her blood sugar from the start. Besides, she's had flu, and you know what infections can do to her. It's a miracle she hasn't—"

Mum was cut off. By me. "Shut up!"

"Anastasia," my father said warningly.

"You shut up, too!" I cried, even though

I know that neither of my parents is fond of that term. No one likes to be told to shut up.

Mum and Dad just stared at me.

I went one step further. "And get out of here. Right now. I'm not kidding."

A look of surprise, then anger, then confusion crossed Mum's face. "Stacey."

"I mean it. Get out. I thought maybe all three of us could be together for fifteen minutes without an argument, but I suppose not."

Dad stood up slowly. "You were not", he said in a low voice, "brought up to speak to *any*body that way, young lady. Whether you're ill or not."

"I know," I replied after a few moments. I glanced at my mother. She was crying. And both she and Dad were gathering their things together, putting on their coats. But they looked as if they were moving in slow motion.

I watched them until they were almost ready to leave. Just as they were about to walk out of the door, I spoke up. "I'm sorry," I said. "I'm *so* sorry. But you two should listen to yourselves sometimes."

Mum dabbed at her eyes with a tissue. My father fumbled around for a handkerchief. I couldn't believe it. I'd made *him* cry, too. For a moment, I felt the anger rise up all over again: I had the power to move two adults to tears, but not to make them act civilly towards one another.

I pushed the anger away. "Can you," I said to Mum and Dad in a steady voice, "come back on Monday, instead of tomorrow? I need some time to think."

"So do I," said Dad.

"So do I," said Mum.

"Okay. So I'll see you on Monday?"

My parents nodded. Then they left, Mum slightly ahead of Dad. I watched them to see if Dad might rest his hand on Mum's back. Or if Mum might send a flicker of a smile to Dad. But they were isolated, living in separate worlds.

Ordinarily, after a scene like that, I would have given in to tears. I might even have enjoyed them, let them run down my cheeks in salty tracks, not bothered to wipe them away. Not that night, though. I was feeling too angry. And, I realized, too strong. My body was getting better, so I allowed my mind to get better, too.

"Look out for number one," I murmured. Where had I heard that? I wasn't sure. But I did, suddenly, know what it meant. And that's exactly what I was doing – looking out for number one, for *me*. I was putting me first, along with my thoughts, feelings and emotions.

How, I wondered, did I *really* want to spend Sunday? Out of hospital, I answered myself. But that wasn't possible. Okay. Next best thing? With my friends, forgetting about my parents. Well, *that* might be possible. I could find out in just a few minutes, with two or three phone calls.

I dialled Claudia first, praying that she was at home.

She was. She answered on the first ring. "Hi, Dawn," she said.

I paused. "Claud, it's me."

"*Stacey?!* I was expecting Dawn to call me back. She – Oh, never mind. It's a long story. How are you? You sound okay. I mean, you sound *good*."

"I'm feeling pretty good," I said truthfully. "And I was wondering something. I know this is a lot to ask, but would you and Dawn and everyone want to come back tomorrow? Would your parents let you?"

"Come *back*? To New *York*? Well . . . okay. I mean, I suppose so. I mean, yes, definitely, but I have to see if we've got enough money and everything."

I laughed. "I know what you mean. If you could all come, I would *love* to see you. But I know that's asking a lot."

"Not so much," replied Claud. "Let me talk to the others. I'll get back to you."

"Okay," I replied. "I'm going to phone Laine in the meantime. You don't mind, do you? I mean, if Laine comes over for a while tomorrow? I thought it would be fun if we all got together."

"Fine with me," said Claud.

We hung up then, and I dialled Laine's number.

"Hi," I said. "It's Stacey. Um, is my mum back yet?"

"No," Laine answered.

"Oh. Well, she probably will be soon. And she might be upset." I told Laine what had happened earlier.

"Wow," said Laine when I'd finished. "So do you want her to phone you when she gets here?"

"No," I replied. "I really do need to wait a while until I talk to my parents again. But I was wondering if you could come and visit tomorrow. Claudia and everyone might be here, too. If they get permission from their parents, and if they can get past the nurses."

"Great!" exclaimed Laine. "See you tomorrow."

On Sunday I woke up early. *Every*one had permission to visit. (Well, not Mallory and Jessi, but the others. Plus Laine. I couldn't wait.)

I asked a nurse to help me wash my hair in the basin. Then I put on fresh clothes. I even put on some make-up that Laine had sneaked to me a few days earlier. I added jewellery and, when I looked at myself in the mirror, thought I looked like the same old Stacey. The same old reasonably *healthy* Stacey.

By one o'clock everyone had arrived. Laine and my Stoneybrook friends greeted each other happily. (They'd met before.) Then they all found seats (Kristy and Mary Anne refused to sit in the plastic chairs again, so they perched on the bed with Laine, while Claud and Dawn risked the chairs.)

"Guess what?" I said. "I never opened my presents yesterday." I pointed to a corner where one of the nurses had hastily stacked the boxes and packages while my friends were being ushered out of the room.

"Good. Open them now," said Claud.

At that moment, a nurse entered my room.

"Aughhh!" exclaimed Mary Anne in a muffled shriek. "Another blood test?"

"No," said the nurse, smiling. "A guest check. I see you have. . ."

Her voice trailed off as she looked at me. My face was practically pleading with her. Please, please, *please* let everyone stay, it was saying.

"I see that you have," the nurse began again, "exactly two visitors."

"Oh, thank you," I said, letting out the breath I'd been holding.

"You're welcome. Just don't make too much noise, okay?"

"No problem," I replied.

The nurse disappeared. "We're safe," I announced in a loud whisper.

121

"Good. Open the presents," said Claud She piled them on my bed. They tumbled around Laine and Kristy and Mary Anne.

I reached for one. But Claud moved it away. "How about this one?" she asked, handing me another.

"Okay," I said. I looked at the tag. "Why, it's from *you*!"

Everybody giggled.

Claudia's present was a breaded bracelet that she'd made herself.

"Thanks!" I exclaimed as I slipped it on.

That was the beginning of an afternoon of (quiet) fun.

I even managed to forget about Mum and Dad.

14th CHAPTER

Thursday

I sat for Charlotte this evening, and she came down with (in this order) Lyme disease, arthritis, a kidney problem, and a sore throat. It's hard to be annoyed with her, though. I think she really doesn't feel one hundred per cent these days. I also think that's because she's tired. Every night she lies awake worrying about Stacey.

Well, by the end of this evening, her worries were over -- and she had made a miraculous recovery, considering that the last *time I had a sore throat I missed a week and a half of school.*

What cured Charlotte? A phone call from Claudia, that's what. And I should add that anyone who heard from Claud tonight felt better when they got off the phone....

"Mary Anne?" said Charlotte plaintively.

"Yeah?" replied Mary Anne.

"I don't feel well."

It was about eight o'clock on Thursday evening. Mary Anne had been at the Johanssens' for half an hour. When she had arrived, Charlotte was already in her nightdress, sitting on her bed, looking slightly pale.

Mary Anne didn't panic when Charlotte said she wasn't feeling well. She knew what was going on with Char. So she said calmly, "How don't you feel well?"

"I'm sort of achey. And I'm *really* tired. I think my neck is getting stiff. I probably have Lyme disease. We'll know for sure if a rash appears where I've been bitten by the tick. Of course, a rash doesn't always show up. Then you have to get a blood test done or something."

"Char, when was the last time you played in the woods?"

Charlotte paused. "I don't remember," she said after a moment. "But that doesn't matter, you know. Carrot spends lots of time outdoors." (Carrot is the Johanssens' dog.) "He could bring deer ticks into the house. I could have been bitten right here in my bedroom."

Mary Anne didn't know what to say to that.

I could sympathize. When my parents had come back to the hospital (separately) on Monday, I hadn't been sure what to say to *them*. The night before, I had thought of some things I wanted to say, like, "Don't put me in the middle," or, "Let the *doctors* talk about my disease. They're the experts, not you."

But did I say those things? No. I was too chicken. All I could do was apologize over and over again. "I'm sorry," I kept saying. "I don't know how I could have told you to shut up and to get out."

"Well, you were upset," said Dad.

"You weren't feeling well," said Mum.

"That's true. . ." But those weren't the most important reasons behind what I'd said. The important reasons were much more complicated. By Thursday, when Mary Anne was sitting for Charlotte, my parents and I had got over Saturday. We were no longer angry. Mum and Dad had accepted my apologies. But I wasn't much closer to telling them what was *really* wrong than I had been before our argument. However, I was thinking all the time. I knew that when I was ready, I would have plenty to say and that I would say it without getting angry or upset.

At any rate, it didn't matter that Mary Anne had no calming words for Charlotte. That's because Char was *convinced* she had Lyme disease. There was no talking her out of it. Besides, while Mary Anne was still coming up with something to say, Charlotte shrieked suddenly and pointed to the carpet.

"What's wrong?" asked Mary Anne, alarmed.

"I see a deer tick! Right here in my room. Now do you believe me?"

"Where's the tick?" Mary Anne was slightly annoyed.

"Right there," Char answered, still pointing to the rug.

Mary Anne peered at the floor. "That little thing?" Her eyes had finally rested on a tiny black dot working its way from one side of the room to the other.

"Deer ticks are small," Charlotte informed Mary Anne. "No bigger than the full stop at the end of a sentence."

Mary Anne isn't mad about insects, but she examined the moving speck from short range. At last she said, "Char that's not a tick. It's a very small spider."

"How can you tell?"

"It's too big to be a deer tick. Besides, it just *looks* like a spider."

"Oh. Well, can you get rid of it?"

"I won't kill it, if that's what you mean," Mary Anne replied. "But I'll put it outside. I'll set it free."

"Okay," agreed Charlotte. And by the time Mary Anne had put the spider outdoors, Charlotte had another complaint. "You know, I really think I might have arthritis," she said when Mary Anne returned. "My back hurts. People can get arthritis in their backs, you know. . . Or, wait! I bet I have a kidney disease. People sometimes get backaches when they have a kidney infection."

"They also get temperatures." Mary Anne touched Char's forehead. "And you haven't got one."

Charlotte was silent for a while. Finally she said, "Let's read, Mary Anne. Let's read about. . ." Charlotte scanned her bookshelf. Then she asked Mary Anne if there were any new books in her Kid-Kit.

"Just one," answered Mary Anne. She fished around in the box until she found a copy of *The Five Little Peppers and How They Grew*, which is a story about the Pepper family, not a lot of vegetables.

"Ooh, that looks good," said Char.

"It is. I think you'll like it. Do you want me to start reading?"

Charlotte nodded. She snuggled against Mary Anne. But Mary Anne hadn't read more than four pages when Charlotte interrupted her.

"Mary Anne? My throat is really sore."

"Maybe you should gargle," suggested Mary Anne.

"Maybe," said Charlotte. "But I don't know if gargling will help a sore throat."

Mary Anne closed her eyes briefly. Just as she was opening them, ready for yet another talk with Charlotte, the phone rang. Mary Anne ran downstairs to answer it. (She *could* have answered the upstairs phone, but Mary Anne feels funny about going into Dr and Mr Johanssen's bedroom. Or any other grown-up's bedroom, for that matter.)

"Hello, Johanssens' residence," said Mary Anne.

"Hi, it's Claud," said Claudia, "and I've got some news about Stacey."

"News? What's happened?" Mary Anne asked quickly. Was this good news or bad news? Had I had another relapse? she wondered. Were my new injections working the way they should be?

"Okay, get this," said Claud. "Stacey will be home on Saturday."

"All *right*!" cried Mary Anne. "Just two more days. Wait till I tell Charlotte. She will be so happy! You can't imagine."

"Oh, yes, I can!" exclaimed Claudia. "And tell Char that when Stacey returns she'll have to rest for a week, then she can go back to school, and a week after *that* she can start babysitting again."

"Terrific!" said Mary Anne.

"I'm phoning all the BSC members," added Claud, "so I'd better go now."

Mary Anne put the phone down then and raced to Charlotte's room. "Guess what? Guess what?" she cried. "No, you won't guess, so I'll tell you."

"Yeah?" said Charlotte.

"Stacey will be home in two days."

"Aaargh!" shrieked Charlotte. (Mary Anne decided that Char's throat wasn't bothering her *too* much.) "On Saturday? Stacey will be back on Saturday?"

"Yup," said Mary Anne. She told Charlotte what Claud had said about resting, school and babysitting.

"So Stacey can't babysit for me for over two weeks?"

"That's right. But isn't it nice to know she's coming back here?"

"Definitely," said Char. "You know what? We should do something for Stacey. We should give her a surprise party."

"I don't know about a surprise party, since Stacey is supposed to be resting, but we should do something for her. She'd like that."

"Then let's give her an ordinary party. We won't surprise her."

"A small, quiet, ordinary party, maybe," said Mary Anne.

"We could make a sign," suggested Charlotte. "I mean, a banner. Remember the banner we hung up when Stacey and her mum moved back to Stoneybrook?"

"Yup. We hung it in front of her house. We could do that again."

"And then we'll be waiting for her in the front garden when her mother drives her home. Only we won't jump out or anything. And we won't invite as many people as we did the last time."

"That sounds good. And maybe we'll just drag over the Pikes' picnic table and serve fruit juice or lemonade."

"Lemonade without sugar in it," added Charlotte.

"Right," said Mary Anne. "Or with artificial sweeteners. Okay, this sounds good. The party will be quiet and small. I think Stacey will really like it. What should the banner say?"

Charlotte frowned. "Mmm . . . how about, 'We're glad you're home, Stacey'?"

"Perfect!"

"Really?" Charlotte looked very pleased.

"Positively. Do you want to help make the banner?"

"Positively!" replied Charlotte, grinning.

"I should phone Claudia and everyone

and see what they think about this."

"Phone them now," said Charlotte.

"Okay." Mary Anne headed back downstairs.

Charlotte ran after her. "Hey, guess what? My sore throat has gone! And I'm pretty sure I don't have Lyme disease or arthritis, or anything, either."

Mary Anne turned around. She hugged Charlotte. "You don't know how glad I am to hear that," she said.

"Who should we call first?" asked Charlotte, wriggling out of Mary Anne's grasp.

"Claudia, I think," answered Mary Anne. "She's got paint. We'll probably make the banner at her house tomorrow afternoon."

"I'll dial!" exclaimed Char.

So she did. Then she handed the receiver to Mary Anne. Mary Anne spoke to Claud, who loved the idea of welcoming me home. Within fifteen minutes, Dawn, Mal, Jessi and Kristy knew about the party, too. Mary Anne assigned jobs to everyone. My friends couldn't wait for Saturday – and neither could I!

15th CHAPTER

The motorway stretched in front of us. I imagined it was the Yellow Brick Road, and that it led straight to my house.

Saturday had arrived at last. I had been sprung from the hospital. And now that I was out of that bland room with its view of dingy grey, I really did feel like Dorothy in Oz. "Hey, Mum, there are *colours* out here!" I had exclaimed as a nurse helped me into our car.

Mum laughed.

The nurse smiled. "It was nice knowing you, Stacey," she said, "but I don't ever want to see your face here again!" (She didn't?) "Don't worry," the nurse went on, "I say that to all my patients. Stay well, okay?"

It was my turn to smile. "Okay." I paused. Then I added, "I hope *I* never see *your* face again, either!"

Grinning, the nurse turned the empty wheelchair round and started towards the door of the hospital.

"Why do they always make me leave the hospital in a wheelchair?" I complained. "I can walk. I was walking in hospital."

Mum shrugged. "Just hospital policy, sweetie." She turned the key in the ignition and at last I began to leave the hospital behind me.

The morning had been a little bit hectic. Mum arrived early to pack my suitcase, and to put all of my cards and gifts into shopping bags. Then she began to empty a vase of its flowers.

"Mum!" I exclaimed. "Can't we keep my flowers? Can't we take them home?"

"*All* of them?" replied Mum. The room was overflowing.

"Well, some of them," I said. "Maybe we could give the rest to the nurses or to the other kids here."

"Good idea," Mum had answered.

So we'd left two bouquets of flowers at the nurses' office. We had delivered four more bouquets to the kids I'd got to know the best (which wasn't very well), and we took three home with us.

While Mum was running round packing my suitcase and handing out flowers, Dad arrived to say goodbye to me. He knew that Mum would be there, and Mum knew that Dad was coming, so when they found themselves together in my room, they didn't talk, but they didn't argue, either.

"From now on," said Dad, "be sure to tell your mother or me when you're feeling so awful. You know the signs to look for."

"Yeah," I agreed. "I suppose I wasn't being very responsible."

Dad shook his head. "It wasn't your fault," he said.

"Then whose was it?"

Dad shrugged. "What difference does it make?"

"None, I suppose."

A little while later, Dad and I were hugging goodbye.

"I promise that my next visit will be more fun," I said.

"I should hope so," Dad answered, smiling. "This'll be hard to top in terms of rotten holidays."

"There's always the sewage treatment plant," I said. "Maybe we could tour it the next time I come for a weekend."

"Okay," said my father. "Then we'll finish off the day with a ride on a dust cart. We'll try to pick a hot, sunny afternoon so the rubbish will be particularly disgusting and smelly."

"Dad, you are so gross!" I cried.

"That's what fathers are for," he replied, as he left my room.

When he had gone, Mum and I waited around for a doctor to come and give me a final examination. Then we could . . . leave!

Now it was sometime in the early afternoon, and Mum and I were following the Yellow Brick Road back to our house on Elm Street in Stoneybrook, Connecticut. My eyes drooped as we drove along.

The next thing I knew, Mum was gently shaking my shoulder.

"We're almost home, Stace," she said.

"Okay," I replied groggily. Why was Mum waking me up? I would wake up by myself when she parked the car in— "I don't believe it!" I cried.

Mum turned to smile at me, "Everyone's glad you've come back."

"I suppose so!"

We were turning the corner on to our street, and already I could see a bunch of balloons tied to our post box. And standing in the garden was a small crowd of kids. As we pulled closer, I could see all my BSC friends, Charlotte, Becca Ramsey, Jamie Newton, Myriah and Gabbie Perkins and several of Mallory's brothers and sisters.

And then I saw the banner: WE'RE GLAD YOU'RE HOME, STACEY! It had been hung across the front door. "I don't believe it," I said again.

135

Mum pulled into the drive. "Your public awaits you," she said.

Slowly I got out of the car. As soon as I stood up, everybody began yelling and cheering and calling to me.

"Hi!" I cried.

And then there was this rush of bodies. I ran around the front of the car ("Slow down, Stacey," said Mum) and all the kids ran towards me. Soon I was hugging everyone, except the Pike triplets, who said they would die if a girl touched them.

"I'm so glad you're home," said Claudia.

"Oh, me, too!" I replied.

I looked down to see who was hugging my waist. It was Charlotte.

"I didn't really think you'd come back," she said. "But you're all well now."

The truth was, I would never be *all* well, but I didn't think this was the appropriate time to say so to Charlotte.

Mary Anne was standing at a picnic table. She ladled lemonade into paper cups, and the kids passed them round. I sat down on the front step to drink mine – after I'd checked to make sure that it didn't contain any *real* sugar.

"Tired, Stace?" asked Dawn.

"Yeah," I admitted.

So Dawn broke up the party then. She sent the guests home, except for Claudia. By this time, Mum had emptied the car. She had carried the suitcase and shopping bags and vases of flowers inside.

"I think I'm going to lie down for a while," I told Claud.

"Are you going to sleep?" she asked.

"No. Just rest. Come with me, okay?"

Claud nodded. "Okay."

We stepped into my house. I breathed in deeply. "Ahhh. This certainly smells better than the hospital did."

Claudia giggled. "Come along, patient," she said.

"Okay, Nurse Claudia." I turned around. "Mum, Claudia and I are going upstairs!" I called.

"All right," my mother called back.

"I think I'm actually going to get *in* bed," I told Claud as we trudged upstairs. When we reached my room, I opened my window. "Fresh air," I murmured. Then I glanced around. "You don't know how nice it is to see colours other than grey and white."

I opened a drawer and took out a clean nightdress."

"Oh, yes, I do," Claud replied, thinking of her own stay in the hospital after she'd broken her leg.

I changed into my nightdress and crawled into bed. Claudia and I gabbed until I started to fall asleep.

"I'll phone you later," said Claud as she left.

"Okay. Thanks." I drifted off to sleep, thinking, There's no place like home. There's no place like home.

I slept for several hours. When I woke up, I felt well enough to eat dinner in the kitchen with Mum. But after that, I was tired again.

"I think I'll go to bed soon," I told my mother. "But first, can you come upstairs so we can talk?"

"Of course." Mum followed me back to my room, where I crawled under the covers again. She sat on the edge of my bed.

"This is something I've been trying to tell you and Dad for a long time now," I began. I drew in a deep breath. "Okay. Here goes. I am not going to be the piggy in the middle for you two any more."

"The piggy?"

"Yeah. I feel as if Dad's always trying to get information about you from me, and you try to find out about Dad from me. And both of you send nasty messages through me. That's not fair. So from now on, I'm not talking about you to Dad or about Dad to you, and I'm not delivering any messages. I'll phone Dad in a few minutes and tell him all this, too."

"Okay," said Mum, nodding her head. "So far what you've said seems reasonable."

"I also want to apologize," I went on. "I know I've been crabby lately, but I wasn't feeling well. Besides, I suppose I've been annoyed with you two."

"Apology accepted. And *my* apologies to you for making you feel like a piggy.'

I smiled. "Thanks. When I phone Dad, I'll also tell him that I'll visit him more often, and without any arguments. I'll be happy to go to New York when I'm feeling better and when I know I won't be the piggy."

"Fair enough," said Mum.

"One last thing. I have to make a confession." I paused because I could feel tears coming to my eyes. "Um, I'm really sorry about all this, but I think the reason I went into the hospital was that I stopped following my diet." I told my mother about the fudge and the chocolate and everything.

Then I began to cry.

Mum put her arms around me. "Darling," she said softly, "you shouldn't have done that, but the doctors are pretty sure your diet didn't have much to do with the change in your blood sugar level. You haven't been feeling well for a long time now, have you?"

I shook my head. "No, I haven't." I was still crying.

"And you know that being a diabetic, especially with this kind of juvenile-onset diabetes, you're much more susceptible to infections than other people are. Besides, because diabetes can be a nasty disease, once you've got an infection, then you're more open to problems with your insulin. It's a vicious circle. We've been lucky so far, but lately you've had the flu and a sore throat—"

"And bronchitis, remember?"

"That's right. I'd forgotten. Furthermore, you've been incredibly busy. So I'm sure that eating sweets didn't help matters, but I'm also sure that that's not why you got ill."

I had stopped crying. I pulled away from Mum. "Maybe I should slow down a little," I told her.

"Good idea."

"I need to catch up on my schoolwork anyway. And the next time I'm not feeling well, I'll tell you. That way I can see the doctor before I get so ill."

"Another good idea."

"Thank you," I said again. I kissed Mum. "I'm really tired," I told her, "but I've got to do one more thing before I go to bed."

I stood up. Then I went into Mum's room. It was time to talk to my father.

DAWN AND THE BIG SLEEPOVER

The author gratefully acknowledges
Peter Lerangis
for his help in
preparing this manuscript.

1st CHAPTER

"Can I read Rachel's letter first? Can I?"

Vanessa Pike was jumping up and down with excitement. She swung a letter and photo in the air, practically hitting me in the face.

"Me next!" Jordan Pike said.

"Me next!" Margo Pike said.

"Me next!" Adam Pike said.

"Come on, you lot, sit down," Mallory Pike said.

Have you ever babysat for a family of eight kids? Well, welcome to the Pikes' house. Fortunately, sitting for them usually involves *two* of us members of the Babysitters Club. Unfortunately, eight kids is a lot, even for us.

Actually, they're really good kids – most of the time. One of them, Mallory, is a member of our club (more about the BSC later). Mal is eleven and a *great* sitter. She

143

and I were both looking after her brothers and sisters that night.

Who am I? I'm Dawn Schafer. I'm thirteen, and I've lived in Stoneybrook, Connecticut, since the seventh grade. I used to live in California, and if you met me, you *might* say, "I can tell." I have *long* blonde hair and blue eyes, and I'm into health foods and sunshine (not that *every* California girl is like that, but that's what a lot of people think). Anyway, I moved here with my mum and my younger brother, Jeff, after my parents got divorced. Stoneybrook was the town my mother grew up in, and *her* parents still live here. I liked it straight away, but Jeff hated it and ended up moving back to California to live with our dad. (He seems happy now, but Mum and I miss him a lot.) We live in a fantastic old farmhouse that was built in 1795. It has a barn with a secret passage that leads straight to my bedroom! Since my mum remarried, my stepfather and stepsister live with us (more about them later, too).

So that's me. Now back to the Pikes' house. Our heroes were on the horns of a dilemma (they weren't really, but I read that once in a book, and it cracked me up). Adam, Jordan and Byron (ten-year-old triplets); Vanessa (who's nine); Nicky (eight); and Margo (seven) were incredibly excited about the letters and photos they had got from their pen pals. Anyway, if you've been keeping count, you've noticed I left out one Pike. That's Claire, who's five. She's only at nursery school, so she wasn't involved in Pens Across America.

I think I should explain that Pens Across America is a national pen pal programme for second-through to fifth-graders. The schools that take part are called "sister schools". (Why? I don't know. *All* the kids participate, not just girls. It should be "sibling schools" or something.) For a few weeks, the kids at Stoneybrook Elementary School (SES) had been writing to . . . Zunis! "Zuni" is the name of a Native American tribe in New Mexico, and they have a junior school on their reservation. (Their reservation is also called Zuni.)

None of the kids had ever met their pen pals, but it was amazing how close they felt. Take Vanessa. She was *dying* to read the letter from her pen pal, Rachel. You'd think Rachel was a long-lost sister, or something (as if Vanessa didn't have enough sisters).

"Let's see her photograph first!" Margo said.

All of us leaned over the coffee table to look at the photograph.

"She's pretty," Margo said. "I wish my pen pal was smiling." She held out a photo of a girl with a grim expression.

Vanessa shrugged. "Maybe she wears a brace."

"Yuk," was Adam's remark.

"Let's see *your* pen pal, Adam," Margo added. "I bet he's a dork."

"He is not," Adam replied. "He looks just like the kids in your photos."

Margo giggled. "He looks like a *girl?*"

"No!" Adam said gloomily. "I mean, he just looks . . . you know, like a kid." He dug a folded-up envelope out of his pocket, then took out a crumpled school photo of a smiling boy with short black hair. Across the bottom in pen it said, YOUR FRIEND, CONRAD.

"What did you expect him to look like?" Vanessa asked.

"I don't know. . ." Adam said. "Like an Indian, I suppose."

"He wants to see head-dresses and costumes," Byron said. "Like on TV."

"And warpaint! *Woo-woo-woo-woo!*" Jordan whooped.

"No. . ." Adam said, turning red.

"Boys, come on!" Mal called out.

I think Adam *did* want to see head-dresses and tepees and things – and he was feeling guilty about it. Mal had lectured him about stereotyping, and all the kids in his school had learned about how the modern Zunis really live.

"He's a *Native American*, Adam," Mallory said, as if she'd said it a hundred times before, which was probably true. "*Indians* are from India. You should know that by now, especially after three letters."

"I know," Adam said with a sigh. "But Indians – uh, Native Americans – are supposed to have names like, you know, Chief Rocking Horse and Joe Crescent Moon. . ." Adam looked forlornly at his letter. "Not Conrad White."

"Maybe it's short for White Horse," Nicky suggested.

"Or White Smoke Signals," Margo piped up.

I decided to interrupt this conversation. "Adam, a *lot* of the pen pals have English-sounding names. It doesn't mean they're not Native Americans."

"My pen pal's called Wendy Jackson," Margo reminded him.

Nicky nodded. "Mine's Joey Evans."

Suddenly, Vanessa exclaimed, "I thought I was going to *read*!"

"You are!" I said. "Okay, everyone listen up. Presenting. . ." (I gave a little dramatic gesture with my arms) "Vanessa!"

Vanessa held up her letter and started to read. This is how it went:

"'Dear Vanessa,

"'Hi. I really liked your letter. I mostly liked hearing about your family. It must be fun to have triplets in the house.'" Vanessa stopped reading and said under her breath, "That's what *she* thinks."

"Hey!" Jordan blurted out.

She quickly went on, "'My family has twelve people. I'm the youngest. There are my brothers John and James; my sister, April; my parents; three grandparents (the fourth one is dead); my aunts Martha and Connie; and my uncle Bob. My brother John is in California now. He's nineteen, and he's allowed to fight forest fires. My dad says he can make a lot of money doing that. I miss him. I have a question for you. Why don't your relatives live with you? It must be hard to get all the work done.'"

"They *all* live in the same *house*?" Nicky said. "It must be super huge."

"If you'd listen, you'd find out," Vanessa answered. She cleared her throat and continued:

"'Our teacher, Mrs Randall, is really nice. She's an Anglo, like you. She said we should tell you about the way Zunis live – about our houses and our parents' jobs and our customs and stuff. Well, we live in a pueblo. That's like a village, with lots of houses around a plaza. Our houses are called adobe houses, and they're made of clay and wood. They have flat roofs, and they're one storey high. Maybe that sounds strange to you, but it's not. We have electricity and running water and TVs and things like that. We speak Zuni at home with our families. Most of the mums and dads make great jewellery to sell in the shops in town. I asked my mum if I could send you a bracelet but she said maybe next time.

"'Yours truly, Rachel Redriver.'"

Everyone began talking at once:

"See? *She* has an Indian name!" Adam said.

"What's an Anglo?" Claire piped up.

"A white person, I think," Mal answered.

"I'm next!" Jordan called out. He unwrinkled his letter and began to read, stumbling over the big words:

"'Dear Jordan,

"'Mrs Randall is making me tell you about Sha'la'ko. [Jordan had a *really* hard time with that one.] It's a big festival that we Zunis have for the new year. Our new year starts in December. Every year there are eight special Sha'la'ko houses. This year ours is one! My mum has been decorating the house for months. When the sun goes down on the first day of Sha'la'ko, dancers come into all the rooms to bless the house. They dance all night without stopping. They wear masks and feathers and stuff, and we're supposed to throw cornmeal at them for good luck. All the kids are allowed to stay up to watch.

"'Do you have the new Star Wars film there? It's great! What about Nintendo? Let me know which video games you like!'"

Suddenly Jordan started to laugh, then instantly stopped.

"What?" asked Vanessa.

"Nothing," Jordan said, hiding his letter. "That's all he wrote."

"No, there's more," Vanessa insisted, grabbing Jordan's letter. "Come on, let's see it!"

"Hey!" Jordan yelled. "*Dawn*! She's—"

Before I could do anything, Vanessa started reading in a singsong voice. "'PS Y-may eacher-tay ells-smay ike-lay a-hay ow-cay. . .'" She paused for a moment, then her eyes lit up. "Oooh. . ."

"My teacher smells like a cow!" Adam cried out. "That's pig Latin!"

"Ugh! Ugh!" Margo said.

Well, you'd think it was the cleverest thing anyone had ever thought of. All the other kids exploded with giggles – even Claire, who had been pretty quiet since she didn't have a pen pal herself. "Adam, silly-billy-goo-goo," she squealed.

"Did you teach Sam that, Jordan?" Adam demanded. (Sam is Jordan's pen pal.)

Byron looked disappointed. "I thought that was our secret language."

"It's okay, Byron," Jordan said. "Sam's a good kid, and I made him promise not to tell anyone."

Byron nodded seriously (he's the most sensitive of the triplets), and I kept myself from laughing. As if their secret would really be *ruined* because some kids right across the country found out.

"Look, you lot," Mal continued, "your pen pals all sent you pictures. Why don't you think about what you can send *them*?"

That idea must have gone down well, because the kids all fell silent. I wouldn't have thought of that, but trust Mal. Really, she's a perfect big sister. As you can see, she is very practical and clever and cool under pressure. Not to mention creative. Her goal in life is to write and illustrate children's books, and I know she'll be great at it. (The problem is, Mal's convinced her parents will never let her grow up. They still won't let her wear trendy clothes or get contact lenses.)

Anyway, Mal's idea was really catching on. Even Adam was getting into it. He ran into his room and emerged seconds later with a big, felt Stoneybrook badge. "This is what I'm going to send!"

"Me too!" Byron shouted.

"Me three!" Jordan pitched in, smiling at his own joke.

"Wait!" I said. "You can't all send the same thing."

"Yeah, that's boring," Vanessa said.

Margo jumped up. "How about Stoneybrook notebooks?"

"Or car stickers!" Byron added.

Mal nodded. "Stoneybrook souvenirs

would be great – but they're not as special as the pictures they sent you."

"We don't *have* our school photos yet," Nicky said with a shrug.

I butted in. "What kind of things do we have in Connecticut that they might not have out there?"

"Cable TV?" Adam suggested.

"Rain," Nicky said. "Miss Farnsworth told us the weather is always sunny out there."

Vanessa groaned. "Really great ideas, everyone. Did you forget to put in your brains this morning?"

"Whatever you say bounces off me and sticks to you," Adam said.

"We could get something from the shopping arcade!" Jordan blurted out. "Like T-shirts with our pictures on them."

"Or some stationery!" Vanessa said.

Anyway, that's pretty much how it went that afternoon at the Pikes'. That was back when the pen pal programme was fun. When us older kids weren't involved. Simple. Easy.

If only I had known what was about to happen.

2nd CHAPTER

By the time Mrs Pike arrived home from her trustees meeting at the Stoneybrook Public Library, the kids were hard at work writing letters. Adam had decided he'd send the badge, and Nicky would send the notebook. Byron was going to ask his dad if he could take some photos of the family, Vanessa planned to write a poem, and Jordan wanted to tape-record himself playing the piano. Margo was still thinking.

As I walked home, all I could think about were the Zunis. They sounded fascinating. I was dying to know more about their lifestyle, and Sha'la'ko, and a million other things. In a way, I felt a bit sad. I wished it was *our* school that was in the Pens Across America programme.

"Hi, Mary Anne," I said to my stepsister, who was in the living room.

Mary Anne took one look at my face and said, "Don't tell me. The triplets flooded the sink."

"No," I said.

"Nicky broke Vanessa's glasses."

"*No!*"

"Margo was sick."

I smiled. "Mary Anne, do I look *that* tired?"

Before Mary Anne could answer, my mum called out from the kitchen, "Hi, sweetheart!"

One thing I should say about my mum. She's *not* that great a cook. I mean, she can throw together a decent salad, but anything else is "eat at your own risk." The same thing with housework. She sort of loses interest halfway through. And Richard, my stepfather, is exactly the opposite – super organized. I was happy to see him in the kitchen, seasoning some sort of delicious smelling casserole.

"Hi!" I called back, plopping on to the living room sofa. "I'll come in and help in a minute."

"That's okay, darling," my mum said. "Everything's almost ready."

"You and Mary Anne can lay the table in about ten minutes," Richard said.

"Okay," I replied.

Mary Anne was still looking at me with that "I know something's wrong" expression on her face.

"The kids were rowdy, but not too bad," I said. "They were working on their pen pal letters."

Mary Anne nodded. "That project sounds like a lot of fun."

"Yeah," I answered. "The kids love it. And to tell you the truth, I'm really disappointed that *we* can't be in the programme, just because we're older."

"It's a bit like what my dad says sometimes: 'Youth is wasted on the young'." Mary Anne smiled. "Maybe you can write to the Zuni elementary school and ask about finding a pen pal of your own in their middle school."

That wasn't a bad idea. See what a great, stepsister I have? Sometimes I think Mary Anne can read my mind.

Okay. I promised I'd tell you about my stepfamily, so here goes. Mary Anne Spier is my best friend in the world. As you can see, she's a good listener, sensitive and patient. Mary Anne's also very shy and she cries easily. She was one of the first people I met when I moved to Connecticut – *before* she was my stepsister, of course. Back then she wore her hair in pigtails and dressed in little-girl clothes, and had to be home by nine o'clock (in the *seventh grade*). That's because her dad (Richard) set the rules. Mary Anne's mum died when Mary Anne was little, then *Richard's* parents died – so Mary Anne was all he had left, and he was *very* protective of her.

Anyway, guess who my mum used to go out with when she was at Stoneybrook High? *Richard!* When Mary Anne and I found this out, we got them back together and – *ta-da!* – they got married. Richard has relaxed a lot, and Mary Anne is no longer the oldest baby in Stoneybrook. As a matter of fact, she's the only one of us BSC members who has ever had a steady boyfriend. His name was (*is* – Mary Anne broke up with him but he's still alive) Logan Bruno. Mary Anne, by the way, is our club's secretary.

You probably want to know about the other club members. Here goes. First of all, they're the greatest friends I could imagine having. If you've ever moved to a school in the middle of the year, you know how hard it is to meet people. Well, the BSC made me feel totally welcome. Everyone was open and friendly, which was great, because nothing turns me off more than cliques where everyone dresses and sounds alike. Not that there are *never* any conflicts in the BSC, but everyone respects everyone else's personality.

And there are *lots* of different personalities.

Kristy Thomas, for example. She's the chairman of the BSC, and the one who thought up the whole thing. As you can guess, she really knows how to get things done – and she *knows* she knows. What I mean is, she can be a little loud and bossy. (A little? A *lot* sometimes.) She's always full of ideas and can be counted on to be mature and level-headed in any emergency. Which you might not guess if you saw her. She seems younger than thirteen, probably because she's the shortest kid in her year and she doesn't seem to care about boys. Also, she never worries about the way she looks. A polo-neck shirt, jeans, trainers, no make-up – that's Kristy. Her two big interests are children (the main requirement for being in the BSC) and sports. She's even thought of a way to combine the two, by organizing a softball team for kids who don't play in Little League. (A real Kristy idea.)

What a family life *she* has. It makes mine look simple. Really, it's sort of like a fairy tale. . . The Saga of Kristy, Chapter 1: Kristy's dad walks out on the family – just heads out the door and never looks back. He leaves his wife with a newborn baby (David Michael), Kristy, and two older brothers (Sam and Charlie). Chapter 2: Mrs Thomas finds a job and brings up all four kids *herself*. Chapter 3: Six years later, Sam and Charlie are at high school, Kristy is chairman of the most brilliant babysitting organization in history, and David Michael is six. Along comes Watson Brewer, a divorced millionaire. He sweeps Mrs

Thomas off her feet (which is hard to imagine – he's balding and quiet and likes gardening), and they fall in love. Kristy hates the idea of having a stepfamily, but. . . Chapter 4: She finally comes round to the idea and Watson marries her mother. The Thomas family moves across town to Watson's mansion, where everyone has their own room – even Watson's kids, Karen and Andrew, who only live there every other weekend and for two weeks in the summer. Everyone lives happily ever after. Epilogue: The Thomas/Brewer family decides to adopt a two-year-old Vietnamese girl, whom they call Emily Michelle. Now the mansion is beginning to look like a village, so Nannie (Kristy's grandmother) moves in to help take care of the kids. And the saga continues.

You may find it hard to believe, but loud Kristy and shy Mary Anne have been best friends practically since birth. (That's what I mean about the BSC – everyone fits together.)

Now. On to Claudia. Claudia Kishi, that is. She's our vice-chairman. She's Japanese-American and totally stunning, with silky black hair, almond-shaped eyes, and a perfect complexion. She's got a great figure, too, despite the fact that she is a junk food *fanatic*. You can't spend two minutes in Claudia's room without her pulling Hula Hoops or a Mars Bar or a Milky Way out of some hiding place. She's got all kinds of art supplies, too, but those are out in the open. Claudia's main thing (besides junk food) is *art*. You name it, she can do it well – painting, drawing, sculpting, jewellery making . . . even the way she *dresses* is artistic. For instance, she walked into school today wearing a bright yellow, oversized man's jacket with rolled-up sleeves; a wide paisley tie right out of the nineteen-sixties; orange ski pants; ankle boots; and huge hoop earrings – and you know what? On her, it looked totally cool.

Oh, another passion of Claud's is Nancy Drew books. She has *them* hidden around her room, too, because her parents don't approve of them. They think she should be reading classics or textbooks, like her sister, Janine. Janine's a certified genius, with one of the highest IQs anyone's heard of. (She's the kind of person who finds mistakes in the *dictionary*.) She and Claudia get along okay, but they couldn't be more different. Claudia doesn't do very well at school – probably because she always feels she can't compete with Janine. Which is too bad, because Claudia's really bright. Oh, well, she'll become a famous artist one day and then it won't matter what grades she got at school.

Claudia's best friend is Stacey McGill, who is our treasurer. Stacey is as sophisticated as Claud, and she also has a flair for wild clothes and jewellery. They both have boyfriends sometimes, although no one serious. But that's where the similarities end. For one thing, Stacey's got blonde hair and blue eyes, she's an only child, and – here's the best part – she's from New York City! Just like I'm a California girl at heart, Stacey's a real New Yorker. She's got a map of the city on her wall, and something called an alternate-side-of-the-street-parking calendar, with cartoons about car-parking (they're really silly but New Yorkers supposedly find them hilarious). Stacey moved to Stoneybrook when her dad was transferred here (he's a businessman) – then, when he was transferred *again*, she moved back to New York. But less than a year after they had settled into a new flat, her parents told her they were getting a divorce – and Stacey moved with her mother *back* to Stoneybrook. She could have chosen to stay in the city, but she didn't. That was a tough decision for her, but we were thrilled when she came back.

Stacey's life is complicated by one other thing, if you can believe it. She has diabetes. That's a disease in which your body has trouble controlling the level of sugar in your blood. Stacey has to be on a strict diet for life (meaning no sweets) – and she has to give herself daily injections of a drug called insulin. To tell you the truth, I still don't know how she can watch Claudia pull out chocolate left and right and not go totally mad.

There are two junior officers in the BSC – "junior" because they're in the sixth grade (the rest of us are in the eighth grade). You know one of them already – Mal. The other one is Jessica (Jessi) Ramsey. She and Mal are best friends. Both of them love reading and are mad about horses. Jessi's the oldest in her family, just like Mal, but she has only one sister (Becca, short for Rebecca) and one brother (Squirt, short for Squirt). Actually, Squirt's real name is John Philip Ramsey, Jr, but he was really tiny when he was born, and some nurses at the hospital gave him the nickname. Becca is eight and a half and Squirt is just over a year old.

Jessi's big talent is ballet dancing and she wants to be a professional. I have to say, she is good, and she doesn't even get stage fright. Jessi is also the BSC's only black member. The Ramseys are one of the only black families in Stoneybrook, by the way. Some of the people here gave Jessi's family a hard time at first, but fortunately things have calmed down and the Ramseys are much happier.

Well, those are the club members. I'll tell you about the club itself in a little while, so stick around!

Back at our house, Richard was putting plates on the table. Even Mum was hard at work, setting place mats and filling a water jug.

Suddenly I was famished – and feeling a lot more energetic than I had when I got back from the Pikes'.

3rd CHAPTER

That Friday Mary Anne and I cycled to our club meeting as usual. Where were we heading? Claudia's house. Her bedroom is the official meeting place of the Babysitters Club for one very important reason – she's the only one of us who has her own private telephone. (That's also the main reason Claudia is the club vice-chairman.)

It was three days after my job at the Pikes', and to tell you the truth, I had sort of forgotten about Pens Across America and the Zunis. All I was thinking about was the same thing I think about whenever I go to a BSC meeting on Friday: *no school tomorrow*. We also meet on Mondays and Wednesdays (5:30 to 6:00 is our meeting time on all days), but Friday meetings are my favourites. Everyone is so relaxed.

Usually.

I'm dying to tell you what happened at this meeting but first let me explain a few things about the club. Actually, *club* is sort of the wrong word for it, because it's really a business (but I suppose "Babysitters Company" would sound pretty strange). When Kristy thought up the idea for the club we were all in the seventh grade. Back then, BW (Before Watson), Kristy and her two older brothers used to take turns babysitting for David Michael. One day, when none of them could sit, Mrs Thomas phoned to try to find an outside sitter . . . and phoned . . . and phoned, but no one was free. She was on the horns of a dilemma (sorry). Well, that's when something clicked inside Kristy's mind. Wouldn't it be great if a parent could dial one number and reach a whole group of babysitters!

The Babysitters Club was born. Straightaway, Kristy got Mary Anne, Claudia and then Stacey to become the first members. They decided on the meeting times, when people could phone and arrange a sitter. Then the four of them could fill the jobs, and everyone would be happy. To get customers, they put an ad in the Stoneybrook paper and distributed leaflets throughout their neighbourhoods. Well, the rest is history. Kristy's great idea caught on immediately. When I moved to Stoneybrook that January, they had so much business they couldn't *wait* to take on a new member (lucky me). Before long, there were two associate members – Logan Bruno and a friend of Kristy's called Shannon Rilbourne. (They're strictly reserve members we call on if we're all busy) Jessi and Mallory became our junior officers when Stacey moved to New York – and they stayed in the club even when Stacey moved back (once a club member, always a club member).

Kristy, as I said, is the club chairman. She runs the meetings and constantly comes up with new plans and ideas – like a summer play group; a special Mothers' Day event, when we took the kids to a carnival as a gift to our clients; and, of course, Kid-Kits. They're boxes filled with our old games, books, toys, colouring books, paper and crayons. Each of us has one, and we take them on our jobs sometimes. Let me tell you, kids *love* them.

Kristy also thought up the idea of the club notebook. That's our official diary. We have to write about every single job we take – *and* read all the entries. It's how we keep track of our kids' likes, dislikes, new habits, things like that. It's also a record of how each of us has dealt with babysitting problems. Writing in it is not my favourite thing to do, but I realize it helps keep us prepared.

I mentioned already that Claudia is our VC. To be honest, she doesn't do a whole lot at the meetings, but it *is* her phone, and we *do* eat all her junk food, so it is only right that she should be an officer.

Mary Anne is our secretary. She's in charge of the club record book (not to be confused with the *note*book I just mentioned). The record book is a list of clients' names, addresses and phone numbers, a record of how much money we make, *and* our weekly sitting schedule. You can imagine what it's like to keep track of that for seven girls, what with Claud's art classes, Jessi's dance lessons and Mal's orthodontist appointments (just to name a few problems). I'll tell you, it makes me dizzy just to *look* at the book, but you know what? Mary Anne has never – I mean *never* – made a mistake. She keeps track of it all in her tidy handwriting.

As treasurer, Stacey handles the money. She's one of these people who can add and subtract numbers in her head like a calculator, so she's perfect for the job. At every Monday meeting, she collects club subs from us. Yes, subs. We all grumble about it, but we understand how necessary it is. The money goes to group expenses, like helping out with Claud's phone bill, paying Charlie for driving Kristy to and from meetings (Watson's mansion is pretty far away), buying new things for the Kid-Kits, and (if there's any left over) a club pizza party or sleepover now and then.

Stacey is *very* thrifty. She keeps track of every penny and hates to spend it unless it's absolutely necessary.

I like being the alternate offcer. I'm almost like an understudy. If someone can't make a meeting, I get to take over her job. For a while, when Stacey moved to New York, I was the club treasurer. But I'm not a maths genius, so I was happy to return the job to her when she moved back. So far I've filled in for just about everyone.

Our two junior officers, Mal and Jessi, aren't allowed to take evening sitting jobs unless they're at their own homes. So they do a lot of the daytime sitting, and that frees the rest of us for evening jobs.

Okay, now you know all there is to know about the club. Finally I can tell you about our meeting.

Mary Anne and I arrived early that day. Claudia greeted us at the door to her room with her hair in a ponytail on top of her head, held up by a huge hairslide in the shape of a bone, like Pebbles in *The Flintstones*. It made her hair bounce when she moved. She was even wearing a Pebbles-type outfit – a pink, off-the-shoulder blouse with huge polka dots and a ragged bottom over black tights. On anyone else it would have looked stupid or babyish, but on Claudia it looked cool.

As we walked into her room, her clock read 5:23. There were a few schoolbooks on her bed – all closed – and a huge pad of paper where she had been sketching some abstract drawings of a half-human, half-horse (at least that's what it looked like).

"Have you tried these, Mary Anne?" Claud said, reaching under her pillow to pull out some new kind of dark-chocolate caramel.

"Nope," Mary Anne said.

"Have one," Claud offered. Then she lay flat on her stomach and pulled a big bag of pretzels from under her bed. "These are for you, Dawn."

She didn't have to twist our arms. We each got into position on Claud's bed – sitting cross-legged, leaning slightly forwards, and chewing. That's how we sit in most of the meetings. (Stacey and I switch sometimes – one of us sits in Claudia's desk chair, with the chair backwards and our chin resting on the top rung.)

"Any calls?" I asked. Sometimes clients forget when our meetings are and call us at odd hours.

"Nnrrrp," Claudia said with her mouth full.

We immediately started giggling, and I could feel a lump of pretzel starting to go up my nose, which made me giggle even more. That made Mary Anne giggle more. Claudia put her hand over her mouth and made some strange snorting noise that she obviously couldn't help.

Wouldn't you know it was at that moment that Kristy walked in. "What happened?" she said innocently.

Well, you know about giggling. Once you start, everything seems funny. We were rolling around on the bed now, and Kristy looked like she was ready to commit us. She shook her head and climbed into Claud's director's chair.

Before long, Stacey arrived, then Jessi. By that time, we were pretty much under control, chatting and munching. Stacey sat in the desk chair, exactly the way I described. Jessi sat on the floor, leaning over and touching her toes, with her chin practically resting on her knees – and talked to Stacey as if she was in the most comfortable position in the world. It hurt just to look at her.

At 5:29, I could see Kristy's eyes glue themselves to the clock. The instant it turned to five-thirty, she called out, "Order!"

As we quietened down, Kristy looked at the door. "Anyone know where Mallory is?

We all shrugged.

"Dental appointment?" Kristy asked Mary Anne.

Mary Anne checked the record book and shook her head. "Not till next week."

Kristy was the only one who seemed upset. I mean, everyone's human – once in a while, just about each one of us is late.

But just try telling that to Kristy.

She let out a big sigh and said, "Okay, I have an idea for something to put in the Kid-Kits. Stacey, could you check how much money we—"

That's when Mallory came in. Now, usually when someone shows up late, she sort of quietly slips in and sits right down, mumbling "sorry" or something. But Mal didn't do that. She just stood there for a second, her brow wrinkled and her mouth in a frown. Straight away we knew something was wrong.

"Mal?" Mary Anne said with concern. "Are you all right?"

Mallory gave a distracted nod. "I'm fine. Didn't you lot hear what happened?"

Six totally blank faces looked back at her. "No, what?" Stacey asked.

"You know the pen pals' school, in New Mexico?" she said.

We nodded.

"It burned down."

That was the last thing anyone expected to hear. We just stared at her, as if she had just said "the grass is purple", or something else you couldn't respond to.

"*What?*" Kristy finally said.

"Vanessa got a letter from her pen pal," Mal said, sitting on the edge of the bed. "There was a fire at a petrol station near the school. It sort of went up like an explosion and then it spread."

"That's *horrible*!" I said.

"Was anybody hurt?" Claudia asked.

Mal shook her head. "Not seriously. But the school was destroyed, and so were some homes."

No one knew what to say. I only knew the Zuni kids through babysitting with the Pikes. Yet somehow, I couldn't keep my stomach from knotting up. I had listened to all the letters and, in a way, I felt that those kids were my friends, too.

"Vanessa was really upset," Mallory added, "and so were the triplets. I had to calm them down. That's why I was late."

"Wow," Stacey said in a low voice. "I wish there was something we could do."

"Maybe there is," I said.

Mallory looked at me hopefully. "What?"

I didn't know the answer to that question. But I was determined to find out.

4th CHAPTER

It was a Friday night, but it certainly didn't feel like it.

Usually Friday night dinner is one of the best times in our house. It's the beginning of the weekend and everyone's in a good mood. Sometimes there are no more leftovers and no one wants to cook, which means getting a pizza or Chinese food or something. Mary Anne and I usually chatter about five miles a minute. When we're not talking, we're shovelling in food or laughing (I know this makes us sound like pigs, but we're actually tidy about it).

After the BSC meeting that night, though, it was another story. Richard had picked up some vegetarian Mexican food on his way home from work, and instead of wolfing it down happily, we were all pretty quiet and lost in our thoughts.

At least I was. I was thinking about those kids in New Mexico. Mary Anne was probably thinking about them, too, but knowing her, she was also wondering why I was so quiet. Mum and Richard knew something was wrong, and they were trying hard to make cheerful conversation.

It was Mum who broke the ice. "Dawn," she said, "did something happen at school?"

I took a deep breath. Then I told her about Pens Across America, Conrad White, Rachel Redriver and Sha'la'ko. I described our meeting and Mal's news about the fire. Mum listened patiently, nodding with concern. "How awful," she murmured after I'd finished.

"Maybe they didn't have a good sprinkler system," Richard added.

To be honest, that seemed like a pretty strange reaction, but I didn't say so. "I suppose not," I replied with a shrug.

"I know how Dawn feels," Mary Anne said. "It just seems so . . . unfair."

"It is," I agreed. "They're really nice kids, Mum – and they work so hard, and they don't have much money. . ."

"The Pikes are really upset about it," Mary Anne added. "Mal says her brothers and sisters were almost crying. It's as if something had happened to their best friends."

Mum gave us both a sympathetic smile. "It *is* unfair," she said. "But the important

173

thing is that no one was seriously hurt. And they'll rebuild whatever was destroyed." She shrugged. "Life goes on."

"I just wish we could help somehow," I said.

"You can," Richard said. "Maybe not the kids in New Mexico, but certainly the Pike kids – cheer them up, encourage them to write supportive letters."

"Yeah," I said, twirling a forkful of refried beans so that the melted cheese wrapped around it. "I think you're right."

Richard *was* right, I realized. I vowed that I'd phone Mal after dinner, and I started feeling a little better. The conversation picked up and things seemed to get back to normal. It was my turn to load the dishwasher that night, which took only a few minutes, since we had eaten a takeaway. Afterwards I quickly made my call to Mal.

"Hi, Mal!" I said.

"Oh . . . hi," came Mal's voice. After we'd chatted for a bit, she asked, "Um, now what are they going to do about the stuff they were going to send?"

"What?"

"You know, the souvenirs to the pen pals? The badges, the notebook. . ."

"Oh!" I said. "Send it all. It'll make them feel better."

"Yeah?"

"Yeah! Don't you think?"

"I don't know, it just seems a little weird. I mean, if I was one of the Zunikids, and my house burned down, and I got a badge in the post... You know what I mean?"

"Oh. Yeah."

I didn't know what to say. I hadn't thought of it that way. Sending cute little souvenirs would make it seem as if we weren't taking their crisis seriously. I was trying to think of something positive when Mal said, "I have to help get Claire to bed, Dawn. I'll talk to you tomorrow, okay?"

"Okay, bye!"

"Bye!"

So much for cheering up the Pikes.

I went to my room, feeling like a real idiot. I didn't have one comforting thing to say to the Pikes – but even when I did, I still wouldn't be helping the Zuni kids. One thing kept sticking in my mind: compared to the Zunis, we were probably *rich*. Surely there had to be something the people in Stoneybrook could do. Something we could give them.

But what? And how?

I tried to imagine being one of the kids whose homes were destroyed. What would I need straight away? That was easy enough to answer: a place to sleep, food, clothes and money.

There wasn't much I could do about the first problem. I supposed (and hoped) that the families had moved in with friends temporarily. That left food, clothes and money – and I knew we could help out with those.

My plan began to take shape. There were three parts to it, and as I thought of each one, I got more and more excited. I talked it over with Mary Anne later that night.

She was in her room, lying on her bed, her face deep in a Judy Blume paperback I had lent her called *Tiger Eyes*.

"Guess what?" I said to her, barging in.

"Hmmm?" came her voice from behind the book.

"Mary Anne, this is important! Can I talk to you for a minute?"

"Mmm-hmm." She was still behind the book.

This was getting frustrating. "You want to know what happens to the man in the hospital? It turns out he's really—" I started to say.

Mary Anne slammed down the book. "*Dawn!* Don't spoil the ending!"

"I had to get your attention *somehow*," I said, plopping down on to her bed.

"Well, I suppose *you're* in a better mood," Mary Anne said with a raised eyebrow. She sat up, curling her legs underneath her. "Okay, what's so important?"

"I know how to help the pen pals."

Suddenly Mary Anne looked interested. "Really? How?"

"It's simple! First of all, SES could have a food collection – you know, the kids go door-to-door, collecting cans and boxes, things that won't spoil. Then there could be a big clothing collection, and finally, some sort of fund-raiser!"

"Fund-raiser?"

"Yeah! I don't know how much money we can get, but anything's better than nothing, right?"

"Wait a minute," Mary Anne said in her practical voice. "What kind of fundraiser?"

I shrugged. (To tell you the truth, I was kind of hoping she'd be more excited.) "I don't know, I'll work something out. But what do you think of the *idea*?"

"It sounds great, Dawn. But it's, you know, a pretty big project. A lot of teachers will have to get involved. Do you think they'll want to do it?"

"Of course they will," I said confidently. "I'm not worried about that part."

"Great," Mary Anne said. I couldn't tell if she meant it, though.

The truth? I *was* worried about it. I felt like a big balloon with its air being squeezed out.

That night it took me a long time to get to sleep.

The next day, Saturday, I did something I would never normally do. I phoned a teacher at her home. Not only that, it was a teacher I didn't even know.

Well, I knew *of* her, actually.

Let me explain. I was excited about going to SES with my plan, but I didn't want to wait till Monday. Besides, even if I did wait, when would I get a chance to go there? Their school day is about the same as ours, so I couldn't go after school. I decided I might as well act right away. But here was the problem: Remember when I said I moved to Stoneybrook in the seventh grade? You guessed it – I never went to SES, so I didn't know any teachers.

That's when I decided to call Mrs Besser. She was my brother Jeff's teacher. I probably wouldn't have remembered her name, except that Jeff used to go around the house yelling, "No more Mrs Besser!" when he was about to move to California.

Opening the phone book I felt excited, but pretty scared. I tried to imagine how I would feel if I was a teacher and some strange pupil called me on my day off. I didn't think I'd mind, but adults can be funny about things like that.

Anyway, there I was, at the *B* section of the phone book. I was half hoping there would be a hundred Bessers so I'd be forced to wait – or *no* Bessers. But there was only one:

BESSER, J. 555–7660

I took a deep breath and tapped out the number. By the third ring I had just about lost my nerve. I was going to hang up when a man's voice answered, "Hello?"

"Hello," I said, my mouth suddenly drying up. "Is Mrs Besser there?"

There was a short silence. "Uh, yes," the man said. Then he must have put his hand over the phone, because the next words were muffled. But I could still make them out: "Darling, it's one of your *kids*!"

Which made me feel even stranger. At first I felt a little insulted. Did I really sound that young? Then I worried that Mrs Besser wouldn't talk to me if I wasn't one of her pupils. *Then* I remembered what a troublemaker Jeff had been – and I was *sure* she'd hang up the minute she heard my name!

"Hello!" came a woman's voice.

"Hi, Mrs Besser. Um, I'm Dawn Schafer. You had my brother Jeff in your class?"

"Oh, *hello*, Dawn!" (What a relief. She sounded happy.) "Yes, your mother used to talk about you. How nice to hear your voice. How's Jeff?"

I knew my mum had had conferences with Mrs Besser about Jeff, but why did they talk about *me*? I wondered. "He's really happy," I answered. "He loves California."

"Oh, that's great. I suppose sending him there was a wise decision after all."

"Oh, yes, it really was." We were getting off the track, so I decided to dig right in. "Um, Mrs Besser, I wondered if I could talk to you about something."

"Of course."

"It's about the Pens Across America programme. I don't know if your class is participating in it. . ."

"We are, yes." Mrs Besser was sounding curious now.

"Well, I heard about what happened—"

"Terrible, wasn't it?"

Now was my chance. "Well, that's why I was calling," I said. "I have some ideas on how to help them."

"I see."

I went over all three parts – the food collection, the clothing collection and the fund-raiser. Mrs Besser listened silently. When she asked about the fund-raiser, I was honest and said I didn't know what it would be yet.

Without seeing her face, I couldn't tell how she felt – but she didn't exactly sound ecstatic. She let out a long "Hmmm. . ." and then said, "Sounds interesting, Dawn. I'll bring it up in the staff room on Monday."

I was dying to know how she felt, but I didn't want to come right out and ask. So I said, "Do you think they might go for it?"

"Well, if *I* have any say in it, they will," she answered. "I mean, after all, what's the point of a pen pal programme? They're supposed to be *pals*, right?"

"Right," I agreed.

"And if I allow my kids to let down their friends, I'm not doing my job, right?"

"Right!"

"What's your number, Dawn? I'll phone you on Monday evening and let you know what happens. If the idea goes down well, we'll talk about how to organize it."

I was so thrilled, I could barely get my own phone number straight. When I had hung up, I let out a whoop of joy. Imagine me, Dawn Schafer, organizing a huge help campaign. It was like something Kristy might do.

Kristy.

Suddenly I realized something that would make my idea even better. Why not get Kristy interested? This would make a perfect project for the whole BSC.

So I phoned her. Luckily for me, she was at home. And when I told her my plan, her reaction was exactly as I would have predicted.

"We have to have an emergency meeting as soon as you hear from Mrs Besser," she said. "We have to work out what the fundraising drive is going to be, where and when we're going to have all these things, how we can get the kids excited – all that kind of stuff."

"It'll be fun!" I said.

"Yup," Kristy answered. "Be sure to phone me immediately, okay?"

"Okay."

It was typical Kristy – taking charge. I was glad but a little uncomfortable. Kristy meant well, but I hoped she wasn't going to make it seem like it was *her* idea.

Hey, relax, I told myself. The important thing was helping the kids, not taking credit for it.

Well, it turned out that the SES teachers were really enthusiastic about the idea. Mrs Besser didn't even wait to phone me at home. One of the senior teachers at *our* school found me during lunch period and said that Mrs Besser had phoned and asked him to tell me the plan was on.

I hope he didn't think I was rude when I yelled "yea!" and ran off to find Kristy.

By the end of the school day, Kristy had contacted everyone in the Babysitters Club. Our Monday night meeting was to start half an hour early, at five o'clock. We were going to plan Operation Help.

I got to Claudia's fifteen minutes early. I was so excited I couldn't even think of eating snacks. Besides, I spent the whole time talking to Claud about my plan. One by one, the others arrived. Mary Anne informed us that Jessi and Stacey had babysitting jobs right up to the usual meeting time, but by 4:58, everyone else was there.

I could feel my heart racing as Kristy called out, "Order!"

5th CHAPTER

As it turned out, I didn't need to worry about Kristy taking credit for my idea. This is the way she opened the meeting:

"Okay, some of you know why this special meeting has been called. But for those who don't, I'll let Dawn explain." She turned to me. "Dawn?"

I was happy to be the one with the big idea for once. And everyone listened carefully as I explained my plan.

Mal was especially excited. "Are we going to vote on this?" she asked when I'd finished speaking. "I vote yes."

"I vote yes," Mary Anne added.

"Me, too!" Claudia said.

Kristy cut them off. "Wait a minute! Is there a motion to put this to a vote?"

Claudia groaned. In a weary, impatient voice, she said, "I motion we put this to a vote."

"Put *what* to a vote?" Kristy said. "You have to be specific."

"*Kristy!*" Claudia said, rolling her eyes. "I motion that we vote whether the Babysitters Club should help out with Dawn's plan, okay?"

"Seconds?" Kristy said.

"I second the motion," Mary Anne called out.

"All those in favour, raise your hands," Kristy said.

Everyone's hand shot in the air.

"It's unanimous," Kristy announced.

"Yea, Dawn!" Mal exclaimed.

"Great," I said. "I'll phone Mrs Besser and ask her to tell her pupils."

"And I'll get my brothers and sisters to tell their teachers," Mallory added.

"That's still not enough," Kristy said. "There are four whole grades, and each grade has a lot of classes. . ."

"How about making a leaflet?" I suggested. "Mrs Besser could make copies, then we could post it around the school."

"I'll make it!" Claudia chimed in. She took a drawing pad off her bedside table. "Okay . . . what should I put in this?"

"Who, what, when, where, why," Kristy recited. "*Who* is all the kids in the Pens Across America programme."

"*What* is a door-to-door food-and-clothing collection," I said. "All canned goods, dry goods, old clothes, shoes—"

"The clothes should be clean," Mary Anne said. "We should mention that."

"Clean clothes," I agreed. "*Why* is the fire at the Zuni reservation."

"The *tragic* fire," Claudia added.

"*When* is something we have to ask the teachers about," Mal added.

"Where's *where*?" Kristy asked.

"What?" Claudia said.

"Where," Kristy repeated.

"Where's what?" Mary Anne said.

I started giggling. I couldn't help it. It was beginning to sound like a comedy routine.

"Where's *where*?" Kristy said. "I mean, where should the kids bring the clothing and the food? They'll have to drop it off somewhere."

"We can use my barn," I said. "I'll ask Mum and Richard. I'm sure they won't mind."

"Great," Claudia said. "I'll pencil it in."

"I have an idea," Mallory said. "If we really want to get kids excited about this plan, we should have prizes or awards—"

"Or maybe a big party for everyone who participates," Mary Anne said. "That way it's not so competitive."

Mallory nodded. "You mean, like a school picnic."

"I heard of a school where the kids became teachers for a day," Kristy said. "That might be fun."

186

Then I had a great idea. "How about a big sleepover?" I said. "We could use the gym, and maybe some of the school staff could participate."

"I like that," Claudia said. "Can you imagine, all those little kids in pyjamas?"

The whole night was taking shape in my mind. "We can serve pizza for dinner," I said, "then afterwards maybe organize some games – you know, a basketball shooting contest, a singalong—"

"Red Rover," Mal added.

"I Spy," Claudia said.

"Right," I said. "If we wanted to hand out awards, we could have a ceremony. Let's see. We'll ask the kids to bring sleeping bags, and maybe we can use rubber mats as mattresses. In the morning we'll make pancakes or something – it'll be so much fun!"

"Yeah," Kristy said, nodding. "And also not too expensive, apart from the food."

"Maybe we can ask a pizza place to donate pizzas for the cause," I said.

"We could try," Kristy replied. "All right, all in favour of the sleepover?"

Again everyone raised hands. Mal raised two.

"Okay, that's that," Kristy said.

"I'll mention it in the leaflet," Claudia said.

Suddenly Kristy looked deep in thought. "Wait a minute, I've just thought of something. Do you really think a lot of kids'll read the leaflets?"

"Oops. . ." Mal said. "Some of them can barely read."

"We have to make sure they *all* know," Kristy said.

"We should notify parents, too, right?" Mary Anne said. "And what about the rest of Stoneybrook? So it won't be a total surprise when kids come knocking on doors."

"Oh. . ." I said, trying to think of answers.

"And what about the fund-raiser?" Kristy said. "We haven't decided exactly how the kids are going to earn money."

Everyone stopped talking for a while. You could almost hear the thoughts tumbling around inside our heads.

Finally Mal said, "I think we should let them come up with their own ways."

"But they're just *kids*," Claudia said.

"My brothers and sisters are just kids, too," Mal said. "But remember what they did when our dad lost his job?"

"That's right," Claudia said with a smile. "I'll never forget Vanessa styling kids' hair in the school playground."

"And Nicky's paper round," I said, "and that 'company' the triplets created for doing odd jobs in the neighbourhood."

"They really managed to pull that off," Mal said.

The phone rang, just as Jessi and Stacey raced into the room. I'd almost forgotten where we were – and what time it was.

Five thirty-two. The special meeting was officially over. Claudia grabbed the receiver. "Hello, Babysitters Club," she said. "Oh, hi, Mrs Braddock!. . . Uh-huh . . . just a minute, let me check."

For the next half-hour, we were pretty busy making appointments and juggling schedules. We never did resolve all of Kristy's questions that afternoon.

But still, I was incredibly excited. It would be a lot of work, but my plan was going to become a reality.

6th CHAPTER

                      Wednesday

Dawn, your idea is fantastic! I was so excited after Monday's meeting, I wanted to blurt it out to everyone. It was really hard to keep it a secret that night when I babysat for Charlotte Johanssen. But then I had to sit for her again last night, and you know what happened.

    Anyway, there's one thing you need to know about Charlotte. Her new favourite books are the "Freddy the Pig" series (be prepared — she's addicted to them). She's been talking about them endlessly, but last night she started talking about her pen pal. The rest is history. I never would have thought Char would be the one to solve our problem — except, knowing her, I shouldn't have been so surprised....

In case you're wondering what Stacey meant, let me explain.

Charlotte Johanssen is really clever. She's eight, but she was moved up into the fourth grade. Charlotte used to be quiet and shy, but gradually, she's become more outgoing and talkative.

There were two reasons for the change in Charlotte. Number One: moving up a grade, which made school more interesting for her (she was bored to tears before). Number Two: Stacey! She and Charlotte have got really close, and Dr Johanssen (Char's mum) says that Stacey helped bring Charlotte out of her shell.

That Monday *and* Tuesday, both Johanssens were busy (Char's mum had to do casualty shifts at Stoneybrook General Hospital, and her dad had to work late on an engineering project), and Stacey got both sitting jobs.

On Tuesday evening, Charlotte worked out something that none of us could – a way to make sure *all* the SES kids knew about my plan.

The evening started out normally. Charlotte was showing Stacey how her body language could affect Carrot, the Johanssens' dog.

Carrot was sitting by the fireplace, lazily looking round the living room. Charlotte and Stacey were on the sofa. "Now watch," Charlotte said. She let her shoulders slump, she pouted her lips, and she let her hair fall in front of her face.

Carrot cocked his head to the side, then trotted towards Charlotte. When he began licking her face, Charlotte laughed. "You are such a clever doggy!" she said. "You want a—"

Without finishing the sentence, she stood up as if she were going to run to the kitchen.

Carrot yelped happily and sprinted into the kitchen.

"See?" Charlotte said, smiling. "I didn't have to say anything!"

"That's great, Char," Stacey said as they followed Carrot.

Charlotte got Carrot a few dog biscuits, then said, "I'm starving, Stace. Can we have a snack, *please*?"

"So *that's* why you got Carrot to come in here," Stacey said with a laugh. "Well, all right. Your mum said we could have a few crackers, but that's it."

Charlotte made a face. "You mean those hard ones with no salt?"

"Those are the only ones in here," Stacey said, pulling out a bag that said CRACKERS AU NATUREL – LOW SODIUM. "Besides, there's salt *in* them, just not *on* them."

"Oh," Charlotte said. She took a cracker from the bag and plopped down in a kitchen chair.

Stacey sat opposite her and placed the open bag on the table, next to a neat pile of yellow, lined paper and envelopes. Judging from the big, scrawly, fourth graderish handwriting, Stacey realized they were letters from Charlotte's pen pal, whose name was Theresa Bradley. "Have you heard from Theresa?"

"Mm-hm," Charlotte said with her mouth closed. The pretzel crunched loudly as she chewed. Then she swallowed and said, "Her house caught fire."

"Oh, that's *terrible*," Stacey said. "Is she all right?"

Charlotte nodded. "Do you want to read the letter?" She took the top sheet off the pile and handed it to Stacey.

"Thanks," Stacey said. She read aloud:

"'Dear Charlotte,

"'I really liked your letter. I haven't read any Freddy books yet. Guess what happened? There was this big, huge fire! It started at this petrol station, then it burned our school down! Our house was on fire, too. I couldn't believe it! We're okay because we were outside. My dad and my uncles got fire extinguishers. They sprayed inside the house. The fire went out, but a lot of things were burned. Now our house is being repaired. We have to live with my aunt and uncle's family. My aunt was a teacher at the school and she lost her job.

"'Some of my clothes were in the washing machine. Those didn't get burned. I wear them every day now. Our TV and

VCR burned, too. My aunt and uncle have a TV but not a VCR.

"'Things aren't too bad. Sometimes it's fun to have so many people around. But my brother wakes up with nightmares sometimes, and my grandmother and my mum cry a lot.

"'My cousin says we're lucky. She's at high school. She wishes her school had burned. My mum was furious when she heard this. She said our education is the most important thing we have. I don't think we're lucky, either. I miss school.

"'Write to me at my aunt and uncle's house. I wrote the address on the envelope. Bye.

"'Your friend, Theresa.'"

Well, Stacey's heart just about broke as she read the letter. (Mine did, too, when she told us about it at the Wednesday meeting.)

"Isn't that sad?" Charlotte said.

Stacey nodded. "Yeah, it really is."

Char's brow was wrinkled, the way it gets when she's upset about something. "What would happen if my house burned down, Stacey?"

"Oh, Char, you don't need to worry about that—"

"Could we move in with you?"

Stacey didn't know what to say. "Well, I suppose – of course, I mean, Mum would—"

"Because we haven't got any aunts and

uncles in Stoneybrook, and I don't want to move away. I would be so lonely."

Charlotte was fiddling nervously with her pretzel, so Stacey reached out to touch her hands. "It's okay, Charlotte. Nothing like that is going to happen."

That's when Stacey decided to tell her about my plan – even though we had all promised not to tell anyone until we actually got started. Stacey thought it might help Charlotte feel better. (Later on, we all agreed she did the right thing.)

"Char," she began. "Can you keep a secret?"

Charlotte perked up. "A secret? About what?"

"Well. . ." Stacey leaned forward and lowered her voice, sounding mysterious. "Dawn thought up this plan to help your pen pals. Only the members of the Babysitters Club know about it. We want everyone in your school to be part of a food-and-clothing collection – you know, going door-to-door and collecting stuff to send to your friends. We're also going to ask kids to try to raise money on their own. Do you think that's a good idea?"

Charlotte's eyes lit up. "Yeah! When—"

"Wait. I didn't tell you the best part. There's going to be an enormously huge sleepover in the SES gym for everyone who helps out."

"Wow! That is *so* fantastic!"

"But don't tell anybody," Stacey said. "We want to work out a good way to spread the word fast – to the school, the parents, the whole town!"

"Ooh! Are you going to have a big assembly?"

"Well, something like that—" Stacey cut herself off. She couldn't believe none of us had thought of an assembly.

"That would be so much fun, Stacey!" Charlotte went on. "You lot can announce it to the whole school, then we'll tell our friends and parents. And our parents can tell *their* friends."

Stacey grinned. "Char, you're amazing. I can't wait to tell Dawn."

"Really?" Charlotte said, beaming.

"No. I've got a better idea. Since you thought of it, why don't *you* tell Dawn? We can go over to her house right now."

"Okay!" Charlotte ran to the garage while Stacey wrote a note to the Johanssens, in case one of them came back early. Then Stacey followed Charlotte out, closing the door behind her.

Char was already on her bike, and Stacey had ridden hers to the Johanssens', so she hopped on it. "Okay," she said, "let's go, but be careful." (Once a babysitter, always a babysitter.)

Stacey cycled down the drive and on to Rimball Street, ahead of Charlotte. They pedalled fast, making the ride to Burnt

Hill Road in about five minutes (at least that's what Stacey said, but I think she was exaggerating).

Mary Anne and I were both at home. Let me tell you, I have never seen Charlotte so excited. Once, when the younger girls were all involved in a beauty contest, Charlotte was too nervous to recite a section of *Charlie and the Chocolate Factory* for the talent competition. You would never know this was the same person.

"Char, that's a *perfect* solution," I said, and I meant it. "I'll talk to Mrs Besser and arrange the assembly."

"For when?" Mary Anne said. "We all have to be at school, remember?"

"It won't take that long," I replied. "We'll just have to get permission to leave for a little while."

"Do you think you can?" Charlotte asked hopefully.

"Yup," I said. (Even though I wasn't a *hundred* per cent positive, I was pretty sure we could convince our teachers.)

We talked about it a little longer, until Stacey decided it was time to leave. She said that Charlotte kept chattering about the assembly right up until her mum came home, but then she kept the secret and didn't say a word.

Stacey could tell Charlotte was much happier – and not only that, she was probably going to be a big help with our project.

7th CHAPTER

"Kristin Reinhardt?"
 "Here."
 "Jodi Reynolds?"
 "Present."
 "Nicole Rogers?"
 "Here."

I could barely hear my registration teacher, Mr Blake, reading out the register. My brain felt as if it was spinning in my head. It was Friday, the day we were going to have our assembly at SES.

Are you surprised at how fast it happened? I was. I had only talked to Mrs Besser about the assembly on Wednesday. Then she spoke to the SES head teacher, who arranged everything. At ten-fifteen on Friday, all the second-, third-, fourth- and fifth-grade classes were going to meet in the school assembly hall.

To hear me!

That's right – since it was my plan, I was supposed to tell them all about it. I don't mind giving school reports or talking in front of a class, but this was really making me nervous. I mean, *four whole grades*! And as an experienced babysitter, I knew those kids were not angels. It's hard enough to get them to listen to a story, let alone a long presentation.

So these were the thoughts tumbling around in my head – Will the kids listen to me? Will they want to get involved? Will I be so nervous that I say something stupid?

For about the tenth time, I reached into my shoulder bag to make sure the speech I had written was still there.

I didn't even hear when Mr Blake called my name.

I snapped back to reality when I felt Mary Anne nudge me (she sits behind me in registration). Then I heard Ray Stuckey, the class clown, saying, "Earth to Dawn! Earth to Dawn!"

A few people laughed, but I was too nervous to be embarrassed. "Here!" I said quickly.

Mr Blake went on with the register, until he was interrupted by the intercom.

"Attention, please. This is Mr Taylor speaking."

Mr Taylor is the head teacher of the Stoneybrook Middle School. He speaks very slowly, and whenever I hear his voice over the intercom, I feel like going to sleep.

But not this time. This time I knew he was going to be talking about me.

"The following students will be dismissed at five minutes to ten," Mr Taylor went on. "Claudia Kishi, Stacey McGill, Mallory Pike, Jessica Ramsey, Dawn Schafer, Mary Anne Spier and Kristy Thomas. All teachers please be advised."

When I turned to look at Mary Anne, she had a big, excited grin on her face. She didn't look nervous at all. Why should she? *She* wasn't the one who had to do the talking.

"Well, excuse *me*!" Ray said under his breath. "If I join the Babysitters Club, will I get a day off, too?"

"Mr Stuckey!" Mr Blake's voice boomed out.

"Eat your heart out, Ray," I whispered. That is *not* something I would normally say, but I was feeling so keyed up, I couldn't help it.

Registration ended, then came maths and boring, *boring* algebraic equations. I looked at the x's and y's and thought I was reading ancient Greek. I could have sworn the clock on the wall was running at half speed.

The exact moment the clock read 9:55, I raised my hand. Miss Berner, my teacher, nodded at me and said, "Good luck."

I suppose the news had spread to the SMS teachers, too. That made me feel even *more* nervous – as if there was this big audience waiting to hear how I did.

I ran outside, where Mrs Downey, the school secretary, was waiting in an estate car. "Thanks for doing this," I said to her.

"Don't mention it," she said, smiling. "I'm *thrilled* to get away from that computer screen for an hour!"

As I got in the front seat, I heard "Hey, Dawn!" and I looked out of the window to see Claudia and Mary Anne running out of the school entrance.

Kristy and Stacey followed close behind, then Mal and Jessi. They all piled in – Mary Anne next to me; Claudia, Kristy and Stacey in the back seat; and Mal and Jessi in the boot-seats.

We were off. I don't remember much about the trip to the junior school. I was too busy trying to control the flutter in my stomach and the tingle in my fingertips. (I can't imagine how an actor must feel. Like this? And if so, how come actors always look so relaxed?)

The SES car park was pretty full, so Miss Downey dropped us off at a back entrance. There, Mrs Besser was waiting.

"Hi!" she said cheerfully. "You must be Dawn. You look just like your brother."

I don't think so, but everyone says I do. Anyway, I think I nodded and said "Thanks," or something else meaningless.

"I'm so glad you girls are doing this,"

Mrs Besser went on, leading us inside. "The kids will be really excited about it."

We walked through the school cafeteria, which was empty and smelled like overboiled broccoli. Then we entered a long corridor.

"My class is already there, along with a couple of others," Mrs Besser said over her shoulder to us.

That's when I could hear the noise coming from the assembly hall – it was like a playground, only with an echo. Every few seconds, a weary adult voice shouted out, "Turn round, Justin!" or "All right, keep it down!"

Suddenly I wished I had never thought of this plan. I wanted to turn and run.

I looked at my friends and noticed they were all looking at me. Mary Anne quickly took my hand and squeezed it. "You're going to be great!" she said.

I took a deep breath and followed Mrs Besser through a door that led to the backstage of the auditorium. Mrs Reynolds, the SES head teacher, was waiting for us there. She has red hair and a strong, kind face. I liked her right away. Shaking our hands warmly, she said, "Is there anything you need?"

Everyone sort of stared blankly, until I replied, "No, I think we're just going to talk."

She nodded. "This was a very good idea, you know."

"Thanks," I said again. My voice sounded squeaky.

Behind us was a curtain that hid the audience from us. Mrs Besser had walked round it and on to the stage. Now she reappeared, saying, "They're almost all here. Are you ready?"

Feeling numb, I nodded.

Mary Anne squeezed my hand again as Mrs Besser walked back onstage, saying, "Okay, quiet please! Take your seats!"

As soon as the kids calmed down, we followed Mrs Reynolds on to the stage. There was a podium with a microphone in the centre of it. Behind the podium were nine chairs, arranged in a semicircle. Mrs Reynolds gestured for us to sit down.

We did, and I made the mistake of looking into the audience. I felt that a million pairs of little eyes were staring at our every movement. There was a lump in my throat the size of a basketball.

It's amazing how loud an assembly hall full of kids can be, even when no one's actually saying anything. All the fidgeting, sighing, coughing, hiccuping, burping, swapping seats – it's never *completely* silent.

Mrs Reynolds walked to the podium. "Good morning," she began. "When we called this a special assembly, we really meant *special*. These girls are familiar to some of you. They have something in common with *all* of you – they care about the children in your sister school in Zuni, New Mexico."

Now the kids *really* settled down. Mrs Reynolds went on for a bit, then said, "Now, these girls have school, too, so they'll have to leave straight after assembly. If you have any questions later on, you can ask Mrs Besser." Mrs Besser, who was sitting with us, stood up and smiled. "Now I'd like to introduce you to the mastermind of the plan. She'll fill you in on all the details. Here's Dawn Schafer!"

I was on. As I stepped up to the podium, clutching my speech, I didn't feel much of anything. I caught a glimpse of Vanessa Pike, grinning widely. Mrs Reynolds had adjusted the mike downwards, but I had to adjust it some more. It made a loud *scrawwwk*, and some of the kids laughed.

"Hi, everybody," I said. The sound of my own voice startled me. It boomed out from the speakers on the walls of the main hall, and it sounded high-pitched and mumbly and *awful*!

"Hi, Dawn!" came a voice from the back. I was pretty sure it was Haley Braddock, and I smiled.

"Um, first I'd like to introduce my friends behind me," I said, turning around. "Next to Mrs Besser is Mary Anne Spier. . ."

Mrs Besser said something to Mary Anne, and she stood up. Her face was redder than I'd ever seen it.

"Yea, Mary Anne!" That was a different voice. There was some applause, too.

One by one I introduced the BSC members. Occasionally I heard a cheer from the crowd. I was beginning to relax. Obviously, we had some fans. (Which made sense, considering all the babysitting hours we'd put in!)

Then I began reading from my speech. I mentioned how concerned we were about the Zuni kids, and how the fire had put people out of homes and jobs. At one point I heard a huge, loud yawn. When I looked up, a teacher was pulling a boy up the aisle by his right hand. A few other kids laughed.

Great. I was *boring* them.

I decided to look up from my speech to tell them about the plan by heart. (Hey, if I didn't know it well enough by now, I was in bad shape.) Sure enough, I didn't make any mistakes. As I outlined the food and clothing collections, and the fund-raising, I could see everyone just looking at me. When I urged the kids to spread the word about our project, I could see a few heads nodding.

And do you know what? I was beginning to feel confident. I could tell the kids were interested.

Of course, I saved the best for last. "This is all going to be a lot of work," I said. "And it's always nice to get a reward when you work hard, right?"

A couple of kids answered, "Right!"

"I think your biggest reward will be knowing that you helped your friends," I went on. "But we would like to give you a celebration of your own. Whoever participates in the collections will get to go to a slumber party in the school gym – with food, games, storytelling, contests, you name it!"

Well, all of a sudden they became *kids* again. Some of them bounced in their seats and clapped. Others let out squeals and began talking to their neighbours. Still others raised their hands, as if we were about to *pick* people to go to the sleepover.

A few of the teachers had to shush some kids. I looked at my watch. My speech was over, but I realized we still had five minutes to go. "Um, does anybody have any questions?"

Haley's hand shot up. "Haley?" I said.

"That's the best idea I ever heard, Dawn!" she blurted out. "Can we tell our pen pals what we're doing?"

"I'm glad you asked that," I said. "The answer is no. This is going to be a surprise. If you write to them, don't even give the slightest hint."

Then I called on Valerie Namm, a friend of Charlotte's, whose hand was raised. "Valerie?"

"How long will the collecting last?" she asked.

"About three weeks," I said. "Longer if it's going really well."

The next person I called on was David Michael, Kristy's brother. "When we go to people's houses, can we collect money, too?" he asked.

I looked back at the other BSC members. They were all leaning over to Kristy, who stood up and said, "Of course. Since fundraising is going to be up to you, that can be *your* method."

"Rob," I said, pointing to Rob Hines.

"Can we just go to the party and forget the other things?" he asked.

Three or four boys on either side of him began to laugh.

"No work, no play," I answered.

Then I called on Jordan Pike.

"Hey, Mal," he said, "what's that thing crawling up the wall behind you?"

Mal spun around, and *Jordan's* group of friends began to howl with laughter. That's when Mrs Besser stood up and said, "All right, if you have any more questions – *real* questions – I'll take them for the next few minutes. But first let's have a round of applause for the girls before they leave!"

The kids did applaud – enthusiastically, too. As I led the other BSC members off the stage, I waved to the kids. When we got to the corridor, we all did a little jumping and squealing and giggling of our own.

Inside, through the open door, we could hear Mrs Besser answering more questions.

"You did it, Dawn!" Kristy said, beaming.

"I suppose I did," I said. I was trying not to get too excited, because there was *so* much work to do now. But the truth was, I felt like shouting with joy. The assembly was a success, and we were on our way!

8th CHAPTER

Monday

Well, this doesn't have anything to do with babysitting, really.

Yes it does, Mal. Mal thinks that taking care of thirty-five kids doesn't count as baby-sitting!

I know, Jessi, but this was a carnival. It's a different story. Anyway, it doesn't matter. I was going to write about it, babysitting or not. I think we did a great job, and we ended up raising a lot of money. If it weren't for Goober Mansfield...

I knew you were going to write about him first. You should start with the good things!

It _was_ good!

209

Mal, he ruined the whole day. And it was all my fault.

That's not true. Okay, okay, I know that look in your eyes. Maybe you should write about it.

I'd be happy to. Let's see; it all began at about 10:00 on Saturday morning...

That Saturday was exactly one week and a day after the assembly at SES. Mal and Jessi had somehow managed to organize a carnival in the Pikes' back garden. Booths, lucky dips, a magic show, the works.

Now, carnivals are supposed to be a little wild, but this one . . . well, let's just say things didn't go the way anyone had expected.

It started out great. Every day that week, Mal and Jessi got together and planned all the details with the younger Pike kids and some of their friends. They built stands out of cardboard boxes and used a lot of old stuff the Pikes had around the house. For whatever else they needed, they pooled money with Mal's brothers and sisters.

The kids had plenty of ideas for the carnival. Mr Pike had just put up a basketball hoop outside the garage, so Adam and Byron set up a free-throw contest. (It cost a quarter to try, so I don't know why they called it "*free* throw". All I know is when I asked them, they rolled their eyes as if I was really stupid.)

Nicky and Jordan made a lucky dip bag out of a huge duffel bag, which they stuffed with little prizes like pencils and baseball cards and comic books. Vanessa and Margo took a plastic paddling pool and made a "fish pond". They used Claire's rubber ducks, Lack, Mack, Nack, Ouack, Pack and Quack (named after the ducks in *Make Way for Ducklings*). If you could pick up one of the ducks, using a fishing rod with a big plastic hook, you could win a small prize.

Jessi had invited her cousin Keisha to come up from New Jersey for the weekend to help out. The two of them took Polaroid pictures of people in a pretty spot in front of the Pikes' garden, for a fee. (Whenever they didn't have customers, Jessi went around taking candid shots, which sold really well, too.) Marilyn and Carolyn Arnold, who are twins, organized a hoopla, using plastic skittles. David Michael Thomas made plastic name tags and messages for people, using one of those little rotating things that look like mini versions of the Starship *Enterprise*. Linny Papadakis, David Michael's friend, performed a magic show. The audience entered his "theatre" through a "curtain", which was a couple of strung-up blankets that blocked off a corner of the garden.

So, there the kids were, at ten o'clock on Saturday morning, frantically setting up. There was a steady *slap, slap, slap . . . bonk*! as Adam and Jordan dribbled and shot baskets on the drive (and missed most of the time – the *bonk*! was the ball hitting the rim). Linny, wearing a shiny fake handlebar moustache and a long black cape, was standing outside his curtains and practising his sales pitch. "Come one, come all, to the greatest magic show on earth!" he shouted over and over again. You would not believe the chaos in the garden.

Oh, well, it was for a good cause, right?

Jessi was making sure the garden looked nice, tossing away dead flowers and stray toys that were lying around. Mal was running all over the place, checking the booths. She spotted Vanessa having trouble blowing up the paddling pool. "Vanessa," she called out, "why don't you get Dad or Mum to help—"

All of a sudden she was hit from the right. She stumbled, then looked over to see Adam running across the garden. The basketball was heading for Linny's curtains. "If you boys can't control the ball, I'm not going to let you have your contest!" Mal shouted.

"You can't say that," Jordan snapped back. "You haven't even got a pen pal!"

Mal was trying to decide the logic of that when Jessi leaped in front of her and said, "Say cheese!"

"Jessi, don't!" Mal said, but it was too late. Jessi snapped the shutter, and the photo came shooting out of the front of the camera.

As they watched it develop, Mal groaned. Her eyes were half shut and her lips were curled in a weird, snarly way. "Ugh!" she said. "Throw it out!"

"I *told* you to say 'cheese'," Jessi said.

"Oh, never mind," Mal said. "Have you talked to Boober yet?"

Overhearing, Claire squealed, "Boober the *Fraggle* is coming?"

"*Goober*," Jessi corrected them. "He's going to do three shows – at twelve, two, and four."

"Good," Mal said. "We'll set him up in the drive."

"Oh, no you won't!" came Adam's voice. "*We* need it!"

"The shows aren't very long," Mal said. "Besides, I don't want anybody shooting stupid baskets while the show is on."

"Everybody'll be watching him, anyway," Jessi added.

You must be dying to know who Goober Mansfield is. His real name is Peter, and he's the star of all the high school plays in a nearby town called Mercer. He's even had a part in a professional theatre production of *Shenandoah*. Jessi found out about him in her ballet class. One of her classmates, Julie Mansfield, is Goober's cousin. Julie mentioned that Goober did a dinosaur show at parties in Mercer, and all the kids there loved it.

Well, Jessi got a phone call from him that night. He was so enthusiastic – and funny – that she signed him up.

He showed up at the Pikes' in a minivan at around ten-thirty on the day of the carnival. Mal liked him straight away. He had a round face with a goony smile, and a loose, rubbery body. Just seeing him made her want to laugh. You know how a person sometimes resembles a name? Well, he sort of *looked* like a Goober.

He and two of his brothers pulled a heavy wooden trunk out of the minivan. Mal led them into the garden and pointed to the drive. "Set up over there, next to the basketball hoop."

"*Mal*—" Adam began to protest, but Mal gave him a Look.

Adam and Jordan sulked as Goober began setting up. He pulled out a papier-mâché tyrannosauraus head, a pair of big dinosaur feet made from diving flippers, a couple of strange-looking masks, a portable cassette player and a megaphone.

Just about then, Claire raced up the drive, shouting, "They're coming!"

"Who?" Mal asked.

"People!" Claire said, jumping up and down.

There were shrieks of excitement (from the stalls that were prepared) and panic (from the ones that weren't). Everyone hurried around, doing last-minute things.

"Okay!" Mal called out above the noise. "Get ready!"

Then, finally, it began.

The first to arrive were Linny Papadakis's parents and two sisters. They, of course, went straight to the magic show. A few minutes later, Betsy Sobak and her parents came, then the Prezziosos.

Before long, the garden was full. Mal guided kids to the stalls. Jessi and Keisha clicked away. Goober moved his stuff far enough from the basketball hoop for Adam and Jordan to have their contest. Linny had a steady stream of customers on the magic stall.

At exactly midday, a whistle blew shrilly.

Mal quickly looked at her watch. "Oh! It's time for the show!" She cleared her throat and called out, "Attention every—"

"*Awroooooo!*" She couldn't even finish the sentence before Goober began shouting into a megaphone. "I am a giant duck-bill dinosaur!" he shouted. "Please help me, I'm dying! *Hellllllllp meee! Awrooooooo!*"

He was wearing a scary mask that looked like the Creature from the Black Lagoon, as well as green flipper feet. He wriggled and twisted as if he was in great pain, then fell to his knees. "Helllp meee!"

Kids quickly finished their games. One by one they gathered around Goober and watched, fascinated. Suddenly he stopped yelling and cocked his head. Then he sprang to his feet and roared.

A couple of the kids screamed gleefully, and Goober began laughing. "There, that'th better!" he said in a goofy, lisping voice that reminded Mal of the Cowardly Lion in *The Wizard of Oz*. "What kinda dinothaur would I be if I couldn't thcare people?"

In no time, everyone was watching. Even Adam and Jordan put down their basketballs and stared. Goober impersonated different dinosaurs, talking about their characteristics, when they lived, whether they ate plants or meat, things like that. He even performed an original dinosaur rap song, dressed as a stegosaurus.

When Mal told me about the show, I wished I'd seen it – but mostly because of what happened later.

It was during the second show that the Perkins family arrived. (They live in Kristy's old house, and they're regular customers of ours.) Many of the kids there had already seen the first show, so all the exhibits were busy. Gabbie Perkins, who's almost three, came racing into the back garden with a tennis ball, giggling. Beside her was their Labrador retriever, Chewy (short for Chewbacca).

"Ugh! Is *that* what took over after we became extinct?" Goober's voice boomed out.

Gabbie spun around to see Goober, wearing his tyrannosaurus mask and pointing at Chewy.

Everyone watching the show turned around. Goober took a step towards Chewy.

Gabbie looked half interested, half frightened – but Chewy knew exactly how he felt. He drew back his lips and let out a snarl.

"Say, pal," Goober said in a deep, rough voice. "How'd a little thing like you end up surviving to the twentieth century?"

With that, he leaned down to pet Chewy.

Well, maybe it was that big, ugly mask, or maybe Goober looked as if he was attacking, but Chewy did something no one had ever seen him do before.

He turned tail and ran.

"Chewy!" Gabbie cried out.

"Chewy, *no!*" called Myriah, her older sister.

It turned out that Jamie Newton was a little bit afraid of dogs – and a *lot* afraid of dogs who jumped in front of him without warning.

Jamie's shriek was bloodcurdling. He ran away – straight into Marilyn and

Carolyn's hoopla. Their skittles went flying.

Marilyn ran after the skittles. Mrs Newton ran after Jamie. Myriah and Gabbie ran after Chewy.

And Chewy decided to run into Linny's curtains to hide. He plunged right in, snapping them off the washing line.

The three kids watching the magic show stood up in surprise. So did Linny.

"Hey, you're ruining my act!" Linny shouted.

"Chewy!" Gabbie said.

"Waaaaah!" Jamie cried.

Jessi was mortified. She ran to Jamie's side as Mal helped Marilyn, Carolyn and Linnie.

It didn't take long to get everything back to normal. Jamie recovered and went home. Mr Perkins took Chewy back to his house. The exhibits were set up and Goober continued his show.

It did take a while for Jessi and Mal to recover. For a long time they talked about Goober Mansfield as if he had ruined the day. But Jessi realized one important thing. After all those weird things had happened, the carnival got twice as crowded.

Maybe, despite everything, Goober Mansfield was the best thing that had happened that day.

9th CHAPTER

monday
ystirday was the yard sail at the ffffff Rudowskis. Boy was I glad to read about youre carnavel, Jesi. Dont get me rong ite just make me feel beter, that I wasint the only one who had a tough time. Remeber when I was assined to supervize the sale and I said that if Jocky Rudowsky was involvd it was bound to be a disastr? Well the funy thing was, it wasint even Jocky who mest up.

Claudia's story actually started a week before she wrote her entry. At our meeting the Monday after the assembly, she had a phone call from Mrs Rodowsky.

"Hi, Mrs Rodowsky," she said. "Can we help you?"

I hate to say it, but you could practically hear us thinking "Oh, no!"

I should tell you one thing. Sitting for Jackie Rodowsky is only for the very brave. He is the most accident-prone seven-year-old you've ever met. If there's food on the table, chances are he'll spill it. If there's something on the ground, chances are he'll trip over it. If he has a new outfit on, you can bet there'll be a rip in it by the end of the day. Claudia always wears her most indestructible clothes when she sits for the Rodowskys. If she had a suit of armour, that would probably be better.

"Jackie and Shea were telling me about the plan you girls are organizing," Mrs Rodowsky said, "and Jackie had the most wonderful idea – a garden sale. We can get families to donate things they don't need any more. I'd be happy to volunteer my back garden. And I was wondering if one of you could supervise the sale."

"Oh," Claudia said, trying to sound enthusiastic but imagining Jackie toppling over a table full of china, "that's a great—"

"How does Sunday sound?" Mrs Rodowsky continued. "Do you think that gives us enough time?"

"Uh, yes, I think so," Claudia said. "Let me talk it over with everyone. We'll be . . . happy to help you."

"Great. I'll get the boys to spread the word at school, and I'll contact their teachers. We'll talk later in the week about details."

"Okay," Claudia said.

"Terrific. Bye, Claudia."

"Bye."

Well, no one exactly jumped out of her seat to volunteer to be in charge. In fact, we actually had to choose straws. And of course, Claud picked the short one.

"Wish me luck," she said with a sigh.

Jackie and Shea Rodowsky were incredibly enthusiastic. They asked Claudia to draw an advertisement for the sale, which they copied and plastered all over their school. And they managed to convince tons of kids to make donations. Whenever Claudia wasn't sitting, she'd help Jackie and Shea pick up all kinds of things from their friends. Lamps, old chairs, paintings, boxes of books, appliances, silverware – you name it, they lugged it to the Rodowskys'.

It was the same week that Mal, Jessi and the Pike kids put together their carnival. It was also the same week that the whole *school* seemed to get caught up in a frenzy of giving. I know, because I shared "barn duty" every evening with Mary Anne. Kids were constantly coming over, bringing all kinds of donated clothes and food.

We were impressed with everyone's concern for their pen pals – until some of the kids started asking us for *receipts*! They wanted to make sure they got credit for their donations. When I asked one of them why, he said, "So I can win first prize at the sleepover!" I had to assure them that we were keeping close track of who brought in what.

Claudia noticed how competitive the SES kids were getting, too. Just *how* competitive, she found out that Sunday.

The Rodowskys' garden was every bit as crowded as the Pikes' back garden had been the day before. Claudia and the Rodowskys spent the morning busily piling things on to tables. Even Archie, Jackie's four-year-old brother, helped out.

Jackie and Shea were constantly going into the house and returning with things they hadn't thought of donating, like jewellery and glassware. Ninety-nine percent of the time, Mr or Mrs Rodowsky would scold them and make them put the things back.

At one point Jackie ran to Claudia and whispered excitedly, "We got the blender!"

"The blender?" Claudia repeated.

"Yeah," Shea piped up. "Mum and Dad never use it, but Dad didn't want to give it up."

"And I made him feel guilty about not donating to such a good cause," Shea added with a grin.

"They also gave us an old toaster," Jackie said, "and a juice extractor, and a waffle maker, and these glass bowls we've *never* used." He reached over to a table and picked up a heavy glass bowl, wedged in among a lot of appliances. "They're in really great shape, too. Look—"

The edge of the bowl caught on a plastic knob on the toaster. The toaster tipped, nudging a pile of plates. "No!" Claudia shouted.

Too late. The plates fell off and crashed onto the Rodowskys' drive. Two of them smashed immediately.

When the toaster fell, it smashed all the others.

"Oh," Jackie said, his mouth hanging open, "sorry."

"Uh, Jackie," Claudia said, stooping to pick up the toaster, "maybe you should get a broom from the garage, okay?"

"Yeah," Jackie said, backing away, "okay."

"Watch it!" Claudia warned, her eyes widening.

Jackie spun around just in time to miss bumping against another table.

With a sigh, Claud picked up the big pieces of the broken plates. (Now you can see why Jackie's nickname is "the walking disaster".) In a moment, Jackie returned unharmed with the broom, and they swept up the rest of the mess. Then Claud went back to setting up the garden. She had to hand it to those boys – they had carefully labelled everything with prices, even sorted things into categories.

By one o'clock (opening time), the garden was ready.

And nobody came – except for Mary Anne and me, but we don't really count. Claudia could feel her heart sink.

But it didn't sink far. By one-twenty the place was hopping. Claudia got so busy she didn't know what had hit her.

Well, the sale wasn't even half an hour old when Mrs Delaney picked up a big, expensive-looking lamp and said, "Hey, that's *my* lamp!"

Not long afterwards Kristy's stepfather, Watson, strolled over with a big smile. "Hi, Claudia," he said. "What sort of literature are you peddling?"

"Some good stuff!" Claudia said, picking up the top book from a pile of old, leather-bound books. "Dusti – Doze –" she stammered, reading a spine that said "Dostoevsky". She quickly looked on the front and read the title instead. "*Crime and Punishment!*"

With a smile, Watson picked up the book and began turning pages. "Sorry, but I have this collection. Precious stuff, too. Why would anyone want to—"

Suddenly his face fell. Watson's name was written in faded blue ink on the title page. He put the book down and opened to the title page of another of the books. "Wait a minute . . . this *is* my collection!"

Claudia didn't know what to say. "Oh . . . I can't imagine what. . ."

"David Michael!" Watson called out, his eyes blazing.

David Michael was at the games table, looking at a jigsaw puzzle. He whirled round. "What?" he asked timidly.

"Come here, please," Watson answered.

David Michael slunk over to him with his head down. "What?" he asked again, quietly.

"Did you give the Rodowsky boys these books?"

David Michael's face was turning red. "Well . . . they – they're so *old*, and you never ever read them and—"

"Watson?" Mrs Brewer's voice interrupted her husband. She was walking towards him, holding a box full of dusty picture frames. "Did you know that this was on the table by the porch?"

Watson glared at David Michael.

"They were in the *attic*!" David Michael protested. "And you *said* you wanted to throw them out!"

"It's not only David Michael," Mrs Brewer said to Watson. "Mrs Kilbourne found a necklace of hers that Maria had donated, and Mrs Kuhn—"

Just then, Shea ran by, wailing. His father was following behind, holding a tennis racket and shaking his head angrily. "Seventy-three dollars," he said to Kristy's parents. "If I hadn't seen someone buying it—"

He must have sensed something was up with Kristy's parents, because he stopped. Watson raised an eyebrow and nodded. "We've had a little surprise of our own," he said.

Poor old David Michael was almost in tears.

Mr Rodowsky scrunched up his forehead. "And Mrs Delaney, and—"

"You'd better believe that's my radio!" another voice boomed out. "Your father bought it for me for our first wedding anniversary!"

It was Mrs Addison, scolding her daughter Corrie.

Watson, Mr Rodowsky, and Mrs Brewer turned to each other slo-o-owly, their eyes wide and their mouths slightly open. Claudia nearly cracked up.

The next thing they knew, Mr Rodowsky was standing on a chair, saying, "Attention, everybody! Attention!"

The crowd calmed down. Mr Rodowsky put on a brave smile and said,

"It has come to my attention that certain items at this sale might not be . . . uh, *authorized*. I think some of our collectors have been a little overzealous. I want to offer my apologies, and I hope this won't dampen the spirit of giving. Perhaps we should take a few moments to sort out the sale items from the . . . nonsale items before we go on. And I assure you, if anything is missing, I'll be responsible. Thank you."

There were a few chuckles from the crowd. The first voice Claudia heard was Mrs Delaney's: "You know, the lamp is a little clunky-looking anyway. I'll let it go."

"Well, I *do* want my radio," Mrs Addison said, then added, "so I'll give you ten dollars for it. . ." She handed a ten-dollar bill to Mrs Rodowsky, who was behind the table. A smile crept across her face. "After all, it's for the kids, right?"

Most of the parents began chattering with each other and laughing. Watson tapped the book a few times and said, "I'll buy these back for fifteen dollars." He gave a small grin. "Non-negotiable."

Claudia breathed a sigh of relief. Moments before, she had imagined the whole project falling apart. But it didn't. In fact, it was a big success and raised a lot of money. There were a few more misunderstandings, a few parents dragging their kids home, clutching jewellery or coffee-pots. But for the most part, the parents were very understanding. They may have been annoyed, but they acted like . . . well, adults.

10th CHAPTER

"That's a big box!" I said to Buddy Barrett as he dragged a cardboard box up our drive.

"Yup," he said. "I can lift it, too."

He did, and his knobbly knees shook with the strain.

"Very good, Buddy," I said. "Why don't you put it down and slide it into the barn."

"Okay."

I helped him pull the box in. It was *heavy*. Buddy lives only a couple of houses away, but I was amazed he had struggled to get the box to the barn himself.

"There!" I said, shoving it into a corner. "You know, you're pretty strong for an eight-year-old."

"Yeah," he said, beaming.

"Do you want me to give you a receipt, Buddy?" I asked, hoping he'd say no.

He nodded eagerly.

For what felt like the hundredth time that day, I grabbed my clipboard from the floor. I had reached the last page of a thick pad of receipts.

Originally, when I had agreed to let my barn be the storage area for the contributions, I thought Mary Anne and I would have an easy job. All we had to do was sit there while kids came and dropped off an occasional box or two. Easy, right?

Wrong.

The carnival and the garden sale had whipped up an unbelievable amount of support for our programme. On some days, kids had to stand in line when they brought things to the barn.

It was Friday, almost a week after the big weekend, and I felt as if I was ready to drop. I lifted out the things in Buddy's box and wrote them down on my pad:

3 prs women's shoes
2 prs women's sneakers
Lt blue sundress
Silk nightgown
Terrycloth robe
4 prs kids' overalls
4 jars tomato sauce
Assorted canned goods
4-lb box, powdered milk
Case powdered baby formula

"Buddy," I said, "are you sure your mum wants to get rid of a whole *case* of baby things?"

"Yeah!" Buddy said. "Marnie grew out of that stuff a long time ago."

"And your mum *said* you could take it?"

Buddy rolled his eyes. "*Dawwwwwn*, are you going to give me a receipt or not?"

I was too tired to get into an argument. I quickly scribbled a receipt and Buddy went off. Three more kids came, and I went through the same routine with each. One of them was a kid named Rob Hines. He had been to the barn three times that week.

At a quarter to nine, people stopped coming (finally!). I was sitting on a box, gazing round, when I realized I had spent all this time collecting this stuff but had never really *looked* at it.

And there was a *lot* to look at. About half of the stuff had come in on Mary Anne's days, so I really was seeing it for the first time.

A lot of it was pretty junky, to be honest – stuff I would be embarrassed to send to New Mexico. There were fashions that were prehistoric, like a polyester pale blue jump-suit with stretched-out pockets. There were shoes that were so old and worn, you could tell exactly what the people's feet looked like and how they walked.

But there were also some pretty nice clothes, and some things that were quite beautiful. I ran my fingers down a gorgeous, silky nightdress with what looked like a hand-painted flower pattern on it. There were some designer dresses I would die to wear. Someone had brought his-and-hers running shoes that looked as if they hadn't been worn.

I began snooping round the food section, too. There were mostly cans of tuna, soup, beef stew, and boxes of cereal and flour and raisins. Sensible things – nutritious, inexpensive, and long-lasting. But mixed in with them were six-packs of chewing gum and chocolate bars, tins of biscuits, a box of imported chocolates, a huge jar of cocoa, three jars of caviar. . .

Caviar?

What was that doing here? Who in their right mind would send caviar to people who needed necessities? For that matter, why would anyone send hot cocoa to people who lived in the desert? And the imported chocolates were wonderful, but not exactly necessary.

It seemed funny to me that most parents would donate practical food and clothing while others would give things that were so useless.

Unless the parents hadn't donated them.

Suddenly the nice stuff didn't seem so . . . *nice*. My eyes travelled over a grey flannel man's suit, hanging near the window. I went to it and opened the lapel.

A tailor's receipt was sticking out of the inside pocket. I pulled it out and read the words scrawled on it.

Under the name HINES was last Wednesday's date.

Mr Hines had bought a suit last week, had it tailored, and then turned round and given it away?

Something was very wrong. And after what had happened at the garden sale, I had a feeling I knew exactly what.

The next morning, Saturday, I voiced my suspicions to Mary Anne over breakfast.

"You know," she said, "I was starting to think something funny was happening, too."

"Why didn't you say anything?" I asked.

"I didn't want to *assume*. Besides, I imagined how happy the pen pals would be when they saw such nice things. . ." She shrugged and sighed. "I suppose it was just wishful thinking."

I nodded. "Well, we still don't know for sure, right?"

"Right. Innocent until proven guilty."

"So what should we do?"

Mary Anne took a bite of her grapefruit and thought about it for a moment. "I think we should talk to some of the kids."

"You mean, go to their houses? We can't do that."

"We won't have to, Dawn. The ones who are doing it are probably the ones who keep coming back. They're going for the prizes." She smiled. "We'll just wait for them."

As if on cue, the Hines family drove up. We were *really* in luck. Not only were we going to see Rob, but his parents, too. We met them at their car and walked with them to the barn.

Poor Rob. The minute Mary Anne said, "Thank you for your incredible generosity, Mr and Mrs Hines," I could see him start to squirm.

Mr Hines chuckled. "Oh, no problem. It's nice to know everything will be put to good use."

"Donating the suit was especially nice," Mary Anne continued, gesturing to the grey flannel suit.

I watched the colour drain out of Mr Hines's face (not to mention Rob's). "Why – I – what's that doing here?" he spluttered.

Rob looked back at the car, as if he could make a getaway.

"*Rob*," Mrs Hines said.

"Um . . . I . . . I suppose I just took it by mistake. . ." Rob said.

Mr Hines was now rummaging through a box under the suit. "And my new brogues! I was looking for them yesterday!"

"But you never wear them," Rob said weakly.

"That's not the point," Mrs Hines replied. "The clothes don't belong to you."

Rob hung his head. "I'm sorry."

Mr Hines sighed. "I'm awfully sorry, girls. I suppose this'll have to be an exchange. I'll take back my good clothes and leave you with a couple of bags." There was an embarrassed smile on his face. "I'm afraid what we're leaving won't be quite as nice."

"Anything's welcome," I said.

After the Hineses had left we had a few more confrontations. Fortunately, not too many kids had pulled the same trick.

But trust Mary Anne to work out a solution to the problem.

Permission slips!

Now, instead of just taking an inventory and writing out receipts, we also had to check each kid's slip, which was made up by Mary Anne and looked like this:

(The lines at the bottom were for a list of donated items and a signature.)

I (we) _____ hereby acknowledge that as parent(s) / guardian(s) of _____, I have agreed to donate the following items to be sent to the SES sister school in Zuni, New Mexico:

_____
_____

Mary Anne wrote out the first slip, and Richard took her to a shop in town to make copies. From then on, we didn't let any kid drop off boxes without a slip (if they didn't have one, we'd send them home, box and all).

It worked. The kids weren't so . . . *ambitious* after that. And to be honest with you, there were moments when I wished we hadn't been, either.

The collections and the fund-raising were fun, but I was totally exhausted.

11th CHAPTER

Thursday

Yesterday, I sat for Matt and Haley Braddock while their parents were at a church committee meeting. I was sort of hoping to take a break from the pen-pal project. I didn't expect to be part of a last-minute fund-raiser.

I also didn't expect to be spending time with Madame Leveaux, Queen of the Gypsies.

"Don't you think it's a great idea, Mary Anne?" Haley said. "I know I can raise money. Please let me be Madame Leveaux. All I have to do is sit in front of the house and tell fortunes. Please please please please please?"

"It *is* a great idea," Mary Anne said, "but it's so elaborate. By the time you get ready, I'll have to leave."

"I'm just going to use my Hallowe'en costume!" Haley insisted. "All the stuff is in my room. And I know exactly what to say. I've been practising!"

"You have? Whose fortunes have you told?"

"I posted one to my pen pal."

"From Madame Leveaux?"

"Please, Mary Anne," Haley said, ignoring the question. "It's two whole days to the sleepover. I could make so much money . . . you know, for the pen pals."

"Mm-hm," Mary Anne said. She could sense that Haley had her sights set on a prize, and this was a last-ditch effort. On the other hand, Haley *had* been working hard on the project, and she was so determined. . .

"Well, okay," Mary Anne said. "But promise me you'll be happy – whether you make a lot of money or not."

"Yea!" Haley shouted, clapping her hands and jumping up and down. "Oh, I knew you'd be nice, Mary Anne!"

Haley turned to her brother, Matt, who had just come into the room. Matt was looking at her expectantly, waiting for her to tell him what was going on.

Matt was born deaf. He's attended a special school for the hearing impaired in Stamford since he was two. Haley talks to him by using Ameslan, or American Sign Language. It's beautiful to watch – all these quick, delicate finger movements – but it's very hard to learn. Of all of us babysitters, only Jessi has learned to use it well.

Haley signed to Matt with an excited expression on her face. Matt smiled and immediately ran down to the basement. Haley disappeared into her bedroom.

For about two minutes, Mary Anne had some peace.

Then Haley emerged, dressed in an outrageous gypsy costume, something like the genie's outfit in *I Dream of Jeannie*. A fringed, sheer, black veil covered her face.

"Greetings!" she said, rolling the *r*. She began doing her idea of an exotic dance – wiggling awkwardly with her hands over her head, palms together.

Mary Anne burst out laughing.

Haley stopped and said, "Vhat? You dare to laugh at zee famous *Madahm* Leveaux?"

"Who are you supposed to sound like?" Mary Anne asked.

"Thees eez zuh vay vee speek een Trannnsylvania," Haley replied.

"Transylvania? Leveaux is a *French* name!"

"I moved vhen I vas a very leetle girl."

"Oh, *that* explains it," Mary Anne said.

"What do you think?" Haley said in her normal voice. "Pretty good, huh?"

"Definitely . . . one of a kind," Mary Anne replied. "Now let's hurry. Your parents come back in about an hour."

"All we need now is a sign," said Haley.

She ran into the study and brought back a piece of paper and some Magic Markers. Mary Anne drew a big sign that looked like this:

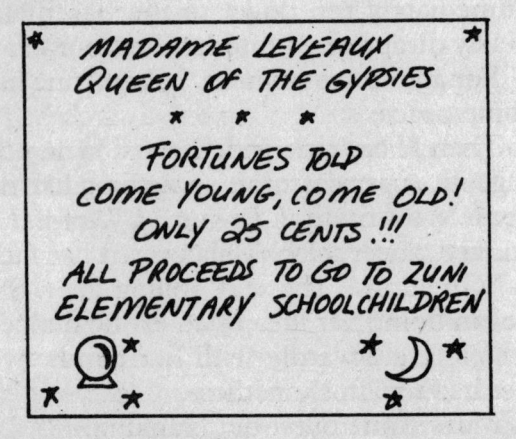

```
*  MADAME LEVEAUX        *
   QUEEN OF THE GYPSIES
       *   *   *
        FORTUNES TOLD
    COME YOUNG, COME OLD!
     ONLY 25 CENTS.!!!
   ALL PROCEEDS TO GO TO ZUNI
   ELEMENTARY SCHOOLCHILDREN
     ◯ *            * ☾ *
   *    *             *
```

By that time, Matt was back from the basement with two folding chairs. He nodded and smiled when he read the sign.

"Perfect!" Haley squealed. "Ooh, this is going to be so great – I mean, zees veel be a vonderful opportunity for zee great *Madahm* Leveaux."

"Come, *Madahm*," Mary Anne said, imitating her accent. She led the two Braddock kids out of the front door. Mary Anne held the table and a chair, Matt held another chair, and Haley held the sign (plus a pack of playing cards she'd found in her room).

Mary Anne set up the table by the pavement. Then Haley began spreading the playing cards on top in neat piles, as if she knew what she was doing. Matt signed something to Haley and ran back inside.

She shook her head, annoyed.

"What did he say?" Mary Anne asked.

"He promised to help," Haley replied, "but now he wants to practise catching fly balls while we're waiting for customers."

Matt emerged again, wearing a New York Mets cap and a baseball mitt. He quietly threw the ball high in the air and caught it, sometimes sprawling on the ground for dramatic effect.

Before long, Haley had a customer.

Mrs Barrett, Buddy's mum, came walking past with her two girls, Suzi and Marnie. The minute she saw Haley, she flashed a dazzling smile.

"Well, well," she said, "who do we have here?"

"I am zee great *Madahm* Leveaux!" Haley announced. "As eet says on zee sign!"

"So it does!" Mrs Barrett said. "It is a great honour to meet you, Madame."

Suzi tried to curtsey, but Marnie just stood there, staring blankly at Haley and clutching her mum's hand. (Suzi's five but Marnie's only two.)

"Zee honour eez mine," Haley said. She gestured grandly to the empty folding chair, which Matt pulled backwards as if he were a waiter in a fancy restaurant. "Please, one of you have a seat and I vill look into your future! Suzi? Marrrrnie?"

"Can I Mummy?" Suzi said excitedly.

"Okay," Mrs Barrett said, letting go of Marnie and reaching into her purse for some money. "And then it's your sister's turn."

Marnie grabbed her mum's skirt. She didn't look excited at all.

As soon as Suzi sat down, Haley placed her right hand on Suzi's forehead. "Shavoom, shaloom. . ." she chanted. "Mmmhm. Ah-hah!" With her left hand, she began shuffling the playing cards around. "Very eenteresting!"

"What? *What?*" Suzi pleaded.

"You have a brother no?" Haley asked.

"Yeah, Buddy," Suzi said. "You know him, Haley!"

"Haley? Who eez Haley? I am zee great *Madahm* Leveaux!"

"Oh. Sorry."

"Yes. Vell, I see your brother in a very beeg room, with . . . large hoops and nets in it."

"A gym!" Suzi said.

"Jeem . . . yes, jeem!" Haley replied. She shuffled the cards some more. "I see some sort of . . . party, and many children wearing pyjamas and eating pizza. . ."

"The sleepover!" Suzi said.

"Ah, yes, zat must be it," Haley took her hand away from Suzi's head and sat back. "You see, M*adahm* Leveaux has correctly predicted zee future! Next, please."

"Hey, that's not fair, Haley!" Suzi said. "You knew about it already!"

"Sweetheart. . ." Mrs Barrett said soothingly.

"I want our money back!" Suzi cried out, standing up.

"Suzi, it's all right. Let Marnie have her fortune told, and maybe we can come back later for another try. Buddy's waiting for us." She pulled Marnie towards Haley.

"Ah, *Madahm* Leveaux *loves* zee leetle ones!" Haley said.

The feeling was definitely not mutual. "No!" Marnie shrieked. Her face turned bright red and she burst into hysterical crying.

Mrs Barrett sighed and lifted Marnie to her shoulder. "That's okay, baby," she said. Then to Mary Anne and Haley, "Sorry, girls. I think we'd better go."

The Barretts left. Matt, who had been looking concerned about Marnie, shrugged and went back to catching fly balls.

"I think the veil scared her," Haley said.

"These things happen," Mary Anne replied. "And by the way, Haley, it's okay to make things up. You don't have to be accurate."

"Okay," Haley said.

Things went well for the next hour or so. Haley was great. As more people came, she grew more confident. Mary Anne said she was such a ham that it was hard not to laugh. The kids loved her and their parents seemed to get a kick out of her, too.

Then Mary Anne spotted Alan Gray, Justin Forbes and Pete Black walking across the street. She rolled her eyes and hoped they'd stay there.

Why? Well, first of all, Alan Gray is about the most immature boy in the eighth grade. He once spent hours at a party putting yellow M&M's in his eyes and saying he was Little Orphan Annie. He also has a crush on Kristy, which drives her absolutely *crazy*. Justin's claim to fame with the Babysitters is that he once made a joke call to Stacey, saying he was from the Atlanta Pig Farm. Pete actually isn't so bad, but when he's with Alan the immaturity sometimes rubs off.

Mary Anne was sure that if they came over to see "Madame Leveaux", the boys would *really* act stupidly and she'd never be able to get rid of them. So she hoped they wouldn't see Haley. Anyway, they were

walking fast, laughing about something.
"Let's call them over," Haley said.

"Uh, let's not," Mary Anne replied.

"Why not?"

But it was too late. Alan saw them and said, "Hey, look!"

Sure enough, the boys ran across the street. Alan read Haley's sign, pronouncing her name, "Madam Levy-oox."

"It's Luh-VOH," Haley said. "And vhat may I do for you boys?"

They laughed when they heard her accent. "I want my fortune told!" Alan said, plopping down in the folding chair. "Okay, Madamee Lee-voke-see-odor?"

See what I mean about Alan? He's such a goon. And of course, the other two thought he was unbelievably funny.

"All fortunes are a quarter, please," Haley said, not letting herself be intimidated.

"What?" Alan said. "You wouldn't do mine for free?"

"I've got a quarter," Pete said, pulling one out of his pocket and putting it on the table.

Haley shuffled her cards around, chanting, "Sha-voom, sha-loom. . ."

Alan looked up at his two friends and exploded with giggles.

"For you, zee great *Madahm* sees—" She stopped herself and gasped. "Oh, I do not believe thees!"

245

"What?" Alan said, just calming down from his giggling spell.

"I haf never seen cards like thees in my career!"

"Oh, yeah?" Alan was looking at the cards now, interested. "What do you see?"

"I see you as a young man – very handsome, too—" Haley began.

"Alaaan," Justin said with a sly smile.

"Quiet," Alan snapped.

Haley moved her cards around some more. Her voice rose with excitement. "I see riches, lots of success and great fame. Oh, my goodness! You vill be known throughout zee world as a famous—" She stopped suddenly.

"Famous what?" Alan demanded. "Famous what?"

"I haf given you zee twenty-fife-cent fortune," Haley said solemnly. "For more, you must pay another quarter."

"Oh." Alan quickly took a quarter out of his pocket. "Here, go on."

"Hey!" Pete said. "You *did* have one—"

"I'll pay you back," Alan told him quickly. "Go ahead," he said to Haley.

Haley laid it on thick, telling Alan he was going to be a film star or something. Of course, the boys pretended they weren't taking it seriously, but all three of them insisted on having their fortunes told. Haley ended up collecting two whole dollars from them. She just made up things they wanted to hear, and they were happy to pay for more.

She said she felt guilty afterwards, but Mary Anne told her not to worry about it.

To be honest, I couldn't help but feel proud of her.

Where was *I* on Wednesday? Frantically making last-minute phone calls about the sleepover. It was in *two days*! And there was still so much to do. Where had the time gone? (Well, most of it had been spent in the barn.)

I couldn't wait for Mary Anne to get back from the Braddocks'. I knew her calm, organized mind would ease my nerves. I must have looked at my watch a hundred times.

Finally, she arrived. Mary Anne quickly told me about Madame Leveaux, and then we got started.

"Okay," she said. "Did you talk to the man at the *Stoneybrook News*?"

"Uh-huh," I said. "He actually interviewed me over the phone! He's going to come once at the beginning and once at the end – both times with a photographer."

"Great. How about the pizza place?"

"Yup. They're donating as many pizzas as we need – and they want to bring them when the photographer is here."

"The toy shop?"

"Same thing. They'll donate the prizes, but they wanted to know when the photographer was coming."

"I suppose it's good publicity," Mary Anne said.

"Well, they deserve it," I replied.

"Mm-hm. And the teachers are all coming?"

"Four of them. They're bringing their own sleeping bags. There're also going to be three cafeteria workers in the morning, who are volunteering to cook breakfast — and the supermarket is donating pancake mix and fruit juice!"

"Great work, Dawn!" Mary Anne said. "I suppose you didn't have time to start working on the schedule. . ."

"I've thought about it," I said. "And I think we should organize a clean-up time at night and in the morning, but I don't think we should do too much else."

"No?"

"Don't you think it would be more fun to just let the kids have a good time, without *making* them do things?"

"Yeah, but what if they get bored, or what if they go wild? We should have a plan to fall back on — and if we don't have to use it, great!"

For the next hour or so, we worked on a schedule of games and activities. But even after we'd finished, we couldn't stop talking about it. I don't know *what* time it was when Mary Anne slumped out of my room and went to bed.

The countdown was beginning. I was so excited, I couldn't imagine making it through one more day.

12th CHAPTER

"How do you connect the tape deck to the speakers?"

"Can you bring the ladder over here?"

"Where's Claudia?"

"Yeouch!"

"You *can't* cancel!"

"Hi, Mrs Besser!"

"Over here!"

"Move it to the right!"

Friday was here! (Could you guess?)

It was almost six o'clock, the official starting time of the sleepover. There was so much shouting and running around in the gym, I don't know how we got anything done (and that was *before* any kids arrived!)

By the way, my voice was the one saying, "You *can't* cancel!" I was on the pay phone just outside the gym. Mr Morton, the owner of the Pizza Express, was telling me his special shipment of flour hadn't arrived.

I was so upset, I could barely speak. "What are the kids going to eat?" I said, almost in tears.

"I'm sorry," Mr Morton said. "I understand your problem, but I can't make pizza without flour. And I'm paying two men to hang around and do nothing, so—"

"Isn't there another place where you can get flour?"

"Not this late – and not for thirty pizzas."

"But the kids'll think you let them down, Mr Morton," I said. "They've grown up with your pizza, and they love it so much."

"*I'm* not letting them down," Mr Morton said. "It's . . . circumstances."

I sighed. "I suppose that's just what I'll have to tell them," I said. "Maybe one day they'll understand. Um, there's a pizza place in Mercer that stays open late, isn't there? Do you happen to have their number?"

Mr Morton was silent for a moment or two. Then he said, "You know, maybe I can call Jerry at the IGA supermarket. Would you mind if some of the pizzas were wholewheat?"

"Not at all!" I practically shouted. "Oh, Mr Morton, you're the greatest!"

I hung up and ran into the gym. Just inside the door, Mary Anne was fiddling with wires at the back of a tape deck while two teachers watched. Mal and Jessi were helping Mrs Besser spread wrestling mats on the floor. Kristy was organizing the tables set up for the pizzas and prizes. Stacey and Claudia were putting up decorations – streamers, posters of New Mexico, pictures and souvenirs sent by the Zuni pen pals.

It felt as if seven years had passed since Wednesday night. We spent part of Thursday at SES, arranging final details. (That's when we found out that almost a hundred kids had signed up!) That night Mary Anne and I counted the money that had been collected (more about that later). Then, on Friday afternoon, everything went wrong at once. First the reporter didn't think he'd make it because he was covering some town meeting that ran late. Then Mrs Reynolds wasn't able to get the CD player she had promised, so Mary Anne had to convince Richard to let her bring her tape deck. Then there was the problem with the pizza. . .

Well, I won't bore you with all the details. The point is, now things were *finally* coming together.

Just after six, Watson dropped off David Michael Thomas. I was *so* happy – the sleepover had finally begun!

For the next hour or so, kids poured in, all of them carrying overnight bags. Haley was one of the first, and so were Buddy Barrett and Becca Ramsey. Soon there was a traffic jam of parents and kids by the gym door. Dozens of voices blended together:

"Bye, sweetheart!"... "Don't forget to brush your teeth!"... "Get some sleep, or you'll be tired tomorrow!"... "Where's the pizza?"... "I don't want to sleep on those yucky mats!"... "What if I have to 'go' in the middle of the night?"...

I'll let you guess which were the parents and which were the kids.

Finally, Mr Selden, one of the teachers, had to announce, "Would everyone please move into either the gym or the corridor? We need to keep the entrance clear!"

In a far corner, I noticed some kids rolling out sleeping bags. "Hey, everyone!" I called. "Don't worry about that yet, okay? There's going to be a lot of running around before bedtime!"

"*WHO BUILT THE ARK? NOAH! NOAH!*"

Suddenly a voice blared out of the speakers so loudly that I had to cover my ears. Immediately the volume went down and a timid voice said, "It works!" Mary Anne had finally got the tape player wired up.

"No kidding," Shea Rodowsky remarked, followed by a burst of giggles.

At a quarter to seven, the reporter and photographer turned up. I introduced myself, then let them roam around the room.

The kids thought this was just about the coolest thing in the world. The reporter conducted interviews with a cassette recorder while the photographer snapped away. I overheard one boy say into the mike, "I intend to pursue my ambition to become a neuro – neurolog – neurobiolo – can I start again?"

It was about then that I noticed a little boy whose lip was starting to quiver. "Are you all right?" I asked, kneeling down.

He frowned and nodded his head, but the moment I turned round, he couldn't hold it any longer. "*I want my mummy to take me home!*" he cried.

"Oh, it'll be okay," I said as reassuringly as I could.

"*Ahh wahhh mahhh mahhhmahhh . . . right nowww!*" he said (that's roughly what he said – it was hard to understand him).

One thing about crying, it's contagious. Two or three other kids began to sob softly. Mary Anne went to one, Claudia to another. Then there was an outbreak of tears on the other side of the gym. For a moment I panicked. Were we going to have to send all the kids home – after their hard work? Who was going to eat the pizza?

Fortunately, we only had to call two kids' parents. Those kids left happily, and the rest of them recovered – especially when 7:05 rolled around.

Why 7:05? Because that's when the pizzas came! You could tell they were here the minute the van pulled into the car park. The smell was *incredible*.

And so was the noise. Kids pushed each other to get to the pizzas even before the delivery men had put them down.

"Hold it!" Mrs Besser called out. "Everyone sit down. The pizzas will not be opened until everyone is sitting!"

Reluctantly, the kids obeyed. They watched, practically drooling, as the delivery men brought in boxes of pizza, crates of lemonade, and stacks of paper plates and napkins. Mr Morton supervised them (and managed to get himself into a few photos).

Mrs Besser chose several of the older kids to help us babysitters distribute slices around the room. It was a big job, and if I had a dime for each time someone said "I've finished!" I'd have been rich.

Needless to say, the pizzas disappeared within minutes (except for a few slices with anchovies). They were good, too – especially the ones made with wholewheat flour.

But let me tell you, *no* pizza is good when it's cold and lying on an abandoned, greasecovered plate. And there were plenty of those left – many of them from the kids who shouted, "I've finished." (Thank you very much.)

And guess which seven girls had to clear up?

Actually, we didn't mind much, because it meant that the worst part was over. The toy shop people were due to come any minute with the delivery of prizes. Then the fun could really begin.

13th CHAPTER

The reporter and photographer were long gone by the time the toyshop people came. The toyshop people didn't seem to mind, though.

They certainly were popular with the kids. It was as if Santa had arrived in the room. You could feel a shiver of excitement going through the gym.

As the delivery people left, we did a quick count of the prizes and worked out which ones would go to which kids. Then Mrs Besser called out in her best teacher-voice, "Listen up, everybody. This is what you've been waiting for!"

"Oooh, awards! Awards!" Haley yelled.

The kids stampeded towards us.

As Kristy, Stacey, Mrs Besser and a couple of other teachers helped the kids to spread out, I turned to Mary Anne. I had just realized the one thing we hadn't talked about. "Mary Anne, who's going to give out the prizes?"

"You are," Mary Anne answered matter-of-factly.

"Me?"

"Why not? You've done more work than any of us. Why shouldn't you be the one the kids go crazy over?"

"Yeah, but what am I going to say?" I asked.

"You'll think of something," Mary Anne said. "Just like that day in the assembly hall."

"Yes, but—"

"Go ahead. Everyone's expecting you to do it."

By now the kids were silent – and staring straight at me. So were Kristy, Stacey, Mal, Claudia and Jessi.

I cleared my throat and picked up my master tally sheet, which I had spent all Thursday night working on.

"Uh, welcome to the Awards Ceremony!" I said.

The kids cheered and clapped. It was as if they were on a TV game show.

I decided to play along with it. "Behind me are the prizes you've been waiting for, courtesy of your favourite shop, the Toy Chest!"

More cheers.

"Are you ready, Mary Anne Spier?" I asked.

"Ready!" Mary Anne said, her hands poised over the boxes of gifts.

"Are you ready?" I asked the kids.

"Ready!" came the incredibly loud answer.

"I can't quite hear you!"

"*READY!*"

"Okay, may I have a drumroll, please. . ."

Kristy started drumming her hands on the table. A few kids in the front joined in – and before long, the floor was vibrating.

I finally had to yell, "Okay, stop!"

It didn't work, so I decided to go on, in a soft voice. "The winner for. . ."

Instantly the room was silent. "The winner for most creative fund-raising idea. . . Haley Braddock!"

"Yea!" Haley yelled as she sprang up.

"Let's have a hand for Haley, our own Madame Leveaux!"

The kids cheered, and Mary Anne handed me Haley's gift. "For your continued study of the stars, this fine telescope!"

"Really?" Haley said. She ripped open the box, pulled out a brand-new miniature telescope, and held it in the air. "Oh, thanks, Dawn!"

As she ran back to her seat, I announced, "And now for the person who donated the most clothes. . ."

This time I didn't have to ask for the drumroll.

". . .Rob Hines !"

The ceremony went on like this. There were a dozen main prizes, all of them really nice – a skateboard, roller skates, video games, a sledge, among others. We tried to spread the gifts to as many kids as possible. For instance, the Pikes shared a croquet set.

I was afraid some of the kids would feel sad or bitter about not winning. But the toyshop people had thought of that in advance. They had included a big bag of tiny prizes – badges, stickers, colouring books and puzzles. Everyone ended up getting some kind of reward.

When the awards were over, I thanked everybody and gave a little speech about helping the pen pals. Then, putting aside my clipboard, I announced, "Okay, it's game time! What do you want to play?"

"Red Rover!" someone shouted.

"Spud!"

"Red Light, Green Light!"

"Mother, May I?"

"All right, if you want to play Red Light, Green Light, come to me," I said.

"I'll take the Spud people!" Kristy volunteered.

"Mary Anne and I will do Red Rover!" Stacey said.

"Mal and I will do Mother, May I?" Jessi piped up.

For about an hour, the kids went wild. Then we swapped them over to quieter activities – card games, I Spy and things like that. It was almost nine o'clock.

The children began to wind down. The teachers had thought to bring a huge selection of books for all different age levels. Before long, the gym was divided into small circles of kids. Each circle was being read to by a teacher or a BSC member. I read *One Morning in Maine* by Robert McCloskey, mostly to seven-year-olds. By the time I got to the last line, "Clam chowder for lunch!", I could see a few heavy eyelids.

It was the perfect time to give them the best news of the night. I excused myself and got up. Then I went to my clipboard and announced, "Uh, before you all go to bed—"

There were a few groans, but not many.

"—I think you might like to know the grand total of the money you raised for your pen pals." I made a big deal of flipping through the note pad, then read the figure.

It was a phenomenal total. I couldn't believe it myself when we had added it up. I had made Stacey count it about four times.

There were some gasps and wows, then a few kids began to applaud.

I was proud of the kids, and glad they realized how impressive the total was. I began clapping, too. "Go ahead," I said. "Give yourselves a hand. You deserve it!"

They did, and do you know what? The looks of satisfaction on their faces were almost enough to make me forget about all the days of hard work.

Almost.

It was bedtime, and trying to put a hundred tired junior-school kids to sleep is no small task. We started with the second-graders, and took them to the boys' and girls' toilets, where they could change in the privacy of the cubicles. Some of them were so tired we practically had to carry them. Then we waited patiently while they washed and brushed their teeth – or refused to wash and brush. *Then* we went back for the next lot.

A little before ten, something happened that I don't think I'll forget for a long time. There was a little boy who had been very quiet that night, a second-grader whose name I didn't know. I remembered that he'd brought a few things to the garage that first week – not a huge amount, but a couple of good-sized boxes. I also remembered that he never looked at me in the barn. He seemed embarrassed.

He was very tired after washing, but as I walked with him to his sleeping bag, he looked straight into my eyes. "Is Johnny going to have dinners, too, now?"

"Johnny?" I asked.

"My pen pal," the boy said. "He told me he wasn't having dinners 'cause his house burned up, and he has to stay in a hotel."

"I . . . I hope so," I said.

"I donated lots of dinner food – tuna, and soup, and stuff like that."

"Well, then, the answer is yes," I said, as I helped him unzip his sleeping bag. "We'll make sure Johnny has dinners."

The boy crawled into the bag. As he snuggled into a comfortable position, there was a happy smile on his face. He looked at me again and said, "Thanks, Dawn. You're the nicest girl I've ever met."

14th CHAPTER

"I . . . I . . . I . . . I . . ."

The voice was coming out in frightened little hiccups. I didn't know the girl, but for some reason she had decided to come to me.

It was 10:09, and I had almost finished tucking in the children. "What is it?" I asked, taking the girl's hand. "Don't worry, I'm listening."

"I . . . I . . . I don't want to stay here!"

"Aren't you having a good time?" I asked. She must have been. She'd been running around like crazy all night.

"Uh-huh," she said, nodding her head.

"Did someone hit you?"

"Uh-uh." She shook her head no.

"Then what's wrong?"

She shrugged. "I just want to go home."

"Oh," I said. "You feeling a little lonely?"

She nodded.

"You feel funny not sleeping in your own bed?"

She nodded harder.

"Okay, come with me." I took the girl into the corridor and phoned her parents. They were very understanding and came right away.

When they left, it was 10:21. All of the kids were in their sleeping bags by then. Not that they were *asleep*, of course. Many of them got their second wind as soon as they were down. There were little pockets of giggling conversation all over the room. Every once in a while, someone would say "Sssshhh!" and the talking would stop – for a few seconds.

This went on until eleven or so. By that time, most of the kids were asleep or almost asleep.

Me? I was ready to drop, too. I was standing (barely) with the teachers and the rest of the BSC members under one of the basketball hoops.

It was the first chance I had had to talk to Mrs Besser all night. "Congratulations, Dawn," she said, smiling broadly. "I've never seen anything quite like this come off so well. I only wish your brother could have been here to see it. He would have been proud."

I nodded. I wished Jeff had been there, too. It was hard not to miss him at a time like this.

Mrs Besser turned to all of the BSC members. "You all deserve nothing but the highest praise."

I was tired, but not too tired to smile. "Thanks," I said. "But if it wasn't for you, this would never have happened."

Everyone agreed with me. Mrs Besser returned my smile and said, "Do me a favour. Would you mind staying exactly the same age for a few years until I have a child old enough to be babysat for?"

We laughed. Some of the kids turned in their sleeping bags to see what was going on.

"We'll see what we can do," I said. I paused. "I don't know about anyone else, but I'm *tired*."

"Me, too," said Mary Anne, Claudia and a couple of teachers.

It was our turn to use the toilets to change in, which was fun, like summer camp, but we kept quiet to avoid disturbing the kids.

Sometime around 11:20 I fell asleep.

At 11:31 I heard a girl say, "I have to go to the toilet!"

"Go ahead," Mary Anne's sleepy voice replied.

"I can't," the girl said.

"Why not?"

"I'm afraid!"

When I heard footsteps, I dozed again.

But not for long. "*I* have to go to the toilet!" someone else announced.

"Me too!"

"Me too!"

The second voice came from nearby. Wearily I rounded up three kids. Wearily I marched them to the toilets. Wearily I walked them back.

I tried to go to sleep again – several times. Just when I would be starting a wonderful dream, some crisis would occur.

At 11:52, Jordan Pike got into a fight over where he and another boy had the right to put their feet while they slept.

At 12:06, a girl had a screaming nightmare. That wasn't funny. While Stacey calmed her down, two other kids began to cry and had to be comforted.

I don't know *when* these things happened: Buddy Barrett started sleepwalking, and Mr Selden followed him patiently all around the gym without waking him up. (For some reason, you're not supposed to wake up a sleepwalker.)

A fifth-grader got cramp.

A second-grader had an . . . *accident* in a sleeping bag and woke up crying.

Someone had eaten too much pizza (Fortunately, a teacher got him to the toilets in time!)

Throughout the night, there were cluster of kids wanting to be taken to the toilet – one would speak up, and the rest would follow.

Needless to say, when morning came, none of us had slept much.

The supermarket delivery people came around 5:30, and we let them into the cafeteria, which was down the hall.

About twenty minutes later, the cafeteria volunteers arrived. They went quietly to work.

I think I will never forget the smell of pancakes that started seeping into the gym. I'm not a big fan of pancakes, but smelling them that morning made me weak with hunger.

It also started rousing the kids. You'd think they had had the deepest, most peaceful night's sleep in their lives.

It was a new day, and they were raring to go, to say the least.

"I'm hungry!" one kid called out.

"Where's the TV?" another demanded.

Another started laughing, exclaiming, "Look at Jimmy's *hair*!"

The boy named Jimmy, whose curly hair had gone wild in the night, furiously tried to press it down.

A group of boys ran around with their sleeping bags tied around their necks like capes, shooting imaginary space-age weapons.

Somehow, us older people managed to arrange them into groups for washing time. Then, of course, they had to dress themselves in the cubicles, which was another adventure. Some of them took *for ever*. Some didn't want to be seen in clothes that had become so wrinkled overnight. Others teased their friends for no good reason.

I thought the pancakes would turn to rocks by the time we got everyone to the cafeteria.

They didn't. In fact, they were incredible – *much* better than the meals I'd had in my junior school. The kids had a choice of plain, blueberry, strawberry, or buttermilk pancakes. There was plenty of syrup and butter. And there was orange, apple and grapefruit juice, and lots of milk and coffee.

"My, you look slightly less than perfect!" Stacey said to me with a teasing smile.

"I feel as if I've been run over by a bus," I replied.

Stacey held out a glass of orange juice. "Here, you have some of his. It'll wake you up."

I shook my head. "No thanks."

My eyelids felt as if they weighed about a ton. And I really needed to be wide awake, because breakfast was like – well, you can imagine what breakfast for a hundred kids was like.

"Hey!" Vanessa Pike suddenly shouted. A pancake had ended up on her head, and a few kids were covering their mouths and laughing. I took her away to the girls' toilets.

By the time I got back, every teacher and babysitter had his or her hands full.

"Ugh!" cried a group of girls, pulling their trays away from a huge syrup spill on a table.

Splat! Jackie Rodowsky landed on his backside when he slipped on some spilled grapefruit juice.

"Hey, look at me!" Byron Pike was entertaining a group of boys by putting two strips of pancake under his nose to look like a moustache.

"Charlene took my orange juice!" a girl started shouting.

"Well, you took my seat!" That must have been Charlene.

This went on . . . and on . . . and on. . .

Until Claudia poked me in the ribs. "Dawn, do you see what I see?"

I looked up. A smiling man and woman were peering through the cafeteria door.

"Daddy! Mummy!" a second-grader called out.

"Parents!" I said, like someone stranded in the desert might say "Water!"

As more and more parents came, the chaos started again. Kids returned their trays (or didn't), went back to the gym, lost their things, had trouble packing their things, mixed their things up with someone else's, you name it.

In the midst of all of this, the reporter and photographer came back to do a follow-up report – which delayed things even more.

The Barretts were the last parents to arrive and the last to leave. As we watched them walk Buddy out to the car park, we stood at the door and waved.

Then it was time for *our* celebration.

"Whoopee!" Kristy shouted. "We did it!"

All seven of us babysitters somehow managed to embrace each other. The teachers stood round us, smiling.

Then we looked back into the gym.

Strewn around the floor were sweet wrappers, shoelaces, toothbrushes, plastic cups, underwear – even a couple of pizza crusts that had been overlooked.

But you know what? Tired as I was, I suddenly felt full of energy. All I could think about was this: My great plan – every last complicated part of it – was over. And boy, had it been a success!

As I cleaned up the remains of the sleepover, I could hardly feel my feet touch the ground.

15th CHAPTER

As soon as we had cleared up, my friends and I gathered at my house with the teachers and bundled everything up to send to Zuni. We loaded up cars and Mrs Reynolds' minivan, packing as tightly as we could, and *still* we had to make three trips.

The postal costs came out of the money we'd collected, but we sent the rest in a cheque directly to the head teacher of the Zuni school (super sleuthing on Claudia's part – she found his name in one of the Pike kids' letters, then called New Mexico information for his home address).

A week later, we heard from him. The letter came to SES and went like this:

To the children of Stoneybrook, Connecticut:
I have been an educator for twenty-seven years. As an English teacher and an administrator, I have guided my children to speak

clearly with well-chosen words. But for the first time in my life, I find that words are inadequate to express my feelings – our feelings.

Many of us were rendered speechless by your generosity and unselfish donation of time. The gifts of clothing and food were distributed where needed, and are already being enjoyed. The money has helped enable us to obtain financing for the construction of a new school.

But the rewards of your work go beyond the gifts themselves. Our children have been inspired by you to do fund-raising of their own. They are planning various activities right now, and the community seems to be throwing its support behind them..

The government, perhaps partly as a reaction to the positive efforts we are displaying, agreed today to grant us substantial disaster funding.

With luck, our school will be built and stocked with supplies by the beginning of next school year.

We hope to be left with a reserve fund for an exchange trip with our brothers and sisters in Stoneybrook, Connecticut.

Once again, thank you all.
Fondly,
    Joseph Woodward

Pretty nice, huh? I felt shivers when I read it. Especially the part about "brothers and sisters". I hope there really will be an exchange trip sometime – and I hope a few older kids will be asked to go along to help!

Anyway, in the weeks after the sleep-over, there was a lot of pen pal correspondence. Charlotte showed me a great letter from Theresa Bradley.

> Dear Char,
> Rember in my last letter when I told you my mum was crying alot? Well, when all your stuf came she cryed some more. But now she says its cause shes happy!
> I'm happy, to. Is the letter frinjed rest from you? Its realy nice and I got it. I also liked geting a botle of choclit sauce and those cans of pork and beens, even tho my ant had some. I didn't like the deviled ham but that's ok.
> My couzin says that now she really wishes her school woud burn down, since she saw what hapened to us.
> I still think shes crazy.
> Thank you for being so nice to us.
>   Luv ya,
>   Theresa
>   your best number #1 pen pal

And there was a letter that came to Mary Anne's house in an envelope marked like this:

```
Nancy Green
P.O. Box A7449
Zuni, NM

              Madame Leveaux
              c/o Mary Anne Spier
              173 Burnt Hill Rd
              Stoneybrook, CT 06800

CAUTION: TO BE OPENED ONLY BY
         MADAME LEVEAUX
```

"Um, Haley?" Mary Anne said the night she brought it to the Braddocks'. "Who's Nancy Green?"

"My pen pal," Haley replied. "Why?"

"That's strange," Mary Anne replied, handing her the letter. "Why would she write to you, as Madame Leveaux, at my address?"

"Oh," Haley said, "I – I wrote her a note from Madame Leveaux, you know, as a joke." Haley was starting to squirm. "Well, I didn't want her to know it was from me, so I gave her your address. I meant to tell you, Mary Anne. Really! I just – forgot."

"That doesn't sound like you, Haley," Mary Anne said.

"I know," Haley replied. "I'm not going to do it again. I'm sorry."

275

"All right," Mary Anne said, turning to go. "See you."

"Bye!" Haley quickly closed the door.

As Mary Anne walked home, she couldn't help smiling. What she hadn't told Haley was that she'd opened the letter by mistake and read it already. Haley, as Madame Leveaux, had written to her pen pal right around the time of the assembly. That was when I had asked all the kids not to tell their pen pals about our plans. Haley was dying to tell Nancy Green, but she knew she couldn't.

That didn't mean *Madame Leveaux* couldn't tell her. . .

Anyway, this is what the letter said:

Dear Mrs Leveaux,

You were right. Everything you said, all that stuff about help coming from a mysterious place in the east, it all came true. When I told my friends about your predictions, nobody believed me. Then, the day after your letter came, we got this great stuff from our pen pals. Clothes, food, even a huge cheque to build a new school! I can't believe my pen pal, Haley Braddock, never mentioned anything about it!

Now here are some questions for you.

Did you know our pen pals are in the same exact town you live in? How did you know my address? How did you know about Pens Across America?

Anyway, thank you for sending the fortune.
Please send me another one. My friends and I can't wait!
   Yours truly,
   Nancy Green
P.S. This time, Haley, disguise your handwriting better!

KRISTY AND THE BABY PARADE

The author gratefully acknowledges
Ellen Miles
for her help in
preparing this manuscript.

1st CHAPTER

Okay, I admit it. I was bored.

I hardly ever get bored while I'm babysitting – I love being with kids – but that day was different. It wasn't exactly cold out, but it was sort of grey and dreary. So I'd been indoors all afternoon with David Michael and Emily Michelle. We'd played almost every game in the house at least three times.

"I'm bored!" said David Michael.

"Bowed!" said Emily Michelle. She doesn't speak very well yet, but she can mimic just about anything you say – even if she doesn't have the slightest idea what it means.

Maybe I should stop here and explain a few things, like who I am and why I was sitting for these two bored kids.

I'm Kristy Thomas. I'm thirteen and I'm in the eighth grade at Stoneybrook

Middle School. More than anything, I love to babysit. In fact, it's sort of a business for me and some of my friends – but I'll tell you more about that later.

It's lucky that I love to babysit because I've got a big family that includes quite a few kids who need sitting for. David Michael and Emily Michelle, for example. And then there are Karen and Andrew. . .

Oh, my family's so confusing sometimes. Let me start at the beginning. My original family was pretty ordinary. There were my mum and dad and my two older brothers, Charlie and Sam, me, and my little brother, David Michael.

But just after David Michael was born, my dad walked out on us. He just left. I hear from him now and then, on my birthday (although sometimes he even forgets that) or at Christmas. I think he's living somewhere in California these days. It was hard on us when he first left, but my mum's pretty strong, and she did a great job of holding the family together.

And then, not too long ago, my mum met a really terrific man called Watson Brewer. They fell in love and got married – so now Watson's my stepfather. After the wedding, we moved across town to live in his mansion.

Watson is a real, true millionaire. Can you believe it? But you'd never know it by the way he acts – he's not stuck up or anything. He's just an ordinary person.

And he's a great father to his two kids from his first marriage – Karen (she's seven) and Andrew (he's almost five). They live with us every other weekend and for a couple of weeks during the summer. They're terrific kids.

So anyway, once we'd moved into the mansion, Mum and Watson started to want a baby – and that's where Emily Michelle comes in. When Mum first started talking about a baby, I thought she was planning to get pregnant. But then Watson told us that they were going to adopt a little Vietnamese girl – and that's exactly what they did.

Emily Michelle is two and a half years old, and she's just about the most adorable thing I've ever seen. She doesn't talk much – partly because she's just beginning to understand English. But she's a real sweetie.

David Michael's seven now, and he loves being a big brother. Emily Michelle looks up to him just like I look up to Charlie (he's seventeen) and Sam (he's fifteen).

I haven't even mentioned Nannie yet – she's my grandmother. She moved in with us after we adopted Emily, partly because we needed her help (Mum and Watson both work) and partly because she was tired of living alone. Her husband died years ago.

Nannie's great. She keeps busy and really enjoys life. She has tons of friends, she likes going bowling, and she's always on the go.

There are several other members of my family – but they're not people. We've got a puppy called Shannon – she's a Bernese mountain dog, and she's going to be *huge* some day. And Boo-Boo is Watson's cat. He's old and fat and pretty grumpy – but he's still part of the family. Plus, Karen and Andrew have two goldfish, Crystal Light the Second and Goldfishie.

So there you have it. I think this is a pretty nice family, even if it is a little complicated.

Now, where was I? Oh, right. I was telling you how bored we all were that day. Well, you'd be bored, too, after playing Cluedo, Twister, Shark Attack (that's Emily's favourite), and one lo-o-ng game of Monopoly.

I racked my brains trying to think of something to do. I wasn't about to turn on the TV – I only do that as a last resort – but I couldn't come up with any other ideas for indoor activities. I kept wishing that the sun would come out so we could go outside, but it refused to budge from behind all those clouds.

Should we make biscuits? Nope. Too messy. Mum would be coming home soon, and she'd want to start dinner. Build with Lego? No way. David Michael had told me early in the afternoon that he was sick of Lego.

I got up to put Shark Attack away, and that's when it hit me. I saw all the magazines and newspapers sitting in their recycling bins on the floor of the hall cupboard. Collages! We'd make collages.

"Yea!" said David Michael when I told him my idea.

"Yea!" echoed Emily Michelle. I knew that she'd make more of a mess than a work of art, but I knew she'd have fun, too. She loves messing around with scraps of paper and glue and Magic Markers.

I grabbed a stack of newspapers and magazines and brought them to the kitchen table. Then I got out safety scissors, glue, crayons and markers, and some paper. I sat David Michael and Emily Michelle at the table and told them to go for it.

Pretty soon David Michael was cutting away, his tongue sticking out as he concentrated on not slicing off Darryl Strawberry's head. It only took Emily Michelle about thirty seconds to get glue all over her hands – but I let her go wild, since she was wearing old clothes.

I picked up a recent issue of *Stoneybrook News*, thinking that I might find some interesting things for both of them to cut out. Most of what I glanced at looked fairly boring, though. There was a long story about the new sewage treatment plant, and another about some couple's fiftieth wedding anniversary.

I kept leafing through the paper, looking for good pictures. Then this advert caught my eye. "Calling All Babies!" it said. It was an advert for the Stoneybrook Baby Parade.

The baby parade. I'd forgotten all about it. It's held only once every two years, and I'd never paid much attention to it. I always thought it was pretty silly. It's this big event in which parents dress up their kids in all kinds of wild costumes and try to win prizes. Some of the kids are in buggies, some are in go-carts, and some are on big floats that hold a whole lot of kids. There are all these different categories for different age groups and types of entries.

For example, the advert described Category A, which would include "children in fancy, decorated go-carts; buggies; coaches; or kiddie cars." Category B was for children in "*comic*, decorated go-carts; buggies. . ." You get the picture. Categories C and D were for floats of various sizes.

There would be a grand marshal for the parade, and judges who would pick first-, second- and third-place winners in each division. All children under the age of three were eligible to enter. The advert said to watch out for applications.

I remembered some of the baby parades I'd seen. They were pretty crazy! Every entry has to have a "theme" – and some of the themes are kind of . . . well, imaginative. Like the float one year that was called

"Circus Days". It featured a twelve-foot high elephant on wheels! Or the "Wild West" float I saw once, with a cowboys-and-Indians pageant being acted out on top of it.

Babies in buggies had to have themes, too – they might be dressed up like fairy-tale characters or people from films.

It was pretty silly, all right.

But after I'd read that ad, my glance kept resting on Emily Michelle. She's *adorable*. Have I already told you that? Well, she is. I looked at her glossy, straight black hair cut like a Dutch girl's. I looked at her sparkling brown almond-shaped eyes. I looked at her plump, pink cheeks and at her sturdy little hands (all covered with glue at the moment, but still very cute) and at her round little tummy.

I was getting an idea.

I'm famous for that – getting ideas, that is. Just ask my friends. I don't mean to sound egotistical or anything. It's just something I'm good at. Ideas pop into my head, and a lot of them turn out to be pretty good, really.

I'm sure you can guess what this idea was about. That's right. I was thinking of entering Emily in the baby parade. She'd be bound to win a prize – and it would be so much fun to dress her up and show her off.

I looked at her again. What category would I enter her in? What kind of costume should she have? There was a lot to think about.

"Do you like my collage, Kristy?" asked David Michael suddenly. I shook myself. I'd been thinking so hard that I'd forgotten what we were doing. I looked at David Michael's creation.

"That's great!" I said. And it was, sort of. It had a baseball theme – that is, David Michael had cut out every picture he could find that had anything to do with baseball, and then he'd pasted them all onto a piece of paper, in no particular order. It was about four layers thick, and pictures were hanging off the sides. He'd also cut out words like HOME RUN and RED SOX from headlines. Those were pasted right over the pictures.

"Charlie'll love it," I said. I knew he would, too. He loves anything to do with baseball.

Just then, I heard the front door slam. "Anybody home?" called a voice.

"There's Charlie now!" I said. "That means Mum will be home soon, too. Time to clear up." I looked at the mess Emily Michelle had made, and I sighed. She might be perfect-looking, but she's just like any other two-and-a-half-year-old when it comes down to it.

I helped clear off the table, thinking all the time about the baby parade. Soon Sam came home, and then Nannie got back from bowling practice, and right on her heels were Mum and Watson.

Before long, the house was full of noise and activity as we all helped get dinner ready. As I told you earlier, I love my wild family. But that night, I was glad when dinner was over and I could go up to my nice quiet room to start my homework – and think about my latest idea.

I was sure that my friends would be excited about the baby parade, too. Maybe Jessi would want to enter Squirt! And there are lots of other babies whom we sit for. This could be a great activity for the whole club !

What club?

Oh, I suppose I haven't told you about it yet. Well, it's a long story.

2nd CHAPTER

The club I've been talking about is special. It's special because it's more than a club – it's a business, as I've mentioned before. It's also special because of the people who belong to it. There are seven of us in the Babysitters Club, and I consider each one of the other members my good friend.

Sometimes, I think it's amazing that we're all such close friends – because we're very different. Of course, we have got things in common. We love to babysit, for one. That's probably why the club works so well.

I'm the chairman of the BSC. That's because it was my idea. (Remember how I said that I often have good ideas? Well, this one was the best ever.) I try to run the club in a business-like way, and I know that sometimes it means I come across as a little bossy. But my friends put up with it pretty well.

They're used to me. They're used to the fact that I have (I admit it) a big mouth. It's not that I'm *mean* or anything, but I'm not always as tactful as I could be. They're also used to the fact that I'm not as sophisticated as the rest of them: I'm not interested in clothes (I usually dress for comfort, not for style – which means jeans, a poloneck, and trainers most days) or make-up or any of that stuff.

Boys? Well, until recently I wasn't interested at all. But lately I've developed a crush on this kid Bart, who coaches a softball team in my neighbourhood. I coach one, too. His team's name is Bart's Bashers, and mine is called Kristy's Krushers.

But you know what? I don't think I'm ready for a real boyfriend. Not after seeing what my best friend, Mary Anne Spier, went through with her boyfriend, Logan Bruno.

We all thought they were the perfect couple – but then they broke up. The break-up was sort of Mary Anne's idea, but it was tough on her just the same.

Mary Anne's a truly sensitive person. She's romantic and a good listener and she cries very, very easily. You might think that would mean that she and I wouldn't get on all that well, since I don't seem to have a sensitive bone in my body. Somehow, though, our friendship has survived my big mouth.

Though we're different in terms of personality, we're alike in other ways. For example, looks. We're both short for our age (actually, I'm even shorter than Mary Anne – I'm the shortest girl in my grade) and have brown hair and brown eyes. Mary Anne tends to dress a little more stylishly than I do – there are times when she actually looks cool, which I *never* do.

We've been friends for ever – or at least it seems that way. I used to live right next door to her, before Mum and Watson got married. Mary Anne's mum died when Mary Anne was just a baby, and her dad brought her up all by himself.

Mr Spier tried really hard to be a good father. In fact, maybe he tried *too* hard. For years, he was incredibly strict with Mary Anne. There were all kinds of rules she had to follow, and she could only dress a certain way. It used to drive her crazy. But finally Mr Spier started to loosen up. He didn't even seem to mind that Mary Anne had a boyfriend! (She's the only one in our club who has had one, by the way.)

Mr Spier actually loosened up so much that he started going out with this woman who happened to be his old high-school sweetheart. She also happened to be the mother of one of our other club members, Dawn Schafer!

Dawn's mum had grown up in Stoneybrook, but then she got married and moved to California. Years later, she got divorced, and she and Dawn (and Dawn's younger brother, Jeff) moved back to Stoneybrook. And after she and Mr Spier had dated for a while, they decided to get married!

So Mary Anne's *other* best friend, Dawn, is now also her stepsister. Mary Anne and her dad (and her kitten, Tigger, too) moved into Dawn's house to live with Dawn and her mum.

What about Jeff? Well, he missed his dad – and California – so much that he moved back there. Now Dawn misses *him*, but she knows he made the right decision.

I think Dawn's happy here in Stoneybrook. I know she misses the sunny beaches and the more laid-back life-style of California, but she's adjusted well to life in Connecticut. Dawn *looks* like my idea of a California girl, though. She's a real knock-out, with her blue eyes and her long, long, pale blonde hair. She's got a style all her own, too – my friends and I call it "California casual". She wears lots of cool clothes in bright colours.

By the way, Dawn was always pretty, even as a little kid. She once told me that when she was two years old, her mum entered her photo in a baby contest – and she won first prize!

But Dawn's not at all stuck-up. I don't even think she has any idea how pretty she is. Dawn is – well, she's mellow, that's the only way I can describe her. She does her own thing, and doesn't care much what other people think of her. I admire her for that.

She's been through some pretty rocky times – first her parents' divorce, and then her brother moving back to California, and then her mum's remarriage. (Even though Dawn and Mary Anne are best friends, it took some time for them to adjust to being in the same family.) But she's hung in there throughout all of it, even when the rest of us knew she must be hurting.

One of Dawn's favourite things about Stoneybrook is the house she lives in. Dawn loves reading ghost stories – so what could be better for her than living in a haunted house? You might think I'm kidding, but I'm not. The house is really, really old, and it has a secret passage. We're almost sure that a ghost lives there!

And if it does, maybe Dawn and Claudia can catch it. Claudia Kishi is another member of our club, and her favourite reading consists of Nancy Drew mysteries. She considers herself a pretty good detective.

Claudia is just as gorgeous as Dawn, but in a totally different way. Instead of pale blonde hair, Claudia's is jet-black. Instead of blue eyes, Claudia's got beautiful brown almond-shaped ones.

Claudia is Japanese-American – very exotic and very, very cool. If you want to talk about style, you've got to talk about Claudia Kishi. Nobody in Stoneybrook can put together a wild outfit like Claud can. She's always up on the latest trend, whether it's big black shoes, tie-dyed leggings, or cool hats.

Her parents don't mind the way she dresses (though they'd probably draw the line if she wanted to dye her hair green or get a Mohican or something) because they know it's all part of Claudia's artistic sense, which they like to encourage.

The thing is, Claud's not a great pupil – not because she's stupid, but because she's just not that interested in school. (Her older sister, Janine, *loves* school – she's a certified genius, so that would explain it.) But Claudia's less-than-average grades in English and maths are balanced out by her above-average artistic talent.

Painting, drawing, sculpting – you name it, Claudia's terrific at it. You wouldn't believe the beautiful things she's made. She even makes her own jewellery sometimes – which just adds to her distinctive personal style.

I mentioned that Claud's parents encourage her artistic talent, but did I tell you how they feel about her passion for Nancy Drew books? Well, they don't exactly approve, so Claud has to hide her books.

She's good at hiding things, because she's got another habit her parents disapprove of: eating junk food.

Now, I like to have an occasional Twix as much as the next person, and I won't turn down a Kit-Kat. But Claudia is on another level of junk-food eating altogether. Security for Claud would be knowing that there are some M&M's in her sock drawer, a packet of Munchies in her paint box, and a bag of tortilla chips – the ones with extra cheese? – on the top shelf of her wardrobe.

The funny thing is that even though Claudia is a very generous person, she can't share her junk food with her best friend, Stacey McGill. Why not? Well, the reason isn't all that funny. It's because Stacey has diabetes, a disease in which her blood sugar can get out of control and she has to be very, very careful about what she eats.

Not too long ago, Stacey was really ill – partly because she had gone off her strict no-sugar diet, and partly because her blood sugar had become really hard to control. She was in hospital and everything, and we were all pretty worried about her. But she's fine now. And I think she will be, as long as she takes care of herself. ("Taking care of herself" includes giving herself daily injections of this stuff called insulin, which her body doesn't make any more. Giving yourself injections! Can you imagine? Ugh.)

Stacey hasn't lived in Stoneybrook for that long, even though we all feel as if we've known her for ever. She grew up in New York City – and she's just as sophisticated as you might imagine. Sometimes she and Claudia decide to get really dressed up. They try their best to outdo each other with wild hairdos (Stacey has blonde hair that she gets permed once in a while), crazy earrings, and the coolest clothes this side of the Connecticut state line.

Stacey stays in touch with what's happening in the city because her father lives there and she visits him fairly often. That's right, Stacey's parents are divorced, too. And the split took place pretty recently.

What happened was this. Stacey's family first moved to Stoneybrook when she was in the seventh grade because her dad got transferred to his company's Stamford office. (That's a city near here.) Then, just when we'd made friends with her, he got transferred back to New York and the McGills had to move back there! We were so sad to see Stacey go.

But pretty soon after they'd returned to the city, Stacey's parents began to fight a lot, and finally they decided to separate. Her mum chose to move back to Stoneybrook, and we were all thrilled when Stacey (who was given the choice of coming back here or living with her dad in his flat in the city) came with her.

Let's see. Me, Mary Anne, Dawn, Claudia, Stacey... There are still two other members of the BSC that I haven't told you about. Jessi and Mallory are younger than the rest of us – they're eleven and in the sixth grade at Stoneybrook Middle School. (All of the rest of us are thirteen and in the eighth grade.)

Jessi Ramsey's family has only lived in Stoneybrook for a little while. They bought the house that Stacey used to live in! And when they moved in, they caused a bit of a stir in the neighbourhood. Why? Because they're black. Big deal, right? That's what all of us thought. But a lot of people felt differently. There aren't too many black families in Stoneybrook – and some people wanted it to stay that way.

But you know what? Most people accept the Ramseys now. They're a great family. Jessi's the eldest of three kids: she's got a little sister named Becca, who's eight, and the cutest baby brother called Squirt. (Well, he wasn't actually *named* Squirt – that's just his nickname. His real name is John Philip Ramsey, Jr.)

Mallory Pike is the oldest in her family, too. But her family is a *lot* bigger than Jessi's. Mal has four brothers and three sisters! (Three of her brothers are triplets.)

Being the eldest is sometimes hard on Mal and Jessi – mainly because they feel that while they have lots of responsibilities, they still get treated like babies by their parents. You know how it is when you're eleven. You want to be treated like more of a grown-up, but your parents still see you as a kid. Jessi and Mal did win one round with their parents: they were finally allowed to get their ears pierced. But Mal still has a brace *and* glasses. Oh, well.

Like any best friends, Jessi and Mal have a lot in common (they both love reading horse stories, for example). But they also have a lot of separate interests. Jessi loves to dance – I'm sure she'll be a professional ballerina some day, if she wants to be. She's really, really talented. And Mal is a writer and an artist. She's always keeping journals and sketching and making up stories. She wants to write – and illustrate – children's books when she's older.

So, those are the members of the BSC. I'm sure you can see why I think our club is pretty special – and why I consider myself so lucky to have such a great group of friends.

3rd CHAPTER

Claudia's room. Monday, 5:25 P.M. If that's the time and place, you can bet what kind of mood I'll be in. I'll be feeling great, because it's almost time for the first BSC meeting of the week.

That day was no exception. I sat in Claudia's director's chair, wearing my visor. (I always wear my visor during meetings; it makes me feel more official.) I had tucked a pencil behind my ear, and I was watching the clock, waiting for the others to arrive.

I'm almost always the first club member to reach Claud's room. Why? Because I'm the chairman, and I feel it's my responsibility to start the meeting on time.

We've run the club in a business-like way, right from the start. I think it's part of the reason that we've been so successful. Who could have guessed that such a simple idea would have turned out so well? As I sat and waited that day, I thought back to the very beginning of the club. . .

It was the beginning of the seventh grade. I was still living next door to Mary Anne, and across the street from Claudia, on Bradford Court. Mum and Watson were dating, but I had no idea that they'd end up married.

Even back then, I loved to babysit. But the person I sat for most was my own brother, David Michael. He needed watching every day after school until Mum got home from work. I also sat for him in the evening sometimes, when Mum went out with Watson.

Sam and Charlie watched David Michael, too, so it was rare that Mum had to hire a babysitter from outside the family. But once in a while everybody wanted to go out at the same time. One afternoon Mum realized that she'd need to hire a sitter for the next day. She got on the phone and started phoning round, looking for somebody to bail us out. I'll never forget that night. We were eating pizza and Mum's got cold while she kept making calls.

That's when I got this idea. What if Mum could phone just one number that would put her in touch with a whole group of experienced babysitters? One of them would *have* to be free. I got really excited about it, and I told Mary Anne and

Claudia as soon as I could. What if, I asked them, we formed a club that would meet a few times a week? During those times, parents could call us to arrange for sitters.

They thought it was great idea, but Claud pointed out (and Mary Anne agreed) that three people weren't going to be enough to keep up with the demand for sitters. Claud had just met – and made friends with – Stacey, so we asked her to join, too. By the time Dawn moved to Stoneybrook, we had so much business that we were nearly desperate for another member. So Dawn joined the club.

How did Jessi and Mal get to be members? Well, remember how I told you that Stacey's family moved back to New York for a while, just before her parents got the divorce? When she left, the club just couldn't keep up with all its sitting jobs, so that's when Jessi and Mal joined. Of course, when Stacey came back she was automatically part of the club again.

The club seems to be just about the right size now, especially since we also have two associate members, Shannon and Logan. (I'll tell you more about them later.) They don't come to meetings (there's no way *nine* of us could fit comfortably into Claud's room), but they help us out when we need extra sitters.

You might be wondering how we get all this business I keep talking about. Well, some of it is "word of mouth". Parents we've sat for have been impressed with us and have told other parents to phone us. Also, we advertise. We made up these cool-looking leaflets (Claud designed them), and every now and then we distribute them around the neighbourhood. Once we even put an advert in the *Stoneybrook News* – but we haven't had to do that again. We have as much business as we can handle.

The leaflets explain how the club works. We meet every Monday, Wednesday and Friday from 5:30 to 6:00, and parents can call us then to line up a sitter. Parents love knowing they'll find a sitter, and we love to babysit!

I told you that I'm the chairman, but I haven't explained what everybody else in the club does. This is one club where every member has a job or a position.

Claudia is the vice-chairman. She doesn't exactly have a job to do, but she's vice chairman for a few good reasons. First of all, we meet in her bedroom. Why? Because she's the only member who has her own phone – and her own private line. We could never tie up any grown-ups' lines with all the calls we get during our meetings.

Claud could also be referred to as the refreshment officer, if there were such a thing. She's very generous with her junk food. As soon as each meeting gets under way, Claudia digs out the snacks. She's thoughtful, too. She knows that Stacey and Dawn don't go for junk food (Stacey because of her diabetes; Dawn because she's addicted to health food) so she always makes sure to have some plain, boring thing like wholewheat crackers on hand, to supplement the Hula Hoops and tortilla chips.

Mary Anne is our club secretary. What a job she has! She keeps track of all our appointments in this big notebook that we call the club record book. The information in that book is irreplaceable. The record book has all the names and addresses of our clients (as well as special facts about their pets, their children's allergies, and other stuff). It also includes our sitting appointments.

Mary Anne has another important task. She has to keep track of all our schedules. That might sound simple, but when you start to think about the things we do – Jessi's dance classes, my softball practices, Claud's art classes, Mallory's orthodontist appointments – well, you get the picture. When a call comes in from a parent looking for a sitter, Mary Anne can tell at a glance which of us is free. She's never made a mistake, which is pretty amazing.

Stacey, the maths whiz, is our treasurer. She keeps track of how much money we earn (even though we each keep what we make, we like to know the total), and she also collects our subs every Monday. We *hate* giving up any of our hard-earned money, but we know it's going to a good cause.

Or several good causes, that is. For example, we use some of the money to pay my brother Charlie to drive me to meetings, since I now live so far from Claud's house. And some of it goes towards Claud's phone bill. And once in a while, we go mad and spend some on a big pizza blow-out.

Dawn is our alternate officer. That means that she knows how to do all our jobs, so we're covered if anybody has to miss a meeting. She was terrific as treasurer, for example, during the time that Stacey had moved back to New York.

Mallory and Jessi are our junior officers. Since they're younger, they don't sit alone at night. But they handle a lot of our afternoon and weekend jobs, which is a tremendous help.

Last but not least are our associate members, the ones I told you about who don't come to meetings. One of them is Shannon Kilbourne, this girl who lives in my new neighbourhood. The other is Logan Bruno. Does that name sound familiar? That's right, he's Mary Anne's "ex". He's a good sitter, too. I'm glad we have him and Shannon to fall back on when the rest of us are too busy to take a job.

"Hey, Kristy, aren't you going to call the meeting to order?"

I snapped my head around to see who had spoken. It was Stacey. She sat in Claud's desk chair, grinning at me and pointing at the digital clock. Its big, white numbers said 5:31. I'd been lost in my thoughts and had almost forgotten that it was my job to get things going.

"Thanks, Stacey!" I said. Then I sat up straight, pulled the pencil out from behind my ear, and tapped it on the arm of my chair. "Order!" I said. "This meeting will now come to order!"

Everybody looked at me and giggled. "We've been *wondering* when you'd get round to starting the meeting," said Claudia, who was sitting on the bed between Dawn and Mary Anne. She tore open a bag of barbecued beef potato crisps and passed it to Jessi and Mallory, who were in their usual places on the floor.

"Any club business?" I asked, looking around the room. Stacey held up the manila envelope that we keep our subs in. "Oh, right," I said. "It's Monday. Okay, everybody, pay up!" We groaned as Stacey passed the envelope round, but we all chipped in.

"Hey, Stacey," said Dawn as the envelope went round. "Do we have enough money for some new stickers? My Kid-Kit is all out of them."

I don't want to sound conceited, but Kid-Kits are another of my great ideas. I noticed something once when David Michael had some friends over. Kids sometimes like to play with *other* kids' toys more than their own. So I thought that we could each make up a kit to take with us on sitting jobs. They're boxes we've decorated with glitter and stuff, and they're full of toys and books and stickers and games.

The kids just love our Kid-Kits, especially on rainy days. And when the kids are happy, the parents are happy, and when the parents are happy, they hire us again. Then we're happy! It's very simple.

Stacey doled out some money to Dawn, and to Mallory, who said she needed crayons for *her* Kid-Kit. Stacey frowned as she counted out the change, and I had to stifle a giggle. She's a great treasurer partly because she *hates* to spend our money.

"Okay," I said. "While we're waiting for the phone to ring—" and just then, it did. I almost jumped out of my seat, but I recovered in time to make a grab for it. It was Mrs Perkins, one of our regular clients. She wanted a sitter for that Thursday, and I said I'd call her back. Mary Anne checked the record book and said that Claud was the only one free, so Claud got the job. Once I'd called back Mrs Perkins, I started again.

"Has everyone read the club notebook?" I asked. There were nods all round the room. The club notebook is another of my ideas, and I have to admit that it's not one of my most popular ones. The notebook is where we write up each of our sitting jobs, giving all the gory details so that the other club members can keep up-to-date on what's happening with our clients. Everybody's pretty good about reading the entries, but nobody (except Mal, maybe) really likes to write them. It takes time, but I have to say that it's worth it. I think it helps us to be better sitters.

"I liked what Dawn had to say about her new technique for dealing with temper tantrums," said Mary Anne. "I never would have thought of tucking children into their beds and talking gently to them until they felt calmer."

"It really works, too!" said Dawn.

We talked some more about "tantrum techniques", and then I started to tell the others about the baby parade. But just then, the phone rang again and Stacey grabbed it. She rolled her eyes when she first heard who was calling, so we all knew it had to be Mrs Prezzioso, one of our more "difficult" clients. Then she listened for a long time, saying an occasional "yes" and "I see."

I was dying to know what the call was about. Finally, Stacey said she'd call Mrs Prezzioso back and hung up.

"What did she want?" I asked.

Stacey filled us in. It seemed that Mrs Prezzioso was looking for a regular sitter – two afternoons a week – for a whole month. The Prezziosos have two daughters: Jenny, who's four, and can be a bit of a brat, and Andrea, who's a baby.

"Mrs P.'s going to be on the planning board at Jenny's nursery school, and she needs a babysitter for when she has to go to meetings," said Stacey.

"What's so complicated about that?" I asked.

"Well, here's the thing. She said that since Andrea is a little more active and alert now – she's not a newborn any more, you know – she would want the sitter to have taken an infant-care class. She said one's about to start at the community centre, and she'll pay the fee for it."

"I'd *love* to do that!" I said right away. I'm always up for learning more about how to be a good babysitter.

"Well, that's good," said Mary Anne. "Because you're the only one of us who could take the job." She'd been checking the schedule, and I suppose everybody else had conflicts because of classes and things. "But you know what?" she added. "I think I'd like to take that class, too. I've seen the ads for it, and it looks like fun."

"I wouldn't mind learning more about babies, myself," said Claud. "What if we all sign up for the course? Then we could advertise ourselves as 'infant specialists'! Maybe we'd get some new business."

Wow. That was a great idea – the kind *I* usually had. I tried not to be jealous. "Sounds great!" I said. And by the end of the meeting, we'd phoned the community centre to sign up. All seven of us.

4th CHAPTER

"Oh, wow!" Mary Anne stood looking around the room, her hand over her mouth. We had arrived at the community centre early – I suppose we were eager to see what the infant-care classes would be like.

"Mary Anne!" I hissed, elbowing her. "Stop staring! You've seen pregnant women before."

"Yeah, but only one at a time," she whispered. "A whole room full of them is different. It's sort of—"

"Overwhelming?" asked a friendly voice. A red-haired woman had appeared next to me, and she was smiling at us. "I know. I've been teaching this course for three years now, and I'm still not used to it."

We stood for a moment, taking in the sight of all those round women. They stood in groups, talking and laughing. There were also a few men there – I suppose they were fathers-to-be. Some of them were discussing a poster that was hung on the front wall: NAPPY CHANGING TECHNIQUES, it said, and it listed all the dos and don'ts of changing nappies. It looked like a long list.

I also saw a cluster of parents with young babies in their arms. They seemed to have a lot to talk about with each other.

"You must be the girls who have the club," said the red-haired woman. "I'm Anita. I'm glad you decided to take the course – more babysitters should, but a lot don't want to spend the time."

"I wanted to take it as soon as I heard about it," said Mary Anne. "My name's Mary Anne Spier, by the way. And this is my best friend, Kristy Thomas. She's the chairman of the The Babysitters Club."

I could hardly believe my ears. Mary Anne is usually shy! It must have been Anita's friendly smile that made her feel comfortable so quickly.

"The other members of our club should be here soon," I said. "We're pretty excited about the class. Oh, look!" I pointed to the doorway. A woman had just come in, and she was carrying not one, but two small babies.

"That's Mrs Salem," said Anita. "She had twins a few months ago. Aren't they sweet? Come on, I'll introduce you."

"So this class is for new parents *and* expectant parents?" I asked.

"That's right," said Anita. "And for anybody else who wants to learn more about looking after babies." She led us across the room. "Liz, meet Kristy and Mary Anne," she said. "Girls, this is Mrs Salem."

Mrs Salem smiled at us. She looked pretty tired. She had put both of the babies on a table, in infant seats. "Hi! I like your T-shirts. Do you really belong to a babysitters' club?"

I looked down. I'd almost forgotten that we'd decided to wear our club T-shirts to class. "Yes, we do," I said. "We've been in business for a while now, and we decided that it was time to learn a little more about babies. Your twins are adorable! What are their names?"

"This is Ricky," she said, folding back a soft yellow blanket from one of the babies' faces. "He's the troublemaker. And this," she said, stroking the face of the other one, "is Rose. She's no angel, either."

They were both so, so sweet. When Mary Anne held her finger out to Ricky, he grabbed on to it with his tiny hand and wouldn't let go. Mary Anne squealed. "He's so strong!" she said.

Mrs Salem laughed. "I know. And Rose has got an even tighter grip!"

"Hi, you two," said Stacey, coming up behind us. "Oh, how cute!" She and

Claudia bent over the twins, cooing. Dawn appeared a minute later and joined them.

"Okay, people!" said Anita, clapping her hands. "Let's get started. I'd like everybody to take a seat, and we'll spend a few minutes getting to know each other."

Just as we were sitting down in the small circle of chairs at the front of the room, Jessi and Mal arrived. Jessi slipped into the chair next to me. "Are we late?" she whispered.

"No," I answered. "You're just in time."

"Oh, good," she said. "We got stuck in traffic after my dad picked me up from ballet class. For a while I thought we weren't going to make it."

"Okay," said Anita, once we were settled. "Let's just go around the circle and introduce ourselves. I'd like each of you to say your first name and a few words about why you're here. I'm Anita, and this is my partner, Don," she said, gesturing to a man sitting next to her.

He was really handsome.

He was wearing glasses, and he was quite old – not as old as Watson – maybe the same age as my English teacher, Mr Fiske. I tried not to stare at him as he smiled at us and said hi.

The first person to speak was a cheerful-looking dark-haired woman. "I'm Sue," she said. "This is my husband, John." She pointed to a bearded man sitting next to her. "And I suppose it's pretty obvious why we're taking this class." She patted her belly and giggled. "Junior, here, is going to be arriving soon, and we don't have the slightest idea of how to take care of him. I've brought up plenty of puppies, but I have a feeling that's not quite the same thing."

Anita smiled. "You're right. For example, you don't have to worry about a baby chewing up your best pair of shoes!"

We laughed. If any of us had been feeling shy before, the ice was broken now. The introductions continued. I noticed a lot of interest when we told the group about our club, which made me realize that we were probably meeting a group of potential clients. I hadn't thought of that before. This class was going to be great for the club in more ways than one.

"Welcome all," said Anita. "Now let's get down to work." She turned to the blackboard and wrote out a list of topics we'd be covering in class. "Child Development: Birth to Six Months," the list began. And then, "What Babies Do . . . and Don't Do; Feeding; Changing nappies; Bathing; Sleep Schedules; and Playtime."

"This looks like a lot, I know," said Anita. "But we'll take it bit by bit, and by the end of the course, you'll be baby experts."

"Changing nappies is the worst part!" whispered Mary Anne. "I can never work out how to do it without making a big mess with the talcum powder and everything."

"It just takes some practice," I whispered back.

Anita was passing out some pamphlets. "I think you'll find these helpful," she said. "They contain lots of good information. Now let's talk about babies," she went on. "One of the most important things to remember is that babies are totally dependent on you for their care. But they can't tell you what they need or want – all they can do is cry, and it's up to you to work out what's wrong."

As if on cue, Ricky – or maybe it was Rose – began to wail. Loudly. Mrs Salem picked the baby up and held it. She looked a little embarrassed.

"That's okay, Liz. Let's just take this as an example. What do you think the baby wants?"

"It's Ricky," said Mrs Salem. "And that sounds like his 'I'm hungry' cry. But there's only one way to find out for sure." She pulled a bottle out of the bag by her feet and offered it to Ricky. He turned his head away and kept screaming.

"I suppose that wasn't it," said Mrs Salem. "Maybe he's just restless. Sometimes he likes to be walked round the room. I think he gets tired of looking at the same scenery for too long." She stood up, still holding him. "Could somebody keep an eye on Rose?" she asked.

"I'll watch her," I said.

Mrs Salem started walking, jiggling Ricky a little with each step, and talking to him in a soothing voice. But it didn't take too many laps around the room for all of us to realize that a change of scene wasn't going to be the answer. Ricky just kept on yelling his head off.

"I'm so sorry," said Mrs Salem. Now she looked *really* embarrassed. She jiggled Ricky some more, and said, "Come on, sweetheart. What's the matter? It's okay," in a soft voice.

He wouldn't stop crying.

"Don't worry, Liz – we'll just make a lesson out of this," said Anita, smiling. "What else might Ricky want? Does anybody have any ideas?"

"Maybe he wants a favourite toy to play with," said one of the pregnant women.

"Well," said Anita, "that's a possibility. But he's so young it's not likely that he's attached to any one toy. Right now, he's mainly interested in being held, and in eating – basic things like that. Anybody else?"

Ricky was still sobbing.

"I can't take it!" I heard Claud whisper to Stacey. "How much longer do you think he'll cry?"

Stacey giggled. "I never knew that such

a little thing could make so much noise," she whispered back.

"He's not colicky, is he?" asked Don, who had stood up and walked over to where Mrs Salem was standing.

"Oh, no," said Mrs Salem. "I can't imagine how I would cope if he was."

"What's 'colicky'?" asked Jessi.

"That's when babies have trouble with their digestion, and they get terrible stomach-aches," said Don. "Nobody really knows why it happens to some babies, but when it does, they cry for three or four hours at a time."

"Oh, my lord!" said Claudia.

"But what can you do when they're like that?" asked Dawn.

"Not much," said Don. "It can be really hard on the parents. All they can do is walk the baby round and try to comfort it."

I hope I never have to sit for a baby with colic.

All this time, Ricky had still been screaming his head off. Suddenly, I had an idea. I caught Anita's eye and said, "Do you think he needs a clean nappy?"

"Good idea, Kristy," she said. "What do you think, Liz?"

"That could be it," said Mrs Salem. "He tends to be really bothered by a wet nappy. Rose doesn't seem to care."

"Let's try it," said Anita. She brought Mrs Salem's changing bag over to the changing table that had been set up in the front of the room. Mrs Salem put Ricky down on the table, and his screams grew even louder. Everybody gathered around to watch. Luckily, I was close enough to see well and still be able to keep an eye on Rose.

"Oh, you use cloth nappies," said Anita. "Great. We need to learn how to put on both kinds, disposable and cloth. So many parents are switching to cloth these days. They are much better for the environment, if you're willing to do just a little more work."

Anita changed Ricky's nappy, talking the whole time about what she was doing. And by the time he was clean and dry, his sobs had died down and he was happily blowing bubbles and making gurgling noises.

I could see that this class was going to be a challenge – and a lot of fun.

5th CHAPTER

"This is our son, Ethan," said Anita. She put her arm around a little boy with strawberry-blond hair. He was wearing a T-shirt with a big purple dinosaur on it.

"Hi, Ethan," I said. "I like your shirt!"

"Say hello to Kristy, Ethan," said Don.

But Ethan was feeling a little bit shy. He rubbed one of his sneakered toes against the other and pressed his face into Don's leg.

"That's okay," I said. "Sometimes I feel shy, too." What a cute kid! I'd got used to the idea that Anita and Don were married – that had become clear by the end of the first class. After four weeks, I still had a bit of a crush on Don; so did Stacey and Dawn – in fact, I think of all us BSC members thought he was pretty terrific.

But I hadn't met Ethan before, so this was something new. All at once I saw Don in a different light: he was just another father, someone who would hire me as a babysitter, tell me where the sink plunger was in case the sink blocked up, and go out to the cinema with his wife. My crush disappeared. Just like that. I still liked him, but I was no longer "infatuated", as Mary Anne had put it.

I was pretty dressed up that Saturday afternoon. I'd worn a skirt with my polo neck instead of my usual jeans. Why? Because the class was over, and we were about to "graduate". We would each be getting a certificate that said we had passed the infant-care course.

We'd been told that we could invite people to the ceremony, so the room was pretty full. Kids were running around and screaming, and lots of people were talking and laughing.

Mum and Watson hadn't been able to come, but Nannie and Charlie were there. Our associate members, Shannon and Logan, had come, and I was happy to see Logan and Mary Anne together again.

It must be hard to learn how to be friends with someone you used to go out with.

Claudia's parents and her sister, Janine, were there, and so was Stacey's mum. Dawn's mum and Mary Anne's dad sat together, looking round the room and smiling at the way the kids were playing together.

Jessi's little sister, Becca, was the only member of the Ramsey family who could come. She had got a lift with the Pikes, who had turned out in full force.

I was feeling a little nervous about the graduation ceremony. Why? Well, because we had taken some tests the week before, and we were about to find out how we'd done in them. Anita had said that we'd all passed, so it wasn't that I was worried about failing. It was just that I was really hoping I had done well in the tests. I'd enjoyed the course, and I felt it was important to demonstrate that I'd learned something from it.

I should say that the tests we took weren't called "tests" by Anita and Don. They called them "evaluations", and they warned us not to take them too seriously.

"These evaluations are just to help us be sure you've learned everything you should have from the course," Don had said.

Even though they weren't supposed to matter so much, I did take the tests seriously.

The first one had been a written "evaluation" – a series of questions, mostly multiple-choice.

Here's an example of one of the questions:

You are changing a nappy for six-month-old Rebecca when you hear the phone ringing in the next room. What do you do?

A) Run to answer it. The call could be important, and Rebecca's comfortable on the changing table. She'll wait.

B) Grab Rebecca and make a run for the phone. You might still get there before it stops ringing.

C) Let it ring. You can't leave Rebecca alone on the changing table.

That one was easy. C, of course. But some of the other questions were a little harder. When I finished that test (I mean, evaluation) I thought I'd done pretty well. But there were one or two questions I wasn't so sure about.

Mary Anne and I talked afterwards, comparing answers. She'd had a much harder time with the test than I had – maybe because she grew up as an only child and never had the day-to-day experience with younger kids I'd had, first with David Michael and now with Emily.

The other evaluation had covered what Anita called "practical skills". For that, we'd each had to demonstrate that we'd learned how to do certain things. For example, we had to put a nappy on a doll, following all the steps we had been taught. Then we had to clean the "baby," put on some cornstarch-based powder (the old kind, talcum, isn't so good for babies), and fasten the nappy securely – all the while pretending that the "baby" was real.

Anita and Don watched closely. They'd told us that they would be taking points off for things like squeezing powder straight from the container – we were supposed to shake it into our hands first, so that we wouldn't risk shooting powder into the baby's face. We also had to make sure to keep one hand on the baby at all times, since they'd told us that it only takes a second for a baby to roll off a changing table.

We also had to show that we knew at least three ways to hold a baby safely, and that we knew where the soft spot is on a baby's head. And, we had to demonstrate our burping technique. All of this was done using dolls to stand in for real babies.

I'd been so nervous while I was putting a nappy on the doll that I honestly wasn't sure whether I'd done everything right. We'd been tested with cloth nappies, because they were harder to use. Had I slipped my hand under the nappy when I pinned it, so that I wouldn't prick the baby? Had I remembered to fold the nappy right?

Oh, well. I'd find out soon enough.

"Can we get started?"

I heard Anita talking at the front of the room, but a lot of other people didn't. The noise level was still pretty high.

"Attention, all graduates!" boomed Don above the racket. "Do any of you want your certificates?"

That seemed to do it. The hubbub died down, and everybody took a few minutes to find seats and settle down for the ceremony.

"We're very proud of you," said Anita. "Remember when I told you that you'd be baby experts by the end of the course? Well, I'd have to say that all of you have reached that goal."

"But," said Don, "there were only two people in the class who got every answer correct on their written evaluations and who also got top scores on the practical section."

I leaned forward to hear what he would say next. I didn't even dare to hope that I could be the one of those people. I took a quick look around the room, trying to guess who they might be. I noticed one woman who was due to give birth that very day – Mrs Nielsen. She'd been very good at changing nappies, I remembered. And I knew that Dawn had definitely done well in the practical part of the evaluation. I'd watched her, and she'd done everything perfectly.

"The first person with a perfect score is John Davenport. Can you come up and get your certificate, John?" That was a surprise! Anita smiled at the bearded man who walked up and shook her hand. "Good work, John! You're the first man in any of our classes who has got a perfect score."

"And the other person," said Don, "is one of our younger pupils."

Dawn! I knew it.

"Kristy Thomas, please come forward!" he finished.

I couldn't believe it.

I stumbled up to the front, shook hands with Don, and took my certificate from Anita. All I could say was, "Thanks!" Then I turned to sit down, but I was stopped in my tracks by a burst of applause.

"All right, Kristy!" I heard Charlie yell.

Somehow I found my seat, and I sat through the rest of the ceremony with a huge grin on my face. I felt great! Not only had I learned something new, but I'd really learned it well. I was pretty proud of myself.

It was fun to watch my friends receive their certificates. When the ceremony was over, we went into the next room, where a reception with cookies and orange juice would take place.

"Congratulations, Kristy!" said Dawn. "I'm so annoyed with myself. All I got wrong was one question on the written evaluation – and it was just a silly mistake."

"Well, we all passed, and that's the main thing," I said. "And, it was a lot of fun, wasn't it?" I stood with my friends, laughing and talking about the course.

About five of the expectant mothers came up to us during the reception to congratulate me – and to ask for the club's phone number! Luckily, I'd thought ahead and made sure to bring some of our leaflets, so I had something to give them.

Mrs Salem brought Ricky and Rose over to say goodbye. "I may be phoning you one day," she said to us. "These two know how to wear out their mummy!"

"Of course," said Claudia. "We'd love to sit for you."

I excused myself from the group and joined Anita and Don. "Thanks for being such great teachers," I said. "You really made the course fun!"

Ethan poked his head out from behind Anita's skirt. "Will you babysit for me one day?" he asked me. I suppose he'd got over his shyness.

"Of course, Ethan," I said. "Any time." I smiled at Anita and Don and said goodbye.

My friends and I had decided to hold our own little celebration after the graduation ceremony, so, once the reception was over, we headed for Claud's room, our usual meeting spot.

Claud passed round some brownies she'd made (she had pretzels for Dawn and Stacey) and poured us each some Diet Coke. "Here's to the graduates!" she said, and we "clinked" our paper cups.

We talked some more about the class and the people in it. "Can you believe how huge Mrs Nielsen has got?" asked Stacey. "I can't imagine having a belly that big."

"I wonder if she'll really have the baby today," said Mary Anne. "How exciting."

Suddenly, in the midst of our celebration, I remembered that I'd promised to let Mrs Prezzioso know straight away when I had completed the infant-care course. I reached for the phone and called her.

"That's great, Kristy!" she said when I'd told her the news. "Can you start a week from Monday? I'll need you every Monday and Thursday from three until five, for four weeks all together.

"Okay," I said. "I'm looking forward to it."

"So is Jenny," said Mrs Prezzioso. "And I'm sure if Andrea could talk, she'd say she was, too."

Just as I said goodbye and hung up, I heard Andrea squeal in the background, and I felt a little twinge of uneasiness. I was going to be taking care of a real baby soon.

Was I ready?

6th CHAPTER

When the time came for my first babysitting job with Jenny and Andrea, I did feel ready. I had gone all over my notes and reread every pamphlet and handout that Don and Anita had given us. I was sure that I was prepared for anything that might happen that day. After all, I had sailed through the course, right?

Well, partly right. That day, I found out that looking after an infant is one thing, but that looking after an infant *and* her four-year-old sister is quite another.

"Hi, Kristy, come on in!" said Mrs Prezzioso when she answered the door that afternoon. She was speaking in a hushed tone, and I gave her a curious look. "Andrea's asleep," she said quietly. "She just went down for a short nap. She'll probably wake up in half an hour or so."

"KRISTY!!!" yelled Jenny, flying down the hall towards me.

I caught her and gave her a quick squeeze. "*Shhh*, Jenny. Let's not wake Andrea for a little while, okay?" I whispered.

"Okay," she whispered back. "Can we play Candy Land?"

Mrs Prezzioso laughed. "I told you she was excited about this," she said. "She loves being a big sister – you'll see that when Andrea wakes up. But she also needs plenty of attention when the two of you are alone together."

I noticed that Jenny wasn't as dressed up as she usually is. I suppose Mrs P. doesn't have time these days to create perfect outfits for every occasion. Jenny always used to look like a model in a clothing catalogue. She'd be dressed in prim white dresses with a lot of lace, matching socks, and hair ribbons. But lately she's been looking more like an ordinary little girl.

For that matter, Mrs P. didn't look quite like she used to, either. Mary Anne always said that Mrs P. looked like she had just stepped out of one of those magazines that have articles with titles like "A Dozen Glamorous New Ways to Use Leftover Meatloaf." But that day she simply appeared nice and neat, like any mother on her way to a meeting at her daughter's nursery school.

I suppose having a four-year-old *and* a baby is keeping Mrs P. pretty busy.

She began to run through some hurried instructions as she put on her jacket and searched for her car keys. "I've left some of Andrea's bottles in the fridge – they're all made up and all you have to do is put them in the bottle warmer when you need one," she said. "Her nappies are in the little cupboard underneath the changing table," she went on. "And if she – oh, dear, I'm late," she said, looking at her watch.

"Don't worry, Mummy," said Jenny. "I'll be a good helper. I know how to look after Andrea."

"That's right, sweetie," said Mrs P., bending to kiss Jenny. "You're a wonderful sister and a big help to your mummy and daddy. You be good for Kristy, all right?"

Jenny nodded and gave her mother a hug. "Now can we play Candy Land?" she asked, turning to me.

I laughed. "Okay, Jenny. 'Bye, Mrs P. Have a good meeting."

As soon as the front door closed, Jenny grabbed my hand and pulled me into the living room. She pulled Candy Land off a shelf in a big cabinet.

"Let's bring it outside to play," she said. "I like to play Candy Land out in the front garden, under my favourite tree."

"Oh, Jenny," I said. "We can't. What if Andrea wakes up and we don't hear her?"

"But I *want* to play outside!" she said, looking stubborn. Now *that* sounded like the old spoiled Jenny, the one who was used to always getting her way. I was going to have to be firm.

"Remember what your mummy said about being a good helper?" I asked. "I need you to help me listen for Andrea. And to do that, we'll have to play inside."

"Okay," said Jenny immediately. "I'll set up the game." She pulled out the box and opened it.

Just then, I heard a sound from upstairs. Was that Andrea?

"All ready!" said Jenny.

"*Shhh. . .*" I whispered. "Just a second. Did you hear that?" I heard the sound again, and this time I was sure. Andrea was waking up.

"Yea!" said Jenny. "Andrea's awake. Let's go and play with her."

I headed upstairs to the nursery, with Jenny at my heels. I was surprised at how easily she'd given up her game of Candy Land. (I can't say I was all that sorry to have missed out on it, myself. Candy Land is so boring!) As we entered the room, I saw Andrea lying in her cot, on her stomach. She had pushed herself up with her arms and was holding her head up – a little unsteadily – and looking around as she gave her soft cries.

"Hi, Andrea!" I said softly. "Oh, she's so cute," I said to Jenny.

"I helped choose her outfit for today," said Jenny proudly. "Pink is my favourite colour, and it's hers, too." She walked out to the cot, stuck her hand between the railings, and patted her sister's foot. "Andrea-Bandrea," she said. "Hi-hi!"

I let Andrea study my face for a minute. She looked a bit confused; no doubt she had expected her mother instead of me. But she didn't seem all that upset about it. I'm sure that having Jenny there helped. At least one person in the room was familiar to her.

When I thought I'd given her enough time to get used to my face, I bent down and lifted her out of the cot.

"Do you need a new nappy?" I asked her. She gurgled in reply. I checked to see if she was wet. "Looks like you're okay for now," I said. I was holding her carefully, just the way I'd been taught in class.

Suddenly, she started to cry, and I mean *really* cry. Her screams were so loud that I wanted to cover my ears. But I couldn't do that while I was holding her. Jenny could, though. And she did.

She stood with her hands over her ears, shouting, "Make her stop! I hate it when she cries like that!" Jenny's eyes were scrunched shut, and she looked as if she was in pain.

What a racket.

I jiggled Andrea. I walked around the room with her. I spoke to her in a soothing, calm voice. She kept on screaming. And so did Jenny.

"Jenny," I said, raising my voice so I could be heard over both of them. "That's enough. I don't like the noise, either, but it doesn't help when you start shouting. Let's go downstairs and get Andrea a bottle, okay?"

She took her hands off her ears straight away. "Okay!" she said. "I'll show you how to make it warm." She ran down the hall and I followed, carrying the still-wailing Andrea.

When we reached the kitchen, Jenny ran to the fridge and threw open the door. Wow! Mrs P had left enough bottles to last us a week. I suppose she wanted to make sure that Andrea wouldn't go hungry, but it looked as if she'd gone overboard.

Jenny reached for one of the bottles – and knocked over a bowl of spaghetti that had been left unwrapped on a top shelf.

"Oh, *no*," I muttered. Andrea kept screaming. Jenny looked at me guiltily.

"I didn't mean –" she began.

"That's okay, Jenny." I said. "Tell you what. Let's get the bottle into the warmer, and then you can help me clean up the mess."

Once I'd turned on the bottle warmer (I was really glad the Prezziosos had one, since warming a bottle in a pan on the stove – as we'd been taught in class –

sounded a lot more complicated), I set to work cleaning up the mess in the fridge. It wasn't easy to do, with a crying baby in one arm. Jenny was "helping," but, although she was eager, she made the mess worse instead of better.

I stood up to rinse out a sponge and looked at the clock. Three-thirty. I'd only been there for half an hour! How was I going to last until five?

The bell on the bottle warmer went off just as I wiped up the last of the spaghetti. I sat down at the kitchen table, getting into a good "feeding" position. Andrea was still yelling, but as soon as I put the bottle into her mouth, her crying stopped.

What a relief.

Jenny sat down next to us and watched eagerly as Andrea sucked at the bottle. "See how her eyes open and close?" she said. "Look at her little hands."

Jenny was obviously in love with her baby sister.

Andrea ate and ate. My arm started to fall asleep, but I didn't want to bother her by shifting my position. After a while, Jenny started to squirm in her seat. She was becoming restless.

"Jenny," I said. "After Andrea finishes her bottle I'll strap her into her seat and she can watch while we make cookies."

"Yea!" shouted Jenny. Andrea "startled" at the noise. Anita had told us about that reflex. Babies do it when they hear a sudden sound. Her whole body seemed to jump, and her eyes flew wide open. For a minute I thought she was going to start crying again, but then she relaxed.

When she had finished with her bottle, I put her into her bouncer seat and strapped her in carefully. Then I put out the ingredients for cookies, and Jenny and I began our project.

We were soon interrupted when Andrea started to cry again. She was grabbing at her stomach, and I realized that she must have wind. I'd forgotten to burp her!

Then, just when she had settled down and I had turned back to measuring and sifting the flour, she began to cry again. "What is it this time?" I asked.

"Nappy, probably," said Jenny. The voice of experience. And she was right.

I changed Andrea without a hitch.

But we never got to make the cookies. There was one interruption after another, all afternoon. Jenny was disappointed, but all I could do was apologize. It was just too hard to take care of Andrea's needs and do special things like baking at the same time.

I realized that I had to take it easy. I didn't have to be Super-sitter. I just needed to be a responsible sitter. Next time I would know.

At the stroke of five, Mrs P. rushed in. I hadn't had a chance to finish cleaning up the kitchen, so I started to apologize. " I'm sorry for the mess," I said. "We were—"

"That's okay," she interrupted. "Look at this! Doesn't this look like fun?" She showed me a piece of paper she was waving around. It was an entry form for the baby parade. "I got it at Jenny's school. She's too old to be in it, but I'm *dying* to enter Andrea. She'll need a costume and some decorations for her buggy. . ."

"It does look like fun," I said. "In fact, I was thinking of—"

But she didn't let me finish my sentence. "You'll help me, won't you, Kristy? I won't have time to do much, but I'll be glad to pay you extra if you could help."

"Oh – I – well. . ." I began. I had really wanted to enter Emily, and I didn't see how I could do both. "I'm not sure I'll have the time," I said finally.

"Okay, well why don't you think about it?" she asked. "Let me know in a few days."

I agreed, and after she'd paid me I said goodbye to the girls and headed out of the door. Mrs P. was certainly excited about the parade, I thought. She hadn't even remembered to ask me how the afternoon went!

7th CHAPTER

Wednesday

You know, ever since we took that cource on babys, I've noticed that they can reely be a lot of fun. I used to think that they din't do much at all exsept cry and sleep. Well, in a way that's still true. But now I know some ways to play with them, and I know how to work out why they're crying... Did you lot ever notice how inkredibely cute Lucy Newton has got lately?

Claud was sitting that day for a couple of our favourite kids, Jamie Newton (he's four) and his baby sister, Lucy. Jamie's always been a sweet little boy, and Lucy is just about the happiest baby I've ever known. She's always smiling and gurgling happily, even when she's just woken up.

"Hi, Claudia!" said Jamie, flinging open the door about two seconds after Claud had rung the bell. "I like your earrings!"

Claud, as usual, was wearing some pretty wild earrings that day. And, of course, they were coordinated with her outfit. Here's what she was wearing (I saw her later that day at our meeting): an oversized red blouse with black buttons, green leggings with white, tie-dyed streaks, and black high-top trainers with all kinds of buckles and snaps on them. (The laces were untied, which I suppose is the cool way to wear them. I'd be tripping over them all day, but Claud can pull it off.)

Can you guess what her earrings were? Dangling watermelon slices. Get it? She was dressed like a watermelon, head to toe. And, of course, Jamie loved the effect.

"I'm going to be a pumpkin for Hallowe'en," he said. (Hallowe'en's about three million months away, but you know how kids are. They like to plan ahead for their favourite occasions.) "Maybe you can help me with my costume."

"Of course, Jamie," said Claudia. "I'd love to." Just then, Mrs Newton came into the front hall. She was carrying Lucy, holding her car keys, and trying to put on her coat at the same time.

"Here," said Claudia. "I'll take her." Lucy clung to her mother just for a second, but when Claud made a funny face at her, she burst out laughing and fell into Claud's arms.

"Thanks, Claudia," said Mrs Newton. "I'm just going to run a few errands, but I'll be sure to be back by five-fifteen so you can make your meeting."

"I may take them to the library, if that's all right," said Claudia. She'd been thinking that it would be fun to take Jamie to the children's room and show him the new puppet theatre. She'd heard about it from her mum, who's the head librarian.

"Liberry! Liberry!" chanted Jamie immediately. "We're going to the liberry!" He jumped up and down.

"That sounds great," said Mrs Newton. "Lucy's buggy is on the porch. Oh, and there's a pile of books you could return for me. They're on top of Jamie's chest of drawers. Thanks!" she grabbed her handbag, gave Jamie and Lucy each a quick kiss, and rushed out of the door.

"Let's go, Claudia!" said Jamie, pulling at her hand. "Let's go to the liberry!"

"I'm glad you want to go," said Claudia, "but first we need to make sure Lucy's wearing a clean nappy, and pack a bag with a bottle in it, in case she needs a snack while we're there."

"*I* need a snack, right now!" said Jamie. "I'm hungry. But after that, can we go?"

"Okay," said Claud, and for the next fifteen minutes she was very busy trying to get Lucy ready for their short trip, making a peanut butter and honey sandwich (on toast) for Jamie, and rounding up the library books, which Jamie had *un*stacked from the pile on his chest of drawers.

Then it took another fifteen minutes to dress Jamie and Lucy for the outdoors. Jamie "helped" by shoving Lucy's feet into her zip-up suit and then jamming the zip as he tried to close it. Luckily for Claud, Lucy just smiled and babbled happily, and her dark blue eyes sparkled as she looked into Claud's brown ones.

Claud had a good time pushing Lucy's buggy down the street. Lucy was so cute that everyone who saw her stopped to smile. Some people bent down and asked Lucy questions in baby-talk.

Jamie walked beside the buggy, proud of his little sister and of the attention she was getting. He told anyone who asked how old she was. He never forgot to add his own age, too, Claud noticed, as well as his birthday.

"Maybe I'll get a lot of presents if all those people know my birthday," he explained happily.

When Claud walked into the children's room at the library, the noise almost knocked her over. The room was *packed* with screaming, yelling, jumping kids. She grabbed Jamie's hand and held Lucy closer. (She'd left the buggy at the entrance and was carrying Lucy.)

"What's going on?" she yelled over the noise, when she'd caught the eye of the children's librarian.

"We've just had an after-school session," the woman yelled back. "And it's almost time for story hour. It should empty out pretty soon."

She was right. Claud took her charges over to a corner to read a book to them and wait for the crowd to disappear. After a few minutes the room had grown much quieter. Then she showed Jamie the puppet theatre. He loved it, and started putting on a show about Little Red Riding Hood. Claudia and Lucy watched.

"Now I'm going to get you," Jamie said in as deep a voice as he could manage, waving the wolf puppet menacingly. "Oh, no!" he answered in a high, squeaky voice. He danced the girl puppet backwards. Lucy waved her hands and shrieked with laughter.

The show went on until Little Red Riding Hood had been saved by various characters, including Spiderman. Finally, Claud realized they'd better go home if she wanted to get to the club meeting on time.

"Order!" I said, as the clock on Claud's desk turned to 5:30. All of us were there, sprawled out around the room. Dawn had been showing us a postcard her brother had sent her from Venice Beach, California. On the front was a photo of a roller-skater wearing an outrageous outfit.

"That picture reminds me," I said, after we'd finished discussing club business – and after we'd answered a few job calls. "What kind of costume do you think I could make Emily for the baby parade?"

"I thought you were supposed to be thinking about *Andrea's* costume," said Mary Anne. I'd told friends about how Mrs P. had asked me to help her.

"Oh, I know," I answered. "I just can't decide what to do about the baby parade. I'm not even sure if my mum will let me enter Emily, but I'm dying to. On the other hand, if I don't help Mrs P. with Andrea, she might not even want me to finish the next three weeks of babysitting that she hired me for."

"She wouldn't dismiss you just for that!" said Stacey.

"I hope not," I answered.

"You know," said Claudia, "Lucy Newton ought to be entered in the parade. She is the cutest thing in the universe."

"She is cute," said Jessi. "So's Squirt, for that matter. I bet he could win a prize."

"What about Laura and Gabbie Perkins?" asked Mary Anne. "They'd love to be in the parade, I bet."

"So would Eleanor Marshall," added Dawn. "I sat for her the other day, and she's such a darling. She is so, so sweet."

I felt it coming. An idea. One of the best ideas I'd had yet. "I know," I said suddenly. "How about if we get a whole lot of babies together and enter them as a group in the Float category?" I was excited. "I could help you lot with that, *and* also get Andrea ready for the Buggy Category. That way, we can all enter whatever babies we want! It'll be fun making the float, won't it?" I had got so carried away that I was already assuming we'd do it.

"You know," said Stacey, "I think that's a great idea!"

Everybody else agreed with her, so we spent the rest of the meeting phoning all the parents we could think of to ask their permission for our plan. Of course, Mrs P. was the first parent I phoned, and she was thrilled that I'd be helping her with Andrea's costume. This was going to be the best baby parade Stoneybrook had ever seen!

8th CHAPTER

"So are you lot all ready to hear my great idea for our float?" I asked. I couldn't wait to tell them my plan. I knew they'd love it. It was Saturday morning, and we were all lounging around in the living room at Dawn and Mary Anne's house. We'd decided to have our baby parade planning meeting there, where we could spread out and talk all morning with no interruptions. (Mary Anne's dad was working in the garden, and Dawn's mum had gone off to do some errands.)

I looked round the room at my friends. Nobody had begged me to tell them my idea, but then again, none of them had said I shouldn't. "Okay, here's what we'll do. The theme will be – get this – Take Me Out to the Ball Game!" I scanned their faces to see their reactions to my idea, but I couldn't tell what they thought. "We'll

345

dress the babies in little baseball uniforms and decorate the float like a baseball pitch. It'll be so, so cute!" I went on.

"You've got to be kidding," said Dawn in a flat voice. "That has to be the worst idea I've ever heard. Babies playing baseball?"

I was crushed. But I didn't have time to defend my idea because Dawn kept on talking.

"*I* think we should do something really different, something nobody else in Stoneybrook would ever think about. Like Surfin' USA!" She smiled at all of us. "We'll dress the babies in really cool-looking outfits, put them on surfboards, and decorate the float to look like the ocean."

I rolled my eyes. Why were surfing babies any better than babies playing baseball? I heard Mary Anne giggle. Dawn glared at her.

"I'm sorry," Mary Anne said. "It's just that the idea of baby surfers seems pretty silly to me. I thought we'd do something that was more related to kids, like maybe acting out a nursery rhyme."

"Oh?" asked Dawn. I could tell she was a little hurt that Mary Anne had made fun of her idea. Well, now she knew how it felt. "What nursery rhyme did you have in mind, Mary Anne?"

"Three Little Kittens," answered Mary Anne proudly. "We'd dress up the babies like kittens, and I could knit little mittens for them... And of course, Tigger could be on the float, too."

"I get it," said Stacey. "You came up with that idea just so you could work out a way for your kitten to be on the float. That's ridiculous! This is a baby parade, not a pet show."

Mary Anne hung her head and sniffled. She cries so easily.

"I'm sorry, Mary Anne," said Stacey. "But don't you think that idea is a little childish? I think the judges would be more impressed with something a little more sophisticated."

Mary Anne wiped her eyes with the back of her hand. "Okay, let's hear it," she said.

"What?" asked Stacey.

"Your idea for our float," answered Mary Anne. "Obviously you think you have a great one. Let's hear it."

"Well," said Stacey. She closed her eyes for a moment and then started talking very fast, as if she were nervous that someone would interrupt her. "I was thinking that we could do a float called 'New York, New York'. It could be a model of the skyline. You know, the Empire State Building and all that? And we could dress up the babies in tuxedos and evening gowns."

I held back a giggle. "Very glamorous," I said, trying to look serious.

Claudia didn't bother to hold back *her* giggles. She burst out laughing. "Stacey, I don't believe it. You've gone off your rocker. Babies in tuxedos? We'd be the biggest joke in the parade."

Stacey crossed her arms and sat silently, frowning at the floor.

I looked around the room.

"How about you, Mal?" I asked. Apparently, we'd all come with ideas, so I thought I might as well let everybody have a chance to speak.

"Oh, well I – " she broke off in midsentence, looking as if she'd like to disappear.

"What, Mal?" asked Jessi. "Come on, you can tell us."

"I was thinking of doing *Misty of Chincoteague*," she said in one breath.

"WHAT?" we all said at once.

"*Misty*," she said. "My favourite book. I thought we could act it out."

"What," said Jessi. "Dress the babies like wild ponies?" She raised her eyebrows. I heard a few giggles exploding round the room.

"I don't know," said Mallory, sounding miserable. "I hadn't really thought it out, I suppose."

The giggles got louder, and soon we were all laughing so hard we could hardly breathe. Every time the laughing began to die down, someone would say, "Ponies!" or "Surfers!" and it would start all over again. My stomach hurt, and tears were rolling down my face.

Finally, we managed to get ourselves under control. "Claudia," I said, once I had found my voice. "What about you? We haven't heard *your* idea."

She blushed. "I know," she said. "And now you're never going to. It was just as daft as all the others."

"Come on!" said Stacey. "You've got to tell. *We* all made fools of ourselves. Why should you be the only one who didn't?"

We pestered her until she broke down. "Oh, all right," she said. "It was an idea about babies from outer space – you know, like something you'd see in those supermarket newspapers: 'Woman gives birth to baby from Mars.'"

We were too stunned even to laugh. That had to be the worst idea of all!

"I know, I know," said Claud. "That's why I didn't want to tell you. But listen, I think Mary Anne is on to something. I think acting out a nursery rhyme is a great idea, even if that kitten one isn't the best choice."

I looked around the room. Everybody was nodding. "You know," I said. "I think Claud's right. So what nursery rhyme could we do?"

"We need one with lots of characters," said Dawn. "I mean, we've already got five babies, right?"

"Let's see," I said, checking the list we'd made. "Squirt and Emily, Lucy Newton,

Eleanor Marshall, and Laura Perkins. That's five. I suppose Gabbie didn't want to be in the parade."

"Okay, let's think," said Stacey. The room was quiet for a few minutes.

"All I can think of are rhymes with two characters!" said Mallory. "Like Jack and Jill, or Peter Peter Pumpkin Eater."

"I know," said Dawn. "This isn't as easy as you'd think."

Then somebody called out the idea that we ended up agreeing on. I can't even remember who it was, and neither can anyone else. I don't think anybody wants to take responsibility for it, even though we all thought it was a great idea. At the time.

The Old Woman Who Lived in a Shoe. That was our idea. It sounded like a lot of fun.

"We'll need more than five babies for that one," said Mary Anne.

"But we don't know too many other kids under three," I answered. "Where can we get more babies?" Then I thought of the infant-care course we'd taken. We'd met a lot of babies there! At least some of those new parents would have to be interested in entering their kids in the baby parade.

"Great idea," said Mary Anne, when I'd blurted out what I'd been thinking. "And I even have some of their phone numbers in the record book. We can phone them straight away."

Good old Mary Anne. What an efficient club secretary. We made some phone calls then and there, and before we knew it we had four more babies lined up.

"You will be on the float with them, won't you?" asked Mrs Salem, when I called to see if Ricky and Rose could be involved.

"Of course," I answered. And I said the same thing to the last mother we called, who asked the same question. But, of course, we hadn't really worked out how we were going to dress – or how *we* were going to handle nine babies, for that matter.

"Nine babies is definitely more than enough," said Stacey. "I don't see how we could handle any more than that. And as for what we should wear – one of us can dress up like the Old Woman, and the others can dress like her older children. That way, we'll all fit into the theme."

We agreed, although we didn't stop to decide which of us would be the Old Woman. We'd made enough decisions for the day.

"We can build the float in my back garden, so we can be near all my art materials," said Claudia. "I hope you realize that it's not going to be easy to build a giant float, though."

"Oh, we'll work it out," I said. "I'll ask Charlie if he can help us. I was thinking that he could pull the float behind the Junk Bucket." (That's Charlie's old car.) I knew he'd be glad to help. He's usually pretty good about things like that.

"So we're all ready, right?" asked Stacey. "I have to meet my mum now so we can go shopping."

"All ready," I said.

That showed how much I knew.

9th CHAPTER

On Monday afternoon when I went to the Prezziosos' to sit, Jenny flung the door open before I'd even rung the bell. She must have been waiting for me. "Guess what!" she said. "Mummy's worked out what Andrea's costume should be."

"That's great," I said. "I can't wait to hear about it." I thought she'd tell me about the costume, but instead she heaved a big sigh.

"I wish *I* could be in the parade," she said, "and wear a pretty costume and everything."

"I know," I said. "But you're a big girl, and the parade's just for babies."

She nodded. "Sometimes I wish I wasn't such a big girl," she said wistfully. "Sometimes I wish I was still a baby."

I felt sorry for her. She must have been feeling pretty left out. "But remember," I said. "Big girls get to do all kinds of things that babies can't do, like helping to bake cookies, and—"

Just then, Mrs Prezzioso burst into the front hall. "Oh!" she said. "You're here, Kristy. I didn't hear the doorbell."

"I know," I said. "Jenny—"

But she cut me off. "Did you hear about Andrea's costume?" she asked. "I think it's going to be absolutely precious." She seemed really excited.

"I heard that you chose a theme," I answered, "but Jenny hasn't told me what it is."

"Oh, I know you're going to love it, Kristy," she said, smiling happily. "I've decided to dress her as Queen Andrea!"

Queen Andrea?

I gulped. "That – that sounds wonderful!" I said, trying to seem enthusiastic. It seemed like a pretty weird idea to me, if you want to know the truth.

"And she's going to have a crown, and a long, long dress!" added Jenny.

"That's right," said Mrs P. "Let me show you what I've found so far." She threw open the door to the hall cupboard. "Here's her crown," she said, showing me a gold crown (made of plastic) with fake jewels all over it. "And she's going to wear this big wig, like they wore in the old days." She showed me something that looked like my neighbour's cat.

I didn't know what to say.

"Oh! I'll be late if I don't get going," said Mrs P. suddenly, looking at her watch. "Andrea's asleep, but she should be ready to wake up soon."

I followed her out to the door. She had planned Andrea's costume without my help. I wondered if she still wanted me to work on it. "Is there anything else I should do about getting Andrea ready for the parade?" I asked. I was hoping that she'd changed her mind and didn't need my help after all.

"Oh, that's right!" she said. "I almost forgot. I want you to work out how to make her buggy look like a coach."

A coach. Oh, of course.

"You can use any materials you find in my sewing room," she said. "I'm going to be pushing her in the parade," she added. "And I want her to look fabulous so she'll make a good impression on the judges. I would really, really like her to win first prize in her category. Wouldn't that be fantastic?"

"Fantastic," I echoed. I waved at Mrs P. as she jumped into her car. Wow! She was getting carried away with this parade stuff. And she certainly sounded as if she wanted Andrea to win a prize. I suddenly felt I was under a lot of pressure.

What if Andrea *didn't* win? Would Mrs P. decide that I was a terrible sitter because I hadn't been able to turn the buggy into a perfect coach? Would she fire me? What would that do to the reputation of the club?

Just then, I heard Andrea's cries from upstairs. She was ready to get up. "C'mon, Jenny," I said, trying to put my worries aside. "Let's go and get Queen Andrea."

It turned out that Her Royal Highness had a wet nappy, so the first order of business was to get her into a dry one. Then Jenny decided she was hungry, so we trooped downstairs for a snack. Just as I was clearing up from that, Andrea started to wail, and I realized that she must have been hungry, too.

I got her a bottle and we sat on the sofa while she drank. Jenny jumped around the room, waving her arms and tunelessly singing the theme from *Sesame Street*. "Watch me!" she said, and she bent down to do a somersault.

It was a pretty crooked one, but she stood up proudly afterwards and looked my way. "Very good, Jenny!" I said.

"Look what else I can do," she said, as she took off into a cartwheel. *Bam*! She careered into the sofa.

"Oh, Jenny," I said. "Are you all right?"

"I'm fine," she said brightly. "Don't you think I'm a good cartwheeler? I could do gymtastics in the parade!"

"That's gym*n*astics," I said. "And yes, you're a good cartwheeler. But cartwheels are for outdoors, not for the living room. And as for the parade, remember what I told you? It's just for babies."

Jenny pouted for a minute or two but brightened when she saw that her baby sister had finished her bottle. "Let's put Andrea's costume on her," she said. "Wait till you see how it looks."

She led me to the hall cupboard, and we got out the parts of the costume that Mrs P. had stored there. Besides the crown and the wig, Jenny pulled out a long cloak with fake fur trim, and a big lacy ruff for Andrea to wear around her neck.

We sat Andrea on the living room floor and dressed her up. Boy, did she look funny! The wig slipped down over one eye, and the crown sat crookedly on top. The cloak was so long that she'd have tripped over it – if she knew how to walk. And the ruff? Well, her chin – and half her face – kind of disappeared into it, so that you couldn't see how cute she was any more.

Jenny giggled. "She looks silly," she said.

I agreed, but I thought it might be better if I didn't say so out loud. "I think she looks very nice," I said (lying through my teeth).

Andrea smiled at me, and then, all of a sudden, she gave a little burp.

"Oh, no!" I said. Andrea had dribbled all over the ruff. It was my fault, too. I'd forgotten to burp her after her bottle. I hurried Andrea out of the Queen outfit and cleaned the ruff as well as I could.

Then I decided that I'd better start thinking about how to make that buggy into a coach. "Come on, Jenny," I said. "You can help me work this out." I took Andrea into the sewing room and put her on the floor in her baby seat. That way, I could keep an eye on her while I worked. I gave her some plastic rings and rattles to keep her busy. Then I looked round the room to see what kind of materials Mrs P. had left for me.

"*Somewhere, over the rainbow*—" sang Jenny in a piercing voice. She stood in the middle of the room, with her hands clasped in front of her, just like Dorothy in *The Wizard of Oz*.

"Jenny," I said. She was not only loud, she was totally off-key.

"*We're off to see the Wizard*," she sang, even louder.

"JENNY!" I said.

She stopped short. "What?" she asked. "I'm just showing you what a good singer I am. Maybe I could sing in the parade."

"Jenny, you can't do gymnastics in the parade, and you can't sing in the parade. You can *watch* the parade, but you can't be in it. You're too old!"

Jenny bit her lower lip and stared at the floor. I gave her a quick hug and said, "Let's see what we can do to decorate Andrea's buggy, okay?"

Jenny nodded sadly. "Okay," she said.

I pulled out some bolts of material from the cupboard. There was this stuff with gold sequins all over it, and some other fabric with silver threads running through it. "We could make a canopy out of these," I said. I put them on the floor by Andrea's seat – and noticed she'd thrown down every one of the toys I'd given her. "Oh, Andrea," I said, laughing.

"She doesn't do it on purpose," said Jenny. "Mummy says that she's just not old enough to hold on to things for very long."

"I know," I said. "I'm not angry." I piled all the toys back into Andrea's lap. "There you go, Your Highness," I said.

Andrea smiled at me and said, "Blurg."

"Okay," I said. "So we'll have a gold-and-silver canopy. What else?"

But Jenny didn't answer. She was too busy twirling around the room, her hands in ballerina positions. Every so often she'd stop and do some tap-dance steps, and then go back to her *pirouettes*.

"What are you doing now?" I asked, although I had a fairly good idea.

"Dancing!" she answered breathlessly. "Maybe I can *dance* in the parade."

I rolled my eyes. She just wasn't getting the message. "Jenny," I said, feeling as if I'd already explained it fifty times. "The parade is just for babies. Now be a big girl

359

and help me decorate Andrea's buggy. We can have fun doing it, and then when you watch the parade and see Andrea win a prize, you'll know that you helped." That was dangerous. I was practically promising her that Andrea would win a prize. But I was desperate.

Jenny brightened. "Then it will be sort of be *my* prize, too?"

"That's right," I said

"Okay."

Jenny and I spent the rest of the afternoon creating the most ridiculous-looking "coach" you can imagine. But when Mrs P. came home, she *loved* it!

10th CHAPTER

Tuesday

I love babies. And not just my little brother Squirt, either. I love all babies — their little toes, their soft skin, their goofy smiles. I love to tickle them and make them laugh. I love to give them their bottles and watch them fall asleep in my lap. I even love to change their nappies — because it makes them so happy to be clean and dry. But today, for the first time, I began to wonder if there *might be such a thing as too many babies!*

I think I understand what made Jessi write that in the club notebook. We ended up having a sort of baby convention that afternoon, and it *was* a little bit overwhelming

Jessi was sitting for Becca and Squirt that day, because her parents were both at work and her Aunt Cecelia had gone out to do some shopping. Her first half hour was fine. Squirt was totally captivated by *Sesame Street*. His favourite character is this little guy Elmo, who isn't on very often, so Squirt has to watch carefully in order to catch him.

Meanwhile, Jessi was showing Becca for the six-hundredth time, the five positions for ballet. Becca was doing all right at first, second and third positions, but every time she tried fourth she would get twisted up and fall over.

Becca does not have the same natural grace as Jessi.

But she didn't let it bother her. In fact, every time Becca fell down she would squeal, then she'd giggle, shrug, and get up to try again. Finally, though, she grew tired of the game.

"Let's do something else," she said to Jessi.

Jessi looked at Squirt. He was singing along with the *Sesame Street* song, which meant that the show was ending. "Okay," she said. "How about if we go over to Claudia's? I think they're starting to build the float over there today."

"Yea!" said Becca. Jessi had told her about the baby parade and about the float that Squirt was going to ride on. Becca was excited about the idea. "Maybe I can help to build it," she said.

Of course, Squirt didn't understand at all about the float, but he loves going for walks, so Jessi had no trouble convincing him to go over to Claudia's. He led the way to his buggy, climbed into it, and waited impatiently for Jessi to start pushing.

"Go!" he said, grinning. "Go, GO!" He was hanging on tightly to his favourite toy of the moment, a red plastic fish.

Jessi let Becca push Squirt most of the way. Becca thinks that's the biggest treat. When they reached Claudia's back garden, Jessi saw that Claudia, Stacey, and Mallory were there already, working on the float.

Jessi was a little surprised, she told me later, at the *way* they were working. It was completely quiet in that garden. Nobody was laughing or talking.

"Hey, you three!" Jessi called. "How's it going?" Nobody gave her much of an answer. Each of them was too busy with the job she was doing. Jessi lifted Squirt out of his buggy and, carrying him, walked round to take a look at their projects.

Claudia was bending chicken wire into the shape of a humongous shoe. Jessi said later that she couldn't work out exactly how and where the babies were supposed to fit into the plan. She offered Claud a suggestion, and Claud thanked her and kept on working.

Stacey was mixing paints, for whenever the float would be ready to decorate. She was trying out little dabs of colour on a big sheet of cardboard. Jessi wondered whether she was mixing up *enough* paint – the shoe that Claudia was building looked so big. But all she said was, "I love that orangey-red colour." Stacey looked up and smiled. She had a spot of yellow paint on her nose.

Mallory was sketching costumes for the babies. Jessi leaned over her shoulder. "Those are adorable," she said. "And they look like they'll be easy to make."

"That was my plan," said Mallory, pushing up her glasses with one finger. "And look at this great material I got. It was really cheap, but isn't it nice?" She held out a big bag to Jessi, who peeped into it.

"Nice," Jessi said. "Really nice." The material was a bright pink, and Jessi shuddered at the thought of how those costumes were going to look next to the orangey-red that Stacey had perfected. Talk about clashing!

But she didn't say a thing. Everybody was working so hard. Who was she to criticize them? If only they would *talk* to each other, she thought. But each seemed to have her own opinion on what the float should look like, and none of them appeared interested in what the others thought.

Since Becca was having a good time running around Claudia's back garden, Jessi decided she would hang around for a while. She offered to help Mallory with her costume design, but Mallory shook her head.

"I've got it under control, Jessi," she said. "Thanks, though."

So Jessi and Squirt just sat and watched.

"Hey, what's up?" called Dawn, walking into the garden. Jamie and Lucy Newton were with her. She walked round just as Jessi had, checking on her friends' progress. "Looking good!" she said to Claud. "Nice work, Stace!" she said, looking at the paints. "I love those costumes," she remarked to Mallory. "They'll be terrific."

Dawn joined Jessi underneath a nearby tree. She was carrying Lucy, and Jamie had run off to play with Becca. "Oh, no!" she whispered, leaning close to Jessi. "Do they know what they're doing?"

Jessi giggled. "*Shhh!*" she said. "They're all working so hard—"

"I know," said Dawn. "Anyway, I'm sure it'll be a great float, no matter what."

Squirt and Lucy grinned at each other Squirt waved hello with his red fish.

"Look!" said Jessi. "They like each other. I just realized that this is a great time for them to meet – *before* they're on the float together."

"You're right," said Dawn. She giggled. "Ms Lucy Jane Newton, I'd like you to meet Mr John Philip Ramsey Jr.," she said, holding her nose so that she sounded like a proper lady.

Jessi laughed. "*So* pleased to make your acquaintance she said, holding her own nose and speaking for Squirt.

"Charmed, I'm sure," said Dawn.

"What *are* you all up to?" asked Mary Anne. She had just entered the garden, carrying Laura Perkins. Gabbie and Myriah were following close behind her.

Dawn laughed and explained that they were making sure that Squirt and Lucy had been "properly introduced".

"Oh, in that case," said Mary Anne, "may I present Miss Laura Elizabeth Perkins?" Laura held out her hand to Lucy, as if she wanted to shake. Jessi, Dawn and Mary Anne giggled.

That was when I arrived, with Jenny and Andrea. Jenny ran off to play with the other little kids, who were by then having a great time running around together. I sat down under the tree and "introduced" Andrea to the others. There we were, with all those babies. It was kind of awesome.

I hadn't had a good look at what Claudia, Mallory and Stacey were doing, so Jessi and Dawn filled me in. I thought that maybe I should talk to them, but Mary Anne convinced me not to.

"Let them go on working,' she said. "The float may look confusing, but I'm sure it'll come together soon."

"Besides," said Dawn, "we've got to watch these babies."

"Aren't they adorable?" said Jessi with a sigh, gazing at Squirt and Lucy. They were sitting next to each other, not actually "playing", but still getting along well.

"I just love babies," said Dawn. "This parade is going to be fun!"

Just then, Lucy grabbed Squirt's fish. She had been eyeing it for several moments, and the temptation must have been too strong to resist any longer.

Squirt let out an earsplitting wail.

Lucy smiled and put the fish's tail in her mouth.

"Lucy, darling," said Dawn. "Give Squirt his fish."

Lucy ignored her.

Squirt cried louder.

Then Laura started to cry.

"What is it?" asked Mary Anne. "What's the matter, Laura?" She picked her up and held her close, jiggling her slightly to calm her.

Dawn finally got the fish away from Lucy and gave it back to Squirt. His cries started to die down, but Lucy's grew louder. To distract her, Dawn held her up to look at Andrea, who was sitting in my lap.

"See Andrea?" asked Dawn. "She's going to be in the parade, just like you. Only she won't be on the float. She's going to be in her very own buggy." Of course, Lucy didn't understand a word Dawn was saying, but the distraction seemed to work and her crying finally stopped.

Laura was still crying, however, so Mary Anne decided to check her nappy.

Meanwhile, Andrea was becoming restless, so I decided to try Dawn's "distraction" technique. "That's Lucy," I said, holding Andrea up to see her. "She's going to be riding on a big, big float." Andrea gave Lucy a toothless grin.

Then she dribbled, all over Lucy.

At the same time, Squirt dropped his fish, couldn't reach it and started to cry again.

Laura was still wailing.

Claudia looked up from her chicken-wire sculpture. "Can't you lot keep those babies quiet?" she asked. "We're trying to get some work done here."

I almost blew up at her, but Mary Anne caught my eye and shook her head. She was right, I knew it. We didn't have time for a big fight, not if we wanted to get that float into the parade.

Somehow, we managed to clean up the babies and calm them down – and even enjoy the rest of the afternoon. But, as Jessi said in the notebook, the scene in Claudia's garden did make us wonder if there could be such a thing as too many babies.

11th CHAPTER

Thursday

I suppose you all think I should be apologizing for my behavior in Claud's garden today, but to tell you the truth, I don't think I should have to. I was only being honest. Besides, as the Marshalls' sitter, I think I owe it to them to make sure that Eleanor looks as good as possible on the float. I can't believe the parade is only two days away...

Maybe Dawn really did think she was being honest, but still, she *did* owe us an apology. Or at least she should have apologized to Mallory. But I'm getting ahead of myself here. Let me tell the story as it happened.

Dawn was sitting for Nina and Eleanor Marshall. We used to sit for them more often when the club first started, but then the Marshalls got a full-time housekeeper. Lately the Marshalls have been calling us again, since they cut back on the housekeeper's hours.

Nina is four, and she's a lot of fun. She's at that stage in which she's learning how to have real conversations with people, and some of the discussions she gets into are pretty funny.

Dawn said that Nina once told her about this friend of hers at her preschool. His name, said Nina, was Jimmytony. He was her "boyfriend", and he phoned her up all the time. Dawn thought that Jimmytony sounded like a great friend.

Later, Dawn found out that Jimmytony *was* a great friend – a great *imaginary* friend. Mrs Marshall explained it to her one day. Nina had made him up, all on her own.

Eleanor is two, and she's incredibly cute. She's got blonde, wavy hair with a big cowlick in the front and gigantic blue eyes. She's just beginning to string words into sentences – sort of. For example, if she and Nina are playing with Nina's Barbie, dressing her up for a night on the town, Eleanor will say "Barbie – dress – dancing!"

Eleanor likes to copy her big sister, and she tries to say and do everything Nina says and does, which isn't always easy for her.

Anyway, Dawn was sitting for the Marshall girls that Thursday afternoon. She'd told Mrs Marshall about the float we were making for the parade (of course, she'd already got permission for Eleanor to be part of it), and Mrs Marshall was excited.

"It's too bad Nina is too old to be on the float," said Mrs Marshall, on her way out of the door that day.

Dawn nodded. "I know," she said. "There are other kids we sit for who would like to be in the parade, too. But it'll be fun for Nina to watch her sister go past on our float. Right, Nina?"

Nina nodded. "Can we play hide-and-seek?" she asked, changing the subject.

Her mother laughed. "Well, I suppose *she* doesn't mind that she's not going to be on the float! I'll leave you to your game."

As soon as Mrs Marshall was out of the door, Dawn found herself with Nina pulling her by one hand and Eleanor holding on to the other.

"Hide-and-seek!" yelled Nina.

"Hide! Seek!" yelled Eleanor.

Dawn had never played hide-and-seek with the girls, so she realized that they must have just learned the game and wanted to "teach" it to her. "Okay," she said. "What do we do first?"

"You close your eyes and count to ten while we hide," said Nina.

"Find!" said Eleanor.

"Right," said Nina. "Then you say 'Ready or not, here I come!' and you find us."

"Sounds like fun," said Dawn. "Let's play just in this room, though, okay?" They were in the living room, and she thought it might be a good idea to keep the game small. She didn't want to hunt all over he house for the girls.

As it turned out, she was worried for nothing.

The Marshall girls had their own version of hide-and-seek. Here's how it went: as soon as Dawn finished counting and said "Ready or not, here I come," both girls started to giggle in their hiding places. They weren't very well hidden, either. Nina was standing behind a lamp that was much smaller than she was, and Eleanor was simply facing into a corner of he room, deciding (Dawn thought) that if she couldn't see Dawn, Dawn couldn't see *her*.

Anyway, Dawn began to prowl round the room, thinking out loud about how to find the girls. "Now, where could they be?" she asked herself. "Where are those girls hiding?" The giggles grew louder and then turned into shrieks as the girls, unable to stand the suspense, ran out of their hiding places and flung themselves at Dawn.

"I found you!" Dawn cried, laughing. They played the game five more times, and each time the girls hid in exactly the same spots and Dawn found them just as quickly. It wasn't hide-and-seek the way Dawn had learned it, but Eleanor and Nina were having a great time anyway.

When they'd finished playing, Dawn suggested they go over to Claudia's to see how the float was coming along. "It should be almost finished by now," she said.

But when they reached Claudia's back garden, Dawn took one look around and wanted to run back to the Marshalls'.

The float stood in the middle of the garden, looking like a lumpy, streaky red mountain. Claud is a talented artist, but I'd had the feeling that something as big as a float wasn't going to be as easy to make as we'd thought. Especially since she'd been trying to take all of our suggestions into account. She must have felt confused.

Claudia and Stacey were hovering around the float adding final touches. "Why didn't you mix more paint?" Claudia asked Stacey, as Dawn walked up to them. "This wasn't nearly enough. No wonder the float looks awful."

"I really don't think that the paint is the problem, Claudia," said Stacey. "I mean, look at the shape of this thing. Who would ever guess it was a shoe?" She turned to Dawn. "What would *you* think it was?" she asked.

"I – I don't know," said Dawn. She didn't want to get in the middle of their argument. "It looks fine," she said. "But – where do the babies sit?"

"Don't worry," I said. I had just arrived with Emily. "I have some ideas about that."

"Oh, you do, do you?" asked Claudia, her hands on her hips. "I'm the one who built the float. I've tried to use everyone's ideas, but that's only made it worse. So now I'm just going to do it my way."

"Okay, what's *your* way?" I asked.

"Well –" she said. It was obvious – to me, anyway – that she hadn't even thought about it.

I looked around. By then, Jessi had arrived with Squirt, and Mary Anne was just coming into the garden carrying Laura Perkins. I knew that Mallory was sitting for Jamie and Lucy Newton that day, and that they would probably be coming over, too.

"I know," I said. "How about a dress rehearsal? We can put the costumes on the babies who turn up today and see how the kids look on the float."

Everybody agreed, so I ran up to Claud's room to use her phone. I phoned Mal at the Newtons'. "Can you bring the costumes over here?" I asked her.

"Of course," she said. "They're not quite finished, but we'll get an idea of how they look."

When she walked into Claud's garden, Mallory was carrying Lucy in one arm and a big brown bag in the other. "Here they are!" she said. She put the bag down and pulled out one of the costumes. The colour was even brighter than I had remembered.

I took one for Emily, and Dawn grabbed one for Eleanor. Jessi got Squirt's, and Mary Anne found one that looked like it would fit Laura. Mal started to button Lucy into her costume.

The costumes looked (to me) like little clown suits, with ruffles down the front. I'm not sure what Mallory had in mind when she designed them, but they did look quite cute once we'd got the babies into them.

I lifted Emily on to the float. Dawn put Eleanor down next to her. Straight away, we both noticed how badly the costumes clashed with the colour of the float, but neither of us said anything. We just looked at each other and raised our eyebrows.

Stacey, however, spoke up. "Good going, Mal," she said sarcastically. "Didn't you see what colour the paint was going to be?"

Mallory blushed. "I – I thought this material would be nice," she said. "It was on sale. Besides, *you* didn't ask *me* about *my* plans!"

"Let's not argue about it," I said. "So the costumes clash. Big deal. But Mallory, where are *our* costumes?"

Mal looked at me blankly.

"We're going to be on the float, too, you know," I said. "What are we going to wear?"

She put her hand over her mouth. "I didn't think of that," she said. "But there's no way I can make seven more costumes in two days. I haven't finished these! Everyone's just going to have to make their own."

"Brilliant," I said. "As if *we've* got time."

"Oh, we can whip something together," said Stacey. "What's the big deal, anyway? We're going to look stupid no matter what we're wearing, since we'll all be riding on this lumpy old float that doesn't look anything like a shoe."

Claudia jumped to her feet. "Now, wait a minute," she said. "It would have looked more like a shoe if I could have made it my way instead of listening to all of you lot and your bright ideas!"

At that moment, Eleanor started wailing. After about two seconds, Squirt joined her. Soon all the babies were crying.

Dawn shook her head. "I bet they're crying because their costumes look so stupid," she whispered to Mary Anne.

But Mallory heard her. "Stupid?" she repeated. "I'd like to see you do better!"

She burst into tears. Jessi tried to comfort her, but Mal pushed her away. "You probably think they look awful, too," she said.

Jessi stepped back. "You said it, I didn't."

Soon everybody was sniping at everybody else. The garden was full of crying babies and yelling babysitters. Dawn decided to leave. She was sick of the baby parade and it hadn't even happened yet.

Back at the Marshalls', Dawn spent the rest of the day putting together a new costume for Eleanor. She found a blue party dress that used to be Nina's, and she matched it with a pair of blue patent shoes. She gave Eleanor a new hairstyle – pigtails tied with big ribbons.

"There," she said. "Now you look like a little girl who would be living in a shoe. In that other costume you looked like a clown!"

Eleanor smiled at her and said, "Clown!" (She must have *liked* that other costume.)

But when Mrs Marshall came home, Dawn told her that the clothes Eleanor had on were perfect for the parade. She asked her to make sure that Eleanor was wearing them on Saturday.

12th CHAPTER

When I woke up on Saturday morning, the first thing I did was look out of the window. It was a bright and sunny day, perfect for a parade.

I didn't feel bright and sunny, though.

To be perfectly honest, I was sort of dreading the parade. I knew our float hadn't turned out well, and I was worried about looking after so many babies at once. Of course, I was also worried about Andrea's costume – and the "coach" that I had designed for her.

What would Mrs P. do if Andrea didn't win a prize?

I tried not to think about that. But it was hard to forget the parade. During breakfast, my family kept asking me questions about it.

"Where do you think we should stand for the best view, Kristy?" asked my mum. I suggested a spot.

"Is Slim Peabody really going to be the grand marshal?" asked Watson. "He was one of my favourite stars when I was a kid. I loved to hear him sing those cowboy songs."

Slim Peabody was supposed to be a celebrity, but he sounded like an old has been to me. Why couldn't they have got somebody like Cam Geary to lead the parade? But I held my tongue and just nodded at Watson. "Yup," I said. "Slim's going to lead the parade."

"I heard that the Girl Guides have made a really professional-looking float," said Sam. "Its theme is 'Save the Animals' and the babies are going to be dressed as endangered species."

"Big deal," I muttered. I went on answering everybody's questions as well as I could, but boy, was I glad when breakfast was over.

"Charlie," I said, when I had finished helping my mum and Watson clear up the kitchen. "Can you take me to the Prezziosos' now? I told Mrs P. I'd help her get Andrea ready for the parade."

"Me and the Junk Bucket are at your disposal," answered Charlie. "Chauffeur, float-puller and handyman. All at a special discount rate!" He grinned and held out his hand, rubbing his fingers and thumb together. "Pay up!" he said. "I want my fee in advance."

I gave him the money we'd agreed on. (The BSC members had voted to take it out of the treasury.) It wasn't much. I knew Charlie was really helping me out of the kindness of his heart. "Okay, let's get going," I said.

When we arrived at the Prezziosos', Mrs P. was, predictably, in a tizzy. Andrea's costume was half on and half off – and the half that was off was scattered all over the ground floor of the house.

And then I saw what Mrs P. was wearing. Have you ever had to pretend you were having a coughing fit in order to cover up a giggle that slipped out? That's what I had to do. Mrs P. was dressed up as one of the "Queen's" guards. She was wearing this red uniform (she must have hired it from a costume place) with big black boots and one of those high, high furry black hats that look like an animal nesting on top of your head. Fake medals were pinned all over her chest.

I couldn't even look at Charlie, who was waiting in his car. I knew he could see her from where he was sitting, and I knew if we looked at each other we would burst out laughing.

While Mrs P. ran upstairs to finish dressing, I got Andrea ready. I picked up her ruff from where it hung over a lampshade and slipped it over her head. "There you go, Your Highness!" I said. Then I looked around for the rest of her costume. When she was all ready, I called to Mrs P. to ask where the "coach" was.

"Back porch," she yelled from her bedroom. "But wait a minute. I want you to check something for me." She ran downstairs. "What do you think of my make-up?" she asked.

What did I think? I thought it looked like Jenny had been the make-up artist. "It looks – great!" I said, trying to sound enthusiastic.

"Thanks," she said. "Jenny helped a lot."

I knew it.

After I'd approved Mrs P.'s make-up, I checked on the buggy I'd decorated for Andrea. As soon as I saw it, I knew that Jenny had "helped" with it, too. I had decorated the buggy to look like a small but royal coach, with wheels made out of gold-painted cardboard. A cardboard horse was fastened to the front, and it really did look like the horse was pulling the coach. Then that fancy fabric was draped over the coach, giving it a royal look.

Jenny, however, had added stickers, pasted on every which way. And none of the stickers had anything to do with the "Queen Andrea" theme. There were Care Bear stickers and Teenage Mutant Hero Turtle stickers and Barbie stickers. Jenny had raided her collection.

"It's beautiful, isn't it?" Jenny was standing behind me, gazing at the buggy.

What could I say?

"Beautiful," I answered. "You really went to town with those stickers, didn't you?" I couldn't be angry with Jenny. I could tell that she was proud of what she'd done, and I thought that the stickers wouldn't show up enough to be seen from the reviewing stand.

"Let's bring the Queen's coach round to the front garden now, okay?" I said.

Jenny helped me with the buggy. One of the big cardboard wheels got a little bent, but I was able to fold it back to its original shape. And one of the horse's ears got torn, but I hoped nobody would notice.

I looked over at Charlie, who was still sitting in his car. His arms were folded over his chest. He looked a little impatient. And I had to go home, anyway. I had to get my costume together and dress Emily in hers.

"I think everything's ready, Mrs P.," I called up the stairs.

Mrs P. appeared on the first-floor landing. She was using a curling iron on her hair – why, I don't know, since it was going to be under that big hat – and she waved goodbye.

Thanks for everything, Kristy," she said. "Wish us luck!"

"Good luck!" I called. (They were going to need it.) "See you at the parade," I added to Jenny. She was going to be standing in a special spot, along with Becca and Jamie and some other kids who were too old to march (or ride) in the parade. Our associate members, Logan and Shannon, had been hired to watch the group of children until the parade was over.

Back at home, I rushed around madly trying to work out what to wear. I was supposed to be dressed as the Old Woman. Don't ask me how that had been decided, because I have no idea. Probably, no one else wanted to be the Old Woman.

I put on a frumpy-looking blouse and one of my mum's long skirts. I tied on an old apron. Then I drew some wrinkles on my face with eyebrow pencil. I looked in the mirror. "Not bad," I said, "for a five minute costume."

I wrestled Emily into her pink clown outfit. She didn't seem all that thrilled to be wearing it – in fact, she had started wailing the minute I brought it out. Even so, as soon as she was dressed, I picked her up and headed downstairs. "Ta-daaa!" I said, as I entered the living room, where everybody was waiting.

There was a long silence.

Finally, Mum found her voice. "Very nice, Kristy," she said. "But why is Emily dressed like a clown?"

I shrugged and shook my head. "Don't ask me," I said. "It wasn't my idea." I turned to Charlie. "Ready to take an Old Woman and a clown over to Claudia's?" I asked.

"Ready," he answered.

I headed out the door carrying Emily. My family waved goodbye. They'd be leaving soon, too, to stake out a good spot on the parade route. Watson was bringing the camcorder.

I put Emily into her car seat, and we were off to Claud's house. It was time to hook the float to Charlie's car. When we pulled up, Charlie honked the horn and Claudia ran out. She was wearing a flowery dress that had once belonged to her grandmother, Mimi. I think that was supposed to be her costume.

"I'm all ready, and so's the float," she said. She opened the garage door, and there it was.

"Whoa!" said Charlie when he saw the float. He slumped down in his seat. "You've got to be kidding. I'm supposed to pull that – that *thing* behind my car?"

Claudia put her hands on her hips. "It's not *that* bad, Charlie," she said. "Besides, we're paying you good money to do it."

"Right," mumbled Charlie.

"Okay," I said, jumping out of the car. "Let's get it hitched up. C'mon. It'll look fine."

I was wrong. So sue me.

The float looked as awful as ever once it was hitched to the Junk Bucket. It was just a giant reddish blob with long, snaky things hanging off it.

"What are *those*?" asked Charlie, pointing to one.

"Shoelaces," said Claud, firmly.

"Oh."

That was when I knew for sure that our float was a disaster. "Do you think it's too late – ?" I started to ask Claudia, but she interrupted me.

"To phone the parents of all those babies and cancel?" she asked. "Kristy, are you out of your mind? Of course it's too late. We're just going to have to make the best of it."

Charlie, meanwhile, had gone around to the back of the car and was rummaging in the boot.

"What are you looking for?" I asked him.

"This," he answered, holding up an old, floppy hat that he sometimes wore when he and Sam went fishing. He put it on. Then he slammed the boot shut. He walked round the car and slid into the driver's seat. Next he started to poke around in the glove compartment.

"*Now* what are you looking for?" I asked. I still hadn't worked out why he was wearing that ratty old hat.

"These," he answered, putting on a pair of mirrored sunglasses that someone had once left in his car. "Now I'm all ready," he said, grinning. "There's no way anybody will recognize me now."

"Charlie!" Claud and I yelled together. I knew then how bad the float really looked.

We drove to the parade route (slowly, because the float was sort of drifting across the road) and met the other club members at the spot we'd decided on. All of the babies were there already, and some of their parents were still hanging around, looking rather worried.

None of the club members' costumes had anything in common. (Of course.) Dawn was dressed a bit like a beachcomber, Mary Anne looked like Raggedy Anne (she was using parts of an old Hallowe'en costume), and Jessi was wearing some sort of ballet get-up. Stacey had on an old sweat shirt that said, "New York – The Big Apple," and Mallory was dressed as she normally is.

Then there were the babies in their silly costumes. At least they looked as if they belonged together. Except for Eleanor, who was wearing her party dress.

Our float was a disaster, and each of us thought this was somebody *else's* fault. Within about two seconds, not one member of the BSC was speaking to the others.

What a mess.

13th CHAPTER

I was glaring at Dawn. Why had she dressed Eleanor differently from all the other babies? Dawn was glaring at Claudia – I suppose because of the way the float looked. Claudia was glaring at Stacey.

Everybody was looking pretty angry.

But the parade was about to start, and we were part of the parade, whether we liked it or not.

I passed round the sunblock I'd brought, while Mallory went around fastening the babies' sun-bonnets. So what if my friends and I weren't speaking to each other? So what if our float looked like The Creature From Another Planet? We had to look after those babies.

"Okay, folks!" I heard a voice over the loud-speaker. "Let's saddle up and move 'em out!"

Oh, how corny.

At least *I* thought it was corny. I noticed that Jessi and Mal were gazing in rapture at Slim Peabody. He was sitting on a big white horse at the front of the parade, which was about a block away from where we were. His saddle was trimmed with silver, and he was wearing a cowboy outfit.

"Wow," breathed Jessi, looking at the horse. "Look at that beautiful animal."

Mallory nodded. "He's gorgeous," she murmured.

Then they remembered that they weren't speaking to each other, and their mouths snapped shut.

Working quickly, we settled the babies in bouncers or on the blankets. They were spread around the shoe. I had sort of pictured them peeping *out* of the shoe – but I knew there was no point in saying anything now. Especially since I wasn't speaking to Claudia, anyway.

At least Claudia had realized that we would need something to keep the babies from falling "overboard." She had built a little guardrail around the float. I settle myself behind it, with Emily in my lap. I had promised Mrs Salem that I'd be responsible for Ricky and Rose, too, so they were propped up nearby.

When the float in front of us began to move, I gave Charlie the signal. We were on our way.

Before we had got started, I'd been to busy to be nervous. But now that the float was moving, my stomach felt jumpy. I wondered how "Queen Andrea" looked, and whether she'd win the prize that Mrs P. wanted so badly. I wondered if the float would last the parade route without falling apart. And I wondered if I was going to be able to stand the humiliation of having hundreds of people watch me ride by.

I could barely look at the crowds lining the street. Watson and Mum were there, somewhere, filming the event for posterity. That was one video I knew *I'd* never watch.

As we rolled along, I sneaked a look at some of the spectators. They'd been applauding and cheering for the floats before us, but they looked a little confused by our float. I couldn't blame them. The fact is, that without these big signs that Claudia had made to hang on the sides of the float, I'm sure no one would ever have known what it was supposed to be.

She'd made the signs in a hurry, and it showed. The one that hung from my side of the float said, THEIR WAS AN OLD WOMMAN WHO LIVED IN A SHO. The other one said, THAIR WAS AN OLD WOMANN WHO LIVED IN A SHUE. Nobody had had time to check Claud's spelling.

I thought I heard people laughing, but I trained my eyes straight ahead and tried not to think about it. At least the babies were behaving. Not one of them was crying – so far. And, even though none of us babysitters was speaking to the others, at least we weren't arguing out loud.

It could have been worse.

I tried to relax. I was stuck on that float until the parade was over, so I knew I might as well make the best of it. I looked up ahead, trying to see how some of the other floats were decorated.

The one in front of us was *very* professional-looking. It was a living merry-go-round! From under a canopy dropped a circle of poles. At the bottom of each pole was a grown-up holding a baby – and each baby was dressed in a really terrific animal costume. The circle moved around and around in time to the music that was playing from a tape player in the middle of the float.

The crowd *loved* it.

Behind us was the float Sam had heard about, the one the Girl Guides had made. It was decorated to look like a tropical rain forest, and each of the babies was supposed to be an endangered species. On the front was a big sign that said, SAVE THE ANIMALS. The float looked nice, but I don't think the babies were all that happy. They were wearing these special animal masks as part of their costumes, and a lot of the babies were crying from behind the masks.

When I craned my neck, I could see some of the Single Buggy entries way behind us. I knew that Mrs P. and Andrea were back there, even though I couldn't make them out. I wondered if the other buggies were as wild and gaudy as Mrs P.'s. I had a feeling she'd gone a little overboard with her Queen Andrea idea.

There were also entries in which kids were being pulled along in wagons or pushed in little go-carts. I hadn't got a good look at any of them, except one – Little Miss Muffet. It was really good. It made me wish we'd stuck to a simpler nursery rhyme.

By the time the parade hit the main route, all the bands that were marching with us had begun to play. I could hear a banjo band behind us, and I knew a big marching band was leading the parade. But guess which band was marching nearest to us?

The bagpipe band.

I *hate* bagpipes. Maybe you've never heard them, so I'll try to describe how they sound. Imagine twenty mean cats fighting over a single piece of fish.

That's how bagpipes sound to me.

I looked at Mary Anne. She hates bagpipes, too. I gave her a little smile, but she just glared at me. Her hands were over her ears.

Then I heard a voice yelling over the caterwauling bagpipes. "Hey, Thomas!

What's that you're pulling? It looks like a mutant marshmallow!"

Oh, no. Charlie's friends had spotted him through his disguise. I saw a crowd of boys standing on the pavement. They were pointing at the float and laughing. I suppose they had recognized the Junk Bucket. (Charlie slumped down in his seat, trying to pretend that he somehow wasn't involved.)

"Hey, Thomas!" yelled another one of the boys. "What are you going to do with your prize money?"

Oh, ha-ha.

I could almost see the steam coming out of Charlie's ears. I was going to be hearing about this for a long, long time. I started to work out how many nights I would have to take out the rubbish for him in order to make up for the parade.

Then the worst thing in the world happened.

Just as we were about to go past the group of boys, the crowd parted slightly and I could see that some girls were with them, too. None of them called out to Charlie – but they were whispering and giggling as they looked at our float. Even from where I was sitting, I could see the back of Charlie's neck turning bright red.

I was really in for it now.

The parade seemed to be moving at a crawl. Most parades end before you want

393

them to, but not this one. It seemed to have been going on for years. We crawled past the spot where Watson and Mum were standing. They cheered and waved. Then we passed Shannon and Logan and the kids they were sitting for. We got a big cheer from them, too.

By that time, the babies were tired of being good. Squirt had started to cry when the bagpipes began playing; they'd stopped, but he hadn't. Ricky and Rose were bawling, too.

Dawn had her hands full with Eleanor, who kept trying to escape from the float. Eleanor's party dress was smudged with red paint, and the bows in her hair had come loose.

Babies were crawling all over the float. None of them wanted to stay put. As soon as Stacey or Claudia got one settled, another one would start to take off.

Then Emily complained of a tummy ache. She was carsick. (Floatsick?)

By the time we passed the reviewing stand, I couldn't even bring myself to smile and wave at the judges. I didn't care any more about winning a prize. All I wanted was for the parade to be over.

14th CHAPTER

Finally the parade ended up in the little park near the shopping centre. What a relief! No more riding past all those smiling faces. No more waving.

But the day wasn't over yet.

First, we had to wait for the rest of the parade to reach the park. Then would come the time for the judges to announce their decisions and hand out prizes.

Obviously we wouldn't be winning any prizes – unless they were giving out a prize for "Worst Float". But I did not want to find out who *had* won. Especially in the Buggy Category.

"I'm outta here!" said Charlie, as soon as he'd parked the car. He climbed out of the Junk Bucket and slammed the door.

"But Charlie—" I wanted to make sure he'd be back. Eventually.

"No 'buts', Kristy. I don't want to have anything else to do with this parade. I'll come back when it's all over."

There was no point in arguing with him. "Okay, Charlie," I said. "See you later."

I turned back to see what everybody else was doing. My friends were still sitting on the float. The babies had settled down again. Some of them had even fallen asleep. Each babysitter was holding a baby in her lap. However, nobody looked as though she were ready to make up, and I wasn't about to be the one to start.

We just watched the rest of the parade trickle into the park. There were some amazing floats. On any other day we would have been talking about them, pointing out special things and laughing at the funny ones.

But that day, we weren't talking to each other. So instead, we talked to the babies we were holding.

"Look at that, Emily!" I said, pointing at a float that had just turned in to the park. The theme was *Star Wars*. The float was decorated to look like a spaceship, and there were four babies on board. One was dressed like Princess Leia, plaits and all. Another was supposed to be Luke Skywalker. He was carrying a plastic sword that was bigger than he was. Then there was Hans Solo, looking like a real swashbuckler, and a furry Chewbacca.

"Funny!" said Emily, chuckling. That's one of the words she's just learned.

I pointed out the *Star Wars* float to Ricky and Rose, too – but they didn't seem too impressed. Ricky just yawned, and Rose gave a little burp. They were just too young to appreciate it.

"Hey, Squirt," said Jessi. "Look!" I sneaked a look at the float that Jessi was pointing to.

"Dothy!" said Squirt happily.

"That's right," replied Jessi. "Dorothy and her friends the Tin Man, the Scarecrow and the Cowardly Lion. And I see the Wizard, too!"

It was a pretty great float. Somebody had spent a lot of time making costumes for those babies. I felt even more embarrassed than before when I thought of how quickly I had thrown my Old Woman outfit together.

Finally the floats stopped arriving, and we started to see the buggies, wagons and go-carts roll in. A lot of the babies in those categories were asleep, but you could still get an idea of what their costumes were.

Straight away, I felt ridiculous for having even wondered if Andrea's buggy was too gaudy. People really went to town when they decorated these things! I've never seen so many ribbons, bows, and sequins in one place before. *Now* I started to wonder if Andrea's buggy was too boring! If I hadn't been in public, I would have groaned out loud. I didn't think Queen Andrea had any more chance of winning in her category than we had in ours.

"Wow!" I heard Dawn say. "Look at that, Eleanor." Eleanor was grinning and bouncing up and down. I followed her eyes and saw a mother pulling a wagon that was decorated to look like one of my favourite books: *Good Night Moon*. (It's about getting ready for bed and saying good night to everything in your room. Kids *love* it, and it's a great way to get them to go to bed.)

The wagon was made to look like a little bed, and the boy who was lying in it must have been about two and a half. His favourite toys were around him. And there was a "window" (made out of cardboard and cling film) running up the side of the wagon, with a big yellow moon hanging in it. It was the cutest thing!

After about half an hour, just when I was feeling as if I couldn't possibly sit on that float for another minute, Slim Peabody stepped on to the stage that had been set up and tapped on the microphone. A piercing screech rang out, and everybody quietened down right away.

"Just testing, pardners!" said Slim.

Oh, please.

"We sure are glad you could all come out for this little parade today," he went on, now that he'd got everybody's attention. "Me and Buster were proud to be part of it."

Buster? Oh, that must be the horse's name. Of course. Silly me.

"How 'bout if we give all these little ladies and gents a great big hand?" he asked the audience. The spectators applauded loudly. The park was pretty jammed by then.

I worked out that maybe about six of these people were clapping for us – and only because they knew us.

"I know you're all just rarin' to know who won the prizes in each division," continued Slim.

Yes! I thought. Let's get on with it. I couldn't wait to get off that float and out of my costume.

"But first," he went on, "the parade committee asked me to entertain you while the judges confer."

Oh, no. Anything but—

Slim pulled out a guitar and strummed on it. Then he began to yodel and sing loudly into the mike. "*I'm an old cowhand from the Rio Grande.*"

Maybe way back when Watson was a fan of his, Slim could carry a tune. But I'm here to tell you that those days were long gone. Slim tortured us with about ten more minutes of cowboy songs before one of the judges bounded up on to the stage and politely cut him off.

"Thank you so much, Mr Peabody," he said.

"Call me Slim," said Slim.

"Let's give Slim a big Stoneybrook hand!" said the judge, turning to the audience. I think everybody applauded as enthusiastically as they did because they were hoping Slim's show was really over. I know that's why I was clapping.

"How 'bout an' encore?" I heard Slim ask the judge. He was close enough to the mike so that we all heard it. I held my breath.

"I think these folks are eager to hear about their winners, Mr – Slim," said the judge. Slim waved and headed off the stage. "And now," said the judge, "it's time to announce the winners of this year's Stoneybrook Baby Parade!"

I wanted to die. This was going to be pure torture. Not only were we not going to get a prize, but Andrea wasn't, either. The parade was a complete disaster. I looked around for Charlie. If only he would turn up now and drive me home!

But Charlie was nowhere to be seen.

The judge started to announce the winners. "In the Go-cart Division," he said, "The winner of the Third Prize is Kevin Davis, for his depiction of Rambo!"

There was lots of cheering for Kevin. I'd missed that Rambo cart, and to tell the truth, I didn't care.

The judge went on, announcing third- second-, and first-place winners in all the categories. When he announced the Float Division, I held my breath. What if I was wrong and somehow we had won Third Prize? (I knew there was no chance we'd do any better than that.) I'd have to go up onstage and accept the ribbon in my awful costume.

"And third-place winner is—"

I closed my eyes.

"The Wizard of Oz!" he finished. "Congratulations to the Morse family." The prize-giving went on and on. The merry-go-round won first prize in the floats, and I was glad.

Finally the judge announced the buggy category. I crossed my fingers, my toes, and my arms, wishing as hard as I could that Andrea would win. The judge announced the third-place winner. It wasn't Andrea. He announced the second-place winner. Not Andrea.

"And First Prize in this division goes to Andrea Prezzioso – or Queen Andrea!" said the judge, smiling.

I heaved a great sigh as I watched Mrs P. carry Andrea up to the stage to receive her ribbon. My job was safe – even if the Babysitters Club broke up tomorrow, which looked entirely possible.

As soon as the judging was over, parents started arriving at our float to pick up their babies. They looked pretty relieved to see that their children were still in one piece. I don't think any of them had actually expected to win a prize, so they weren't disappointed.

Mrs P. rushed over to me, smiling happily. "Thank you *so much*," she said. "Isn't it wonderful?" She showed me Andrea's blue ribbon. Andrea was asleep in her buggy. Jenny was holding her mother's hand.

"We won, Kristy!" she said. "Just like you said we would."

Lucky for me.

As the last baby was being picked up, Charlie came back. My ex-friends and I piled into the Junk Bucket and, with the float trailing behind us, Charlie drove us home. Needless to say, there was no talking along the way.

Finally Charlie, Emily, and I were the only ones left in the car. "What do you want me to do with the float?" asked Charlie.

"Take it to the dump," I answered. "Please."

15th CHAPTER

When Charlie pulled up outside our house, I unbuckled Emily from her car seat and lifted her out of the car.

Charlie was still sitting behind the wheel. "Do you really want me to take it to the dump?" he asked, gesturing to the float. It sat behind the car, all lumpy and red.

"I do," I answered. I never wanted to see that thing again.

My brother shrugged. "Okay," he said. He waved goodbye and pulled away from the kerb.

"Make sure it gets crushed in the compacter!" I called after him. Then I took Emily inside. The house was quiet. Mum must have gone out shopping and Watson was in his study. Nannie was sitting in the living room, reading.

"How was the parade, sweetie?" she asked.

403

"Just be glad you had a bowling tournament today and you couldn't come," I answered. "It was a disaster. At least, our float was. Actually, the rest of the parade was pretty good."

Nannie smiled at me. "I'll be glad to look after Emily for a while," she said. "You look tired."

"Thanks," I replied. "I'll just get her out of this costume, and then I'll bring her down to you." I carried Emily upstairs and took off her costume. Emily had certainly been good-natured during the parade. "You're the best, Miss Em," I said, kissing her nose.

She giggled and kissed me back.

I found a clean sundress for Emily and buttoned her into it. She looked happy to be out of that clown costume. I threw the costume into the laundry basket, thinking she might be able to use it next Hallowe'en. Then I took Emily back downstairs.

"Come here, darling," said Nannie, spreading her arms wide. Emily ran over to her, laughing. "Okay, Kristy," said Nannie. "You're free now."

Free to do what I really wanted to do: go to my room and think. I headed upstairs again and changed out of my costume. Then I lay across my bed. I wanted to work out what had gone so terribly wrong with our float. Usually our club projects turn out pretty well, but this one had bombed.

It didn't take me long to understand what had happened. The reason we didn't make a better float was because we hadn't worked *together*. Everybody had gone her separate way, each thinking she knew what was best. We hadn't been communicating at all. And now we were all angry with each other.

It was time to start talking – even if it was too late to save our float. I decided to phone Mary Anne and apologize. Since she's my best friend, I wanted to be sure to make up with her first.

I went to the phone in the hall and dialled her number. She picked up the receiver after one ring.

"Hello?" she said.

"Hi, Mary Anne? It's me, Kristy. I'm calling to apologize. I don't want us to be angry with each other any more."

"This is *so* weird," said Mary Anne. "When you called, I had my hand on the phone. I was going to call *you*."

"Really?" I asked.

"Really," she answered. "Dawn and I made up as soon as we got home. I *hate* it when we're all arguing. And I think everybody else is probably making up, too. It's ridiculous for us to be so worked up about that stupid old float."

I agreed with Mary Anne.

"And you know what?" she went on. "Dawn and I realized that we weren't really that angry with each other. It was more that we were embarrassed – about the float."

"I know what you mean," I said. "It *was* pretty embarrassing, wasn't it?" I started to giggle, and so did Mary Anne. Soon we were laughing so hard we couldn't stop.

"I thought I would *die* when Slim Peabody was singing," I said.

"I know. And what about those bagpipes?"

Suddenly I couldn't remember why we had ever been so angry with each other in the first place.

After I had got off the phone with Mary Anne, I spent some time calling the other members of the BSC. Dawn and Mary Anne had been right; everybody was more than ready to make up.

"Let's talk about this at Monday's meeting," said Stacey, when I called her. "Maybe we can learn something from this."

"Good idea," I said.

That night at dinner, Mum and Watson wanted to talk about the parade. "Wasn't that merry-go-round float wonderful?" asked Mum.

"It certainly was," I said. "Too bad we were right behind it."

Watson smiled at me. "Oh, come on, Kristy. Your float wasn't so bad," he said.

"Yes it was!" exclaimed Charlie. "But now that 'Shoe' is the size of a *shoe box*. It was really satisfying to watch it get crushed."

"I'm sorry those people recognized you," I said to Charlie. I didn't even want to *mention* the girls.

"No big deal," he said. "I'll get over it." He punched me lightly on the shoulder. "Just don't ever ask me to pull one of your club's floats again."

"Don't worry," I said. "I don't think we'll be entering any parades for a while."

By Monday, the parade was just a memory. I spent the early part of the afternoon sitting for Jenny and Andrea. By then, I had got used to looking after both of them – in fact, it was starting to be fun.

Andrea's first prize ribbon had been mounted on the wall above her cot, and Mrs P. was late getting out of the house because she "just had" to show me the parade photos she'd asked a friend to take. She thanked me again and again for my help.

"I was glad to do it," I said. I wasn't lying, either. I'd had fun decorating Andrea's buggy. I may not be as good an artist as Claudia, but I had to admit that I had done a pretty good job on that coach.

When I had finished at the Prezziosos', I headed for Claudia's house. It was time for our club meeting. As usual, I was early, but it wasn't long before the others started to trickle in.

"Hi, Stacey," I said when she stuck her head in the doorway. She smiled at me and sat down at Claud's desk. Claud was already in place on her bed.

Jessi and Mallory arrived together and plopped on the floor. Jessi had a magazine with her, and she and Mal were tearing out the perfume adverts and rubbing the scented paper on their wrists.

"I like this one, don't you?" asked Mal, thrusting her wrist towards me.

I sniffed and coughed. "Nice," I said. "It's pretty . . . strong, though, isn't it?"

"I think it's really *rich*-smelling," said Jessi. "Like what you'd wear if you lived in Beverly Hills or something."

By then, Dawn and Mary Anne had arrived, and Claud was busy rummaging around under her pillow. I had a feeling I knew what she was looking for.

"I *thought* I'd saved something for the meeting," she said, pulling out a bag of mini chocolate bars. "Who likes Snickers?" She passed the bag to Jessi and Mal. "And I've got something here for the health freaks, too," she went on, searching under the bed. "Low-salt Triscuits!" She tossed the box to Dawn.

Just then, I noticed out of the corner of my eye that the digital clock had clicked to 5:30. "Order!" I said. Jessi and Mal put away their magazine. The meeting had begun.

Since it was a Monday, subs were the first order of business. "Cough it up, you lot!" said Stacey happily, passing around the envelope. She just loves to collect that money.

"How much is in the treasury?" I asked.

Stacey counted it in a matter of seconds. I don't know how she does it so fast. "Well," she answered, "we've got enough for a pizza party. But not enough for extra topping. It looks like we spent the pepperoni money on the *you*-know-what."

"The float?" I asked. "You can say it. It's all in the past, now."

"Thank heaven," said Claud. "What a disaster. You know, I've realized something. A big project like that just can't work without cooperation."

"Right," said Dawn. "A little give-and-take."

"Communication!" said Mary Anne.

"Working together," added Jessi and Mal.

"Okay," I said. "So at least *one* good thing came out of the baby parade. We learned an important lesson."

The phone rang then. It was Mrs Salem. She needed a sitter for Ricky and Rose. And not too long after that, we got another phone call. It was Mrs Gold, another mother from our class, wanting to hire us to watch her two-month-old baby.

"I heard from Mrs Salem what a wonderful job you did with the babies on your float," she said to me.

After we'd arranged the jobs, I looked round Claud's room and smiled at my friends. "I suppose that's *three* good things that came out of the parade," I said. "One lesson and two new clients!"